Your Dieting Daughter

‿‿ ‿‿ ‿‿

Your Dieting Daughter

છે છે છે

Is She Dying for Attention?

Carolyn Costin

BRUNNER/MAZEL, *Publishers* • NEW YORK

This book is designed as a guide to understanding eating disorders. The information contained here is meant to enhance the reader's coping skills and knowledge base; it is not meant to be used in place of a formal medical diagnosis or appropriate medical treatment.

The names and other identifying characteristics of patients discussed in this text have been changed to protect their confidentiality.

Library of Congress Cataloging-in-Publication Data

Costin, Carolyn.
    Your dieting daughter: is she dying for attention? / Carolyn Costin.
        p. cm.
    Includes bibliographical references.
    ISBN 0-87630-836-1
    1. Eating disorders in adolescence. 2. Mothers and daughters. 3. Fathers and daughters. 4. Reducing diets. 5. Body image in adolescence. I. Title.
RJ506.E18C67   1997
616.85'26'008352–dc20   96-38423
                                                                                         CIP

Published by
BRUNNER/MAZEL, INC.
19 Union Square West
New York, New York 10003

Manufactured in the United States of America

10 9 8 7 6 5 4 3 2 1

This book is dedicated to my patients
and to my two nieces, Caitlin and Siena,
who come closest to the role of daughters in my life.

Dear Caitlin and Siena,

In your short lives you have already taught me and demonstrated to those around you how to see not just the stars but the spaces between the stars and not with the eyes but with the heart. If there is any gift I give you, may it be for you not to allow yourselves to be measured by numbers or outside things that don't matter, and to remember that just as the snow goose need not bathe itself to be white, neither need you do anything but be yourselves. And finally, let your fears not be not that you are inadequate in any way, but that you are powerful beyond measure.

Carolyn

Contents

ॐ ॐ ॐ

Acknowledgments

๑ ๑ ๑

Among other things that helped me with this book were the gifts of empathy that I got from my mother, perseverance from my father, and the blessing of having so many special people in my life. I am privileged to have had hundreds of extraordinary individuals share with me the deepest part of their souls. My work and this book could not have been accomplished without them all.

There are many individuals who helped with this project, too numerous to mention, but none of my work could ever be accomplished without my trusted and faithful assistant, and guardian angel, Fredda Kurtz, who in a way has dedicated her life to helping me with mine.

Furthermore, at this point in my life, I could never accomplish anything without my incredible gift from the universe, my husband, Bruce.

And finally, last but not least, I am indebted to my own suffering, battle, and victory over an old enemy *and* friend, anorexia nervosa, without whom I would not be the person I am today.

—CAROLYN COSTIN

Prologue:
Dying to Be Thin

ও ও ও

Dear Mom and Dad,

From the day I was born you have given me all and more of yourselves to make me happy, and because of that I am so sorry I have failed you in so many ways. I want to be perfect . . . I feel like I'm trying to get rid of my headache by banging my head against a wall. I wish I didn't have to worry about how I was going to wake up in the morning and feel because of something I have eaten. To be honest I don't even like food anymore, it's easy for me to skip a meal or throw it up. I like the feeling of not being full inside. I wish I could feel the way I did when I was skinny. To get there it's like running down a hall to a door that keeps getting further, and I'm so tired of running. I know that you have thought I have done this for attention because you said that, but believe me the last thing I want is attention on me. And if I could have it any way, I wish you would have never found out only because I want you to be happy and not have to worry. I wish you would have never found out only because I want you to be happy and not have to worry.

ও ও ও

Dear Mom and Dad,

I know that you have a lot of questions. . . . I know that you're both angry and frustrated but so am I. A long time ago you both said that you were educating yourselves on Bulimia and Anorexia and I feel like all you have educated yourselves on was the surface of the disease. You both are not to blame for my eating disorder but I did not arrive at this point alone. . . .

ও ও ও

Dear Mom and Dad,

It's not easy watching your child try to kill herself and be expected to "give her space." There is no book on how to raise children, how to be fair, or what to do when this happens to you. I don't know why I have anorexia/bulimia or if I'll ever be cured.

I do know that I have a lot to be thankful for and a lot to want to live for. I am so sorry for the hurtful way I treated you and the contempt that I had. It wasn't contempt for you that was coming out, it was contempt for myself.

I have met many dieting daughters in my life. I have been one myself. The girls and women whose lives created this book are all dieting daughters who, through internalizing our culture's standards of beauty, sacrificed their spirits for the sake of appearance. Their stories reveal an insidious philosophy of life that has come to haunt us all, a philosophy in which the highest value is placed on image, a "lookism" philosophy, where how you look is more important than who you are. I have spent the last 16 years trying to undo the damage that the lookism philosophy has wreaked, both in my own life and in the lives of others. As I was formulating my thoughts and material for this book, I reviewed several hundred scenes, those that I have personally experienced or witnessed and those that have been described to me by clients or their loved ones, in the hope that I might make sense out of what seems senseless. As a therapist specializing in disordered eating, that is my job. I use the term "disordered eating" because my clients range from the housewife who is desperate, but unable, to lose that last five pounds, to the nine-year-old child who cries about being too fat at 80 pounds, from the 300-pound woman who can't bear to give up her food, to those clients with the clinically diagnosable eating disorders—anorexia nervosa, bulimia nervosa, and binge eating. All of these people have developed "disordered eating," which derives from a disordered sense of self.

Take 16-year-old Sara. Her mother, Beth, called my office over the weekend to tell me Sara had gotten her period back. Beth was elated, because this was a sign that Sara was getting better. But she could not understand why Sara was nervous, anxious, and worried. We talked about it. I explained that Sara needed lots of reassurance, because menstruating is a sign that she is becoming "normal," not so unique, and an indication that she may be closer to the proper weight now, not the 80 pounds she was—and still wants to be. I told Beth that Sara needs to see how unique and special she is without having to starve herself and that it is important to understand how scary this is for her. I explained the need to be careful when expressing excitement about her menstruating. What she needs is for everyone to understand how ambivalent she feels and how scary this is. When I spoke to Sara, I let her know, as I have before, that I do understand. She believes me because she knows I have been there myself. I lost my period for seven years, and that was just one of the things I lost as an anorexic.

And there is little eight-year-old Aron and her mother, Toni, who brought Aron to see me because "she is overweight and yet compulsively eats." Toni makes Aron "diet" lunches for school, but Aron gives them away and trades her belongings for nondiet food. Today, when I asked Aron how she knew she was hungry, she said, "Whenever I see food or think about it." When I asked her how she knew she was full, she told me, "Whenever all the food is gone." When I asked her why she was coming to see me, she said, "Because I am fat. My mom says that when I grow up people will be mean to me and boys won't like me. She said I had to come because I have a problem and you are a talking doctor who can help."

I worry about my upcoming session with 22-year-old Anna and her parents who think she doesn't really have a problem. I can imagine Anna's long, brown hair that looks dull and lifeless and lately has been falling out. I can picture the scene she described to me today. She is driving her car rushed and hurried, music blasting. She pulls up to the familiar fast-food drive-through and, in a monotone voice, orders, "Six hamburgers, six fries and uh, what did they want, oh yeah, three Cokes, two root beers, and one vanilla malt." She can hardly wait. She has the money ready, and when it's her turn, she pulls up, quickly pays, requests ketchup, saying she "got in trouble for forgetting it last time," and drives away. Almost instantly, when out on the road, she starts unwrapping the food and eating it all at the same time. Food spills out on the car seat, but she doesn't seem to notice, and then she eats the food off the seat. Three hamburgers go down almost together. The fries are all over the place, but they quickly vanish as she obsessively stuffs them into her mouth. The other hamburgers go a bit more slowly. As the remaining fries are finished, she opens the malt and takes a long, slow, satisfying drink. She is finally becoming more relaxed. The last of the food is gone. Wrappers are everywhere and five drinks sit; there never was any intention of disturbing them. They were just protection, a shield or decoy, to make it look as though six people had ordered lunch. The "mission" is not over. She drives now in search of a gas station. She spots one, pulls in over to the side. Casually she gathers up all the wrappers and the unopened drinks and puts them all back in the bag. Bag in hand she walks to the bathroom, locks the door, dumps the trash, enters the stall, fingers go down her throat and she throws up her food. A sigh of relief, a glance in the mirror, she is ready to do it again. And her parents think she is fine and just seeking attention.

Our dieting daughters need help and their parents and loved ones need as much help as they do. Having been through an eating disorder myself has been a major advantage in treating young girls and women who are dieting and/or engaged in disordered eating. I understand these dilemmas in more than an intellectual way. Instinctually, I often know what will and will not work, what to say and what not to say. Over the years I have learned that I have something to offer in helping others who want to empathize, understand, and help those suffering from disordered eating. Helping the significant others became a passion that fueled this book. It is written in the hope that I can provide others with the insight that I have acquired from my own experience, from what my clients, their families, and loved ones have taught me, and from my success and failures as a therapist specializing in disordered eating over the last 16 years.

This book is about what you, the reader, can do to understand and to help right what has gone terribly wrong, not just with your daughter or in your own home, but in the lives of all our daughters and their daughters to come. But first, and always, we must begin with ourselves. Therefore, before I begin the book I want to share with you a brief look into my past and my own struggle as a dieting daughter, who was dying to be thin.

ALL THE WAY DOWN—AND BACK AGAIN

Sitting in biology class, 10:10 A.M., almost time for nutrition. I couldn't stop thinking about those big chocolate chip cookies that you could smell baking in the school cafeteria. As usual, Nancy and I were "on diets," and as usual, I knew she would meet me at the snack line to see if we were going to let each other "off the hook." As usual, we did, and giggling we each got a cookie and some breakfast rolls to share. After all, why should we be miserable and deprive ourselves. I and all my friends tried one diet after another, but our favorite was ice cream sundaes after school or burritos during lunch. There were too many other problems to deal with, let alone trying "not to eat." It wasn't that any of us were obese or anything but we could have shed a few pounds to our advantage. At five feet, four inches, and 135 pounds, I was "getting up there," but no one else seemed to care as much as I did. My friend Nancy felt about the same. We were just becoming "sensitive" about life, learning about Kahlil Gibran, J. D. Salinger, evil people like Hitler, and love. I guess we were both pretty disillusioned about the mess of humanity. It was the time of our life when losing a boyfriend was the most miserable experience imaginable, and for our birthdays that year, which were only a few days apart, we bought a big two-layer chocolate cake and ate it all ourselves, teary eyed, but together.

I always knew there was something better out there for me. I knew I had a certain strength and willpower that would really show up somewhere. I was the girl who read her chemistry book with a flashlight on the school bus headed to and from the basketball game. I was the only teenager who preferred her mother to drive her certain places so she could read or study in the car. I had to be the "best." I was never a quitter. I always had to win. My brother refused to play chess with me because it took me so long to make my move. He said I took the game too seriously and that I should be willing to "lose to learn" or to "risk a few pieces in order for long-range advantage." He never understood that I couldn't lose, it didn't seem like an option to me. And he never grasped that to lose a pawn, even for the chance to get his queen, was traumatic because I couldn't count on the future, only on the moment, and each piece seemed so important.

This was the time in my life when I was beginning to realize, as most female adolescents do, that beauty would get you everywhere, and that, for some reason, I really needed to prove something. I felt tough and strong and smart on the inside and showed it, but plain, even ugly, and unnoticed, on the outside. I excelled academically, got into student government and drama, even became the school mascot, but none of that was enough.

I decided I was finally going to do it, I would be the one, among all my friends, who would lose weight. And so diet I did. I was proud of myself, my mother was proud of me. My friends asked, "How did you do it, what diet did you go on?" They said admiringly, "You look so good." These comments helped me continue and then something just snapped. It seemed easy. I felt determined. I had a goal to work toward, a tangible reward, a constant task to occupy me. In those adolescent days with few goals, confused values, and feelings of no purpose, dieting gave me a curious strength. I would always tell myself, "You don't need this tortilla chip or that cookie, or a bite of her candy bar." I reasoned, "These things will always be around, you can have them later if you want." Later took a long time to come.

My friends tried to get me to eat or break my diet: "Come on it's my birthday" or "Just this once for me." But if you had a lot of friends, this meant all the time. If one were going to be tough and strong and true, the rule had to be *never* break the rules. I almost lost some friends over it. In the beginning I think they were mostly jealous of my willpower, but eventually they were frightened and saddened by it.

I didn't see *it* coming. They didn't see *it* coming. Nobody saw *it* coming. At that time, only a handful even knew what *it* was. And so I left for college, at around 115 pounds, I was 20 pounds lighter and 20 times more screwed up than I or anyone knew.

When I was introduced to Debbie, my assigned college roommate, my first thought was that she was thinner than me. She was nice and I decided I even liked her, but I would have liked her more if she were fatter. We were truly an odd couple. She was, by religion and since childhood, a vegetarian, almost unheard of back then. Debbie's vegetarianism made dieting easier for me. Although I didn't convert to vegetarianism immediately, our eating habits were quite peculiar, quite different, and yet very compatible. She didn't want a refrigerator in the room, and neither did I. We both watched our budgets, as well as our diets. In the dining hall, we'd both take salad and veggies and then she'd go for the potatoes and bread and beans—all the things I "couldn't eat." That's how it was, I couldn't. By this time, there was a self-defined mandate imprinted on my brain of "allowables," "watchouts," "rarelys," and "strictly forbidden" foods. But it didn't seem odd to me. In fact, I felt righteous about it. Debbie, having dealt all her life with comments, criticisms, and nagging about her "diet," was very conscientious and respectful about not bugging me about my eating habits. We got along great.

Soon my thoughts, day and night, became obsessed with weight and food and controlling them both. At first, Debbie didn't know of the inner torture I was going through, but slowly she began to understand.

"I'm so damn fat," I said, standing on the bed in the dorm room looking into our mirror. "I'm not going, Look at my legs. I can't believe this," and I started to cry.

"You are out of your mind. You're nuts," said Debbie, "Look at you. You're so damn skinny."

"These pants make me look fat. Look at this, no really come here. Look at this, don't you see, right here on my legs?"

"You are really full of it. Let's go. Wear something else then."

"I just got these."

"Well wear them then, they look good"

"I can't, damn it. I'm sorry, Debbie, just go, go ahead, leave me alone." I wept hysterically on the bed. How could I be fat? I weighed 90 pounds now. I was proud of that. How come I looked so fat?

The next morning I went upstairs, first thing, to borrow someone's scale. It registered 89 pounds, and I felt relieved. I had a better day that day.

I skipped breakfast, as I did most every morning, feeling guilty because it had been paid for in my room and board fees. I just couldn't fit the calories into my regimen. First of all, it was the easiest meal to skip entirely, lunch and dinner being too sociable, almost necessary for interaction and contact.

"I'm worried about you," people kept saying. I loved the comments. It all proved I was thin. I couldn't really see it myself. I can't remember ever really looking too thin—even at 79 pounds, with repeated warnings from my friends and my doctor, cessation of menstruation, and wearing size 1 pants.

Emotionally, I don't ever remember feeling thin enough to let go and eat a meal or even a piece of cake. I always "watched it." I was always on guard, constantly reprimanding myself for slight mishaps or an overextension of my allotted calorie intake. I once even tried to throw up after eating some **forbidden food**. Lucky for me, I couldn't do it.

It didn't matter to me that I couldn't take a bath because I was so bony it hurt to sit in the tub. It didn't bother me that when I slept on my side I had to put a pillow between my knees because the bones had no padding and hurt without it. It didn't make much difference that I was so cold all the time to the point of turning blue and that my hair was falling out. I was thin, and being thin seemed more important than anything else. Now I know it was much more than that.

I was very emotional that year. Someone could walk into my room and ask me how I was and I'd start to cry. I would go for a walk and cry watching the leaves fall from the trees. I called my mother constantly and cried. My mom took me to our family doctor. He told me that my weight was too low but all my blood tests were normal. He told me that even though he couldn't say there was anything wrong with me now eventually problems would show up and I would pay for it later. I gloated about the "nothing was wrong now" part and ignored the "pay for it later" part—and no one knew what to do.

My mother became increasingly worried. I guess everyone was, but me. I thought they were all exaggerating. So what if I sometimes became depressed and tearful, it had nothing to do with my weight. As far as that was concerned, I actually felt fine. I jogged and exercised every day. I did 205 sit-ups every night. The extra five were in case I did a few sloppy ones along the way. Looking back to that time and at my clients now, I am amazed at the power of mind over matter and at what the human body can endure.

On visits home, I took comments like, "What do they feed you at school?" as compliments. I prided myself on eating less than anyone around me. I never wanted to be second best in anything, especially dieting. I was proving that losing weight was something I was good at, best at, admired for. People often asked me, "How did you do it?" or commented, "I'd like to follow you around and eat what you eat for a while." If they only knew. What they didn't see was my obsession with food. While everyone thought

I was doing "without food" and had conquered our society's obsession with food, I was one of the worst offenders.

The truth was that I would wake up in the morning and worry about how I was going to avoid breakfast. I thought about what the dining hall was serving. I checked the menu every week and memorized it. I couldn't stand it when other people passed up food. I'd think, "What a waste, I'd eat if I could." I never thought I could. I felt so obsessed by food that I knew I could never let up on my control over my eating because I would never be able to stop. I would end up obese and disgusting.

At lunch I'd join everyone with my green salad sprinkled with vinegar and maybe half an apple or a little cottage cheese, if I felt a little daring. Then I had to fill my afternoon studying, if not in class, so that I could make it to 5:00 P.M., preferably 5:30, when I had to face dinner. After that, it was easier, with no more routine meals to be dealt with. I was fairly safe until morning, when it started over again. Beginning that year and for seven years after, I did not eat spaghetti, hamburgers, a sandwich, a piece of toast, pancakes, French toast, pizza, bacon, enchiladas, apple pie, lasagna, a chocolate bar, or a soft drink containing sugar. These were poison. There was no reason on earth to eat them. But, if I could have eaten them without the calories, I wouldn't have hesitated about eating every single one.

I was addicted to chewing gum (at times, exceeding more than 12 packs a day), sugarless only. I also, for some reason, always allowed some ice cream. I figured there was no substitute for it (frozen yogurt wasn't around yet) and so it was carefully incorporated into my daily diet. Since I only allowed minimal calories each day, around 600 (over 1,000 was taboo), ice cream sometimes took up a great portion. Therefore, on many occasions, aside from my usual salad, I would choose ice cream over the meat or fish or cheese or whatever else might have been infinitely better for me. I wanted that ice cream. It always seemed worth it. It was my treat or reward for being "so good."

I dreaded school parties or picnics. I dreaded visits from friends back home. I dreaded dealing with food when I went home. I dreaded going out to dinner. I dreaded birthday parties and holidays, all because I had to psyche myself up for "not eating" and for dealing with others who might pressure me to eat. They were all potential situations for my demise or a breakdown; that is, eating too much.

I had an inner voice. It was as if a little man were living inside my head. He plotted out the day's food allowance, he automatically calculated calories of any food that was before me or that was going into my mouth.

He always told me I didn't need this or that food item, and if I ignored him, he punished me with guilt and stomachaches and tears and made me eat even less food for a while and do more exercise.

He made me put my bike on the highest gear so I had to strive hard for what could have been an easy ride. He made me swim laps whenever I got in a swimming pool; to merely play in the pool was to be lazy. He made me keep running until I reached the freeway or the lake or the dorm or whatever landmark he decided would be difficult enough for me. He made me say No, when I wanted to say Yes, study when I wanted to play, starve myself almost to death when all I really wanted was to eat, to live, and to be happy.

It took seven years, but I recovered. I am recovered from the desire to be thin at any cost, from the need to be perfect, and from the illusion that what I look like is more important than who I am. Recovery takes time; it is a process. There was never a point when I said, "Now I am recovered." It is more a sense of looking back and realizing that something very terrible is now gone and something more true to my real self has taken its place. It would be false and misleading to say that as a female in this society I do not have my share of body-image issues, wanting to wear size 5, wishing that 41 didn't mean wrinkles, and even feeling fat sometimes. And, often I order my salad dressing on the side, and drink my cappuccinos nonfat. I even exercise. But I also eat Häagen-Dazs in my bubble bath at night, share bags of M&Ms with my Labrador, Gonner, and I drink, instead of pass up, a glass of champagne. And if the dressing happens to come on the salad … oh well, no big deal. I will no longer sacrifice. I will no longer betray myself or my body in the pursuit of some cultural standard, or in the quest for acceptance or praise for my external qualities. I have found a balance. I have made peace with food, and with myself. It is with our society that I do my battling now. This book is written in the hope that you can help your daughter do the same.

Your Dieting Daughter

♪ ♪ ♪

1

ello ello ello

"My Daughter
Wants/Needs to Diet"

Approximately one third of the U. S. adult population is overweight. [1]

*Fifty percent of females between the ages of 11 and 13 see themselves
as overweight, and by the age of 13, 80% have attempted to lose
weight, with 10% reporting the use of self-induced vomiting.* [2]

*Anorexia nervosa and bulimia nervosa are two of the most life
threatening of all psychiatric illnesses. At least 5%–20% of all
anorexic people will eventually die from the disorder.*[3]

If your daughter wants to diet or if you think she has a problem with her
weight or eating, when and how to intervene is a difficult and tricky dilemma. Consider the various scenarios:

1. What do you do when your normal weight, underweight, or over-
    weight teenage daughter is sitting at the dinner table pushing her
    food around on the plate, picking at it, and not eating much of
    anything?
2. How should you react when you find empty boxes of laxatives,
    diet pills, and numerous candy wrappers stashed in your daughter's
    room?

3. What kind of limits should you impose on your skeletal looking daughter regarding visits to the gym or participation on the track team upon discovering that she is no longer menstruating?
4. What do you say to your daughter when she comes home from school crying because the other kids are making fun of her for being fat?

The following are possible responses to scenario number 4. Which response would you choose?

(a) Reassure her that she is not fat and tell her to ignore the other kids.
(b) Tell her that you will help her go on a diet to lose weight.
(c) Tell her that people come in all shapes and sizes, but it's what's on the inside that counts.
(d) Get her professional help, for example, from a dietitian or eating disorder therapist.

Some of these responses are better than others, but none of them is a sure bet to resolving the problem. You may have thought of other responses not listed here, but the response you select should vary depending on many circumstances, including your daughter's current weight.

For the sake of continuing with our example, assume that your daughter is overweight. You have been trying not to make a big issue out of her weight, but when she comes home crying because the other kids are teasing her for being fat, you can't just sit back and do nothing. You want to respond but you're not sure how. Let's explore the responses listed above in detail.

(a) Reassure her that she is not fat and tell her to ignore the other kids. The first problem with this response is that your daughter will not trust you if you tell her she is not fat and she knows she is. Of course, it all depends on what or whose criteria are used. In any case, you don't want your daughter to think you will lie to her just to make her feel better. It won't work. Second, to tell her to ignore the other kids is to tell her to ignore the world around her. At this age, her peers are her world and what they think of her will mean more than what you think.

(b) Tell her that you will help her go on a diet to lose weight. The idea of helping your daughter lose weight may be a good one, but it is full of dangerous implications. Don't suggest dieting to your daughter without eliciting as much information from her as you can. Make sure that dieting

is what she wants to do and that it is appropriate for her. Offering to help your daughter diet may include you in the category of people who she thinks find her unacceptable the way she is. Furthermore, she may feel uncomfortable with, or even threatened by, your doing the helping. If you become overinvolved, she may hide things from you or stop telling you the truth. You will be in an awkward situation if your daughter doesn't follow your advice or lies to you about what she is eating. If you become overinvested in your daughter's weight loss, it sets her up to "do it for you," or not do it and be against you.

Do not offer to go on a diet with your daughter. In some cases, the team approach may work, but dieting with your daughter is fraught with minefields. Your daughter may experience your involvement as intrusive. Your participation in what she does with her body may take away from her need to separate and individuate from you, which is a crucial element of development. Problems with separation and individuation are often uncovered in individuals with eating disorders. A common mistake is to think that dieting together won't be a problem because, "My daughter and I are very close, we're like best friends." Even if you and your daughter have a good relationship, even if your daughter agrees to let you help her, it is best to let her do it, as much as possible, on her own, or to find help from someone other than you.

If your daughter is overweight, it is unwise to have her on an eating plan that is entirely different from that of the rest of the family. The message given may begin a process of negativity, such as, "I'm unworthy or not good enough." The best idea is for all family members to try to maintain a healthy, active lifestyle. Overall, the idea is to focus on health, not weight or numbers on the scale.

(c) Tell her that people come in all shapes and sizes, but it's what's on the inside that counts. Reassuring responses, such as, "It's what's on the inside that counts," can be useful but probably won't solve the problem. Your daughter will try to take in what you say, but again, what you think matters less than what her peers think. Although reassuring messages should be repeated over and over for young girls, such sentiments probably won't be enough and other action will be necessary. Make sure to ask your daughter how she feels and what she would like to do.

(d) Get her professional help, for example, a dietitian or eating disorder therapist. Professional help may be a good solution, and people often wait too long to explore this option. If you choose this route, there are certain precautions you should take. Your daughter may take this action as

a sign that you find her unacceptable, or, worse, crazy. How you present the idea of getting professional help is very important and will affect your daughter's feelings about it and willingness to follow through. Tell her you want to find someone who can help her achieve her goals in a healthy way. The professional should be a specialist in the field of eating disorders or weight control. If you choose a dietitian, make sure he or she has training in counseling skills. The professional should consult with your daughter, and in this case, since she is only 16, with you and possibly the entire family. An eating disorder specialist will know if your daughter does or does not have an eating disorder and will be able to devise a treatment plan to help. If there is no evidence of an eating disorder, a professional will also know how to help you and your daughter prevent her issues with food and weight from developing into one.

After exploring the various responses, it is clear that the problem of dealing with a daughter who wants to diet, or is already dieting, is fraught with complications and implications that can seem overwhelming. Deciding how to respond to your daughter's weight problem, whether or not she asks for your help, involves addressing your own thoughts, beliefs, and behaviors. Parental attitudes and expectations are critical in influencing young girls who want to diet. In the past few years, parents have increasingly been bringing their elementary-school-age daughters to my clinic for "diet consultations" and/or eating disorder treatment. Sad as it is, legitimate cases of the primary eating disorders, anorexia nervosa and bulimia nervosa, are occurring in younger and younger children.

Another trend is just as alarming: children being brought in for therapy because their parents consider them overweight. Some of these children are overweight by medical standards and do need help with eating habits. However, in all too many cases, the child is not substantially overweight and the parent's concern is unfounded or exaggerated and must be addressed. Parents, especially if one of them is overweight, are doing what they think best by trying to prevent their daughter from suffering the health problems or size discrimination that they have been encountering in their own lives. Keep in mind that you may unwittingly become the first source of discrimination against your daughter if you give her the message that, because of her body size, she is unacceptable.

A father may influence his daughter's opinion about her body and her decision to diet in several ways. A daughter who hears her father make comments about female bodies, even if not directly about hers, learns what is attractive and acceptable. Fathers who are runners or exercise enthusiasts often promote the "no pain, no gain" slogan familiar to athletes and praise their daughters for this kind of thinking and behaving. I increasingly see young girls who, seeking praise from their fathers, are driven into compulsive exercise. Willow, an anorexic girl I was treating, told me that she began running after her father commented that running would keep her from getting fat. As Willow said, "He would come home after long runs, get on the scale and brag about how much weight he lost, and point out that I could do the same." Willow's father, and many others like him, selectively reward their daughters for such traits as running through the pain, working out through exhaustion, and playing only to win. Fathers may be experienced and wise enough to keep this kind of philosophy under control, but their daughters may not be.

A mother influences her daughter's decision to lose weight by displaying her own issues with food, weight, and dieting. A mother who makes negative or critical comments about her own body sets a poor example for her daughter. In trying to protect her daughter from becoming overweight or from being discriminated against, a mother may give an unclear message, making her daughter feel unacceptable the way she is, and thus doing more harm than good. Furthermore, mothers often complicate things by not allowing their daughters to have weight or body image problems on their own. Mothers often want to join their daughters in dieting or to assume their daughter's pain. As one mother wrote to me, "If it is Casey's destiny to be fat, then why am I so scared?"

Parents are automatically involved in their daughter's dieting behaviors for practical reasons. For the most part, it is the parents who will have to supply and cook the proper food, help select and pay for any type of weight loss center or gym membership, find and pay for a dietitian or therapist, and provide emotional support. Parents must also be aware of dieting's dangers. They must be willing to intervene, and capable of doing so, when the dieting has gone too far or the methods used are too extreme. All of this is a formidable task.

Don't despair. This book was created to help you understand and explore the various complexities of the dieting issue and to prepare you to deal with your daughter and our "thin is in" society. Reading this book will help you acknowledge how important it is that you are clear and comfortable with your own relationship to your body, eating, and weight. The best thing you can do for your daughter is to take good care of yourself. "Do as I say, not as I do" will not work. Last, this book is meant to prepare you for a battle against the cultural pressure to be thin at all costs, and to combat the forces, cultural and otherwise, that will be pushing your daughter in that direction.

2

≈ ≈ ≈

Thin Is In

Of the fifty years of Life *covers, though many showed women, only 19 of those were not actresses or models; that is, not there because of their beauty.*

Naomi Wolf [4]

Certain themes, such as concern with weight, fear of rejection and the need for perfection, seem rooted in cultural expectations for women rather than in the "pathology" of each individual girl. Girls struggle with mixed messages: Be beautiful, but beauty is only skin deep. Be sexy, but not sexual. Be honest, but don't hurt anyone's feelings. Be independent, but be nice. Be smart, but not so smart you threaten boys.

Mary Pipher, *Reviving Ophelia* [5]

You can never be too rich or too thin.

Duchess of Windsor

Losing weight may be a reasonable goal for your daughter, but the pursuit of thinness has become an epidemic that is ruining and, in some cases, ending young girls' lives. What you are up against, as a parent, is that our culture and way of life, our lack of knowledge and understanding, all contribute to perpetuating thinness mania. We have a "thin is in" society, where young people, particularly females, are exhibiting the logical extreme of the idea that what you weigh means more than who you are and being stick thin is a measure of success, beauty, and happiness.

Young girls, pick up the message from their parents, the media, and role models that to be thin is not only desirable, it is required. This message lays the groundwork for young girls to pursue dieting as a necessary part of being female.

The "thin is in," society has been a long time in the making; it is not just the simple result of current media messages or faulty parenting. However, there are things we can do, as a society and as parents, to help remedy the situation. We must help our daughters to not fall prey to dieting obsession and oppression. We must help those who can sincerely benefit from weight loss to accomplish it in a healthy way. We must strive to prevent the inevitable occurrences of eating disorders in a society where undue influence is placed on body weight and shape .

You and your daughter are bombarded daily by advertisements for taking weight off and keeping it off. It is a national obsession. From our magazines, our billboards, and our television and film images, we get the message that women's bodies are not their own, but society's, and that to be female one must strive to be beautiful, and being beautiful means being thin. We are wiring our jaws, stapling our stomachs, having the fat sucked out of us, getting tummy tucks, taking urine injections, drinking liquid protein, downing diet pills and fat blockers, and buying every new diet book that hits the shelves, the latest of which has us "entering the zone." One of the most amazing things about all this is that, as far as weight loss goes, what we are doing is not working! Statistics on child and adolescent obesity reveal that 27% of children and 21% of teens are obese, an increase of 54% in the last 20 years. Furthermore, 50 to 70% of obese youngsters will be obese adults. Even worse, 95 to 98% of those who lose weight gain it back! [6] Think about the impression this is making on your daughter who is learning to be female, trying to fit in and figuring out how to be accepted in this world.

If your daughter feels fat, but is not, she is not alone in her distorted and disturbed view. An alarming revelation was brought to light back in 1984 when *Glamour* magazine[7] conducted a survey of 33,000 women in which 75% of those between 18 and 35 said they were overweight. In actuality, only 25% were overweight according to standardized height and weight charts. Furthermore, 45% of the underweight women thought they were too fat. These same *Glamour* respondents chose losing ten to fifteen pounds above success in work or in love as their most desired goal. In the November 1987 issue of *New Body Magazine*,[8] another study reported that 95% of all women ranged from disgusted to disappointed with their bodies. Twenty-nine percent said they would rather be bald than fat, and 25% said they would give up their job, money, even a man, to lose weight.

The thinness trend has not slowed down in the 1990s. In fact, the ideal image portrayed for women is getting even further away from the norm or from reality. While 25 years ago models weighed 8 percent less than the average woman in North America (at five feet, three inches tall, 144 pounds), today's models are 23 percent below that weight and young girls want to be like them.[9] One modeling agency revealed that in its quest for models, of the 40,000 pictures submitted, only four met the agency's criteria.

WHAT GIRLS SAY THEY WANT:

No flaws
Perfect shapes
Straight up and down
No curves
Large breasts
No fat
Five feet ten inches tall, 115 pounds
Size 4, or, at most, size 6
Drop dead gorgeous

Modeling agencies were then asked what they look for in a model.

WHAT MODELING AGENCIES WANT:

Five feet eight inches tall, to six feet
34B bust, 24-inch waist, 34-inch hips
Maybe 35–25–35
36 inches is too big
Long neck
Shorter waist
Long legs
Perfect body

Nina Blanchard Modeling Agency Revealed:

Although males are increasingly included, the message to be thin is directed mainly toward females. From the time of infancy, girls get attention and mirroring responses for how they look, for being pretty and cute, far more often than for tasks they perform. Responses to girls are different from those to boys. "Oh, just look how pretty you are in your little pink party dress," or "What cute little pigtails you have," are the types of comments almost automatically elicited from adults in reaction to little girls. Boys more readily receive praise and mirroring for their performance: "What a great tower you've built," or "Hey, everyone, look how far Jason can throw the ball." Through selective mirroring or responding, young females learn that it is for their appearance that they can most easily get attention, praise, and approval.

Young females turn into adolescent girls who read teen magazines. Teen magazines are filled with advertisements, such as the Gap ad that features a very skinny female model and the statement, "Just the Right Shape." Is the Gap suggesting that any other figure is the wrong shape? Another ad, for a weight-loss product, shows a slim girl in a bikini with the tag line, "Get the Body That Gets the Guys." Even the naming of such items as the women's cigarette "Virginia Slims" contributes to the indoctrination.

It is not only advertisements, but articles as well, that are directed at increasingly younger females. One teen magazine ran an article with this copy: "Instant Swimsuit Makeovers … for bulges, jiggles, droops and sags." The article continued, "For everyone who hesitates before going public in a swimsuit (is there anyone who doesn't?) wishing a stomach didn't stick out so much or a rear end weren't quite so rounded or thighs quite so jiggly…" This article would make any young girl begin to scrutinize her body if she weren't already doing so before reading it.

It has not always been this way but rather has happened gradually with the growth of our industrialized society. Our culture manufactures both the products and the need for those products; advertisers manipulate the trends. Our image of beauty has changed from the more sensuous and curvy Marilyn Monroe to the sticklike Twiggy, who came along in the 1960s. Consider that our Miss Americas, Playboy playmates, ballerinas, fashion models, and movie stars have steadily been decreasing in weight since the 1960s and that Americans are spending $33 billion [10] a year to take weight off and keep up (or should I say, down) with them. In 1961, the

Playboy playmate of the year weighed 137 pounds and was approximately five feet, eight inches tall. The February 1990 playmate was five feet, seven inches tall and weighed 105 pounds! Similar trends are true for Miss America and other beauty contestants. Our female role models have changed from Marilyn Monroe to Kate Moss. Even worse, many of our celebrities themselves admit to suffering from eating disorders. Singer Karen Carpenter died of heart failure caused by her battle with anorexia nervosa. Actress Jane Fonda, now a leader in aerobic fitness, admits to having been bulimic for 15 years. Actress Tracy Gold had to leave her role on "Growing Pains" and was hospitalized for anorexia nervosa. And singer Paula Abdul underwent treatment for bulimia nervosa. Princess Di has admitted to suffering from both anorexia and bulimia. Oprah Winfrey and Dolly Parton dieted in front of millions, inspiring viewers to do the same, and the list goes on and on.

One seldom sees instant makeovers for males. Males, however, are not excluded entirely from society's pressure to look a certain way, and they are increasingly being subjected to a cultural preference for leanness. And, although such cases are rare, men (e.g., Elton John) have admitted to suffering from anorexia or bulimia. The few studies on the incidence of males with eating disorders indicate that somewhere between 1 and 5% of eating disorder cases are male. Because of the nature of this book, the information on males with eating disorders is cursory; refer to Appendix C, "Resources," and, in particular, the book *Males With Eating Disorders*, edited by Arnold Anderson, for more information on this topic.

Media attention and reported cases of males with eating disorders have been increasing. One reason for the lower incidence of eating-disordered males is that males are typically rewarded for what they do more than for how they look. And as far as looks go, the ideal standard for a male can be pursued and achieved healthfully. *Being big* is not a big problem for a man. Fat men are discriminated against far less than are fat women. Leanness may be increasingly stressed as the cultural preference for a male physique, but the main message for males with regard to body image is to have muscles and be strong, which is helped naturally through their genetics and their inherent supply of testosterone. Furthermore (except for the elite body builders, who are only held up as the ideal male image for a very small percentage of the population), males can improve their bodies to approximate the ideal standard by minimal workouts in a gym or by participating in sports, while at the same time eating a healthy and abundant diet.

If you are a female and reading this, you have felt the pressure to be thin, even if you haven't, by some miracle, been sucked in by it. Imagine your daughter's being constantly bombarded, overtly or covertly, by the idea that she must be thin to be attractive, or even worthy. All of this helps to explain why studies have shown that 70 to 80% of fourth graders report being on diets[11] and why females account for approximately 97% of eating disorders.[12] Is it a wonder that today's little girls are picking up on their mother's, big sister's, or some popular celebrity's fears, obsessions, and behaviors regarding food, body, and weight? We cannot begin to address these issues too early.

What is your daughter telling herself? What are the messages she has adopted and internalized? What is going on inside the mind of any young girl dieting to the point of losing, not just weight, but everything she wanted to attain? The next chapter takes a look at the doctrine or rules that have been adopted by young girls today, in their pursuit of thinness.

3

❧ ❧ ❧

The Thin Commandments

Many girls lose contact with their true selves, and when they do, they become extraordinarily vulnerable to a culture that is all too happy to use them for its purposes.... Girls who operate from a false self often reduce the world to a more manageable place by distorting reality. Some girls join cults in which others do their thinking for them. Some girls become anorexic and reduce all the complexity in life to just one issue—weight.

Mary Pipher, *Reviving Ophelia*[13]

To understand the dedication to thinness beyond reason, it is important to understand not only the culture that promotes it, but also the mind-set of a young girl dieting. Even with an understanding of the information presented thus far, it may be hard to comprehend how your daughter can relentlessly pursue something that is so unhealthy, is not working, or is taking up her entire life, not to mention disrupting the family. Who or what is causing her to do these things? Where did she come up with some of these behaviors? Why would she persist beyond the point of reason?

One of the things that go on inside a young dieter's mind is the formulation of and adherence to self-imposed rules. For example, one young girl may demand of herself that she never eat more than 600 calories a day.

Another girl may use the rule that, "eating fat will make you fat, so it must be avoided at all costs." Still another may believe that she is not allowed to eat unless she exercises and so she requires this of herself. With the help of my patients, I formulated a master list of "The Thin Commandments," which encompasses the thousands of variations on the messages, rules, and guidelines that I have witnessed young girls living (perhaps, dying) by. I use this list to explore and expose my patients' rules to themselves, since most of them are unaware that they even have them. It is important to show a young girl how she has adopted certain ideas that may or may not be based on fact, and imposed them on herself. After going over "The Thin Commandments" with a patient, I ask her what rules she might be living by. As a parent, you may have already noticed certain rules that your daughter has adopted for herself that shape some of her behaviors, particularly those related to food and weight. You may want to share both your observations and "The Thin Commandments" with your daughter to help both of you understand better the dieting mentality and each other.

THE THIN COMMANDMENTS

1. If you aren't thin, you aren't attractive.
2. Being thin is more important than being healthy—more important than anything.
3. You must buy clothes, cut your hair, take laxatives, starve yourself, do anything to make yourself be, or at least look, thinner.
4. You shall earn all food and you shall not eat without feeling guilty.
5. You shall not eat fattening food without punishing yourself afterwards.
6. You shall count calories and fat and restrict intake accordingly.
7. What the scale says is the most important thing.
8. Losing weight is good—gaining weight is bad.
9. You can never be too thin.
10. Being thin and not eating are signs of true willpower and success.

It is a complex combination of factors that leads from cultural pressures and self imposed rules to an eating disorder. Following "The Thin Commandments" for dieting may help your daughter lose weight, but it may come to a point at which she can't stop following the rules. In her mind, breaking the rules may mean gaining any lost weight back. It may mean losing control. As you read quotes from other parents' daughters, you will see how the behaviors themselves—following the rules—become the goal. If this is true for your daughter, then she may feel lost and afraid without these rules.

If you aren't thin, you aren't attractive.

"I get so much attention when I lose weight. People notice me who never noticed me before."

"I never got any attention from boys. My girlfriend was skinnier than I was and she got it all. I thought I had everything she did but I wasn't skinny. So I decided I'd lose weight. Now I'm afraid to stop."

Being thin is more important than being healthy—more important than anything.

"I throw up my food to lose weight. My gums have been bleeding, my face is always all puffy now. I know I might wear down the enamel on my teeth too, but I don't really care about all that as long as I'm thin."

"Everyone says I don't eat enough to be healthy, but I don't really care. I have stomach and chest pains sometimes and it scares, me but it scares me worse to get fat."

"I don't care how I lose weight, I may not be around after 30 years old anyway. Today I want to be thin, and that is all that matters to me."

You must buy clothes, cut your hair, take laxatives, starve yourself, do anything to make yourself be, or at least look, thinner.

"Even though after several months I haven't really lost weight, taking laxatives makes me look thinner. I actually weigh less the next day. I can feel my wrists and they're thinner. My rings slide off my fingers easier. It's like tricking myself, but at the time I feel relieved that I look thinner."

"Everything I do—cocaine, drinking, exercise—has to do with trying to lose weight."

"I try on at least six or seven outfits every morning, I have to have the one that makes me look thinnest. It can take me three hours to get ready in the morning because of this, but I can't stop. I can't leave the house until I'm satisfied that I look as thin as I possibly can."

You shall earn all food and you shall not eat without feeling guilty.

"I went on this diet that trained me to feel guilty if I ate. I convinced myself that I have to exercise if I want to eat. It's like I brainwashed myself and don't know how to reverse it."

"I feel so guilty if I eat. I never ever eat in front of people. I can't even stand for my family to watch me eat. I feel like I'm undisciplined or weak or something if I have to eat. It's as if I think I should be above and beyond that. The problem is, then I binge when I'm alone and I feel guilty about that, too."

"I have to earn every bite of food or I feel guilty. Mostly I have to earn it through exercise. I have to burn the most calories I can. Standing burns more than sitting, and moving more than standing. I always try to move. I shake my legs when sitting in class. I run in place, do exercises in bed, get hall passes to get out of class, and go run up and down the bleachers. I get up at night and do jumping jacks and go walking at 2 o'clock or 3 o'clock in the morning. If I don't do these things, I won't allow myself to eat."

You shall not eat fattening food without punishing yourself afterwards.

"Certain foods are bad. I feel so bad if I eat them. I don't allow myself to have them. If I do, I have to take laxatives or throw up because then it seems like I'm getting the food out. It helps me get rid of my anxiety about how much I ate. I always tell myself I can't eat anything else for at least 24 hours for being so bad."

"Throwing up is kind of like a punishment for breaking my rule. It's a pleasure to eat certain things and I don't think I deserve it, so I have to punish myself. I hate doing it. Some girls like it, but I hate it. I don't know what else to do. I feel like I can't stand myself if I don't."

"I make these diet promises in my diary with consequences that are always really bad, so bad that I won't dare break the promises. One time I wrote that if I ate anything before Saturday, my brother would die, another time I wrote that if I ate anything but frozen yogurt for a week, Mike would break up with me. I know it works too, because one time I wrote that if I ate anything for three days my pet hamster would die and I broke that promise and he died—so I know it works. I make promises all the time because it keeps me from eating."

You shall count calories and fat and restrict intake accordingly.

"I became a calorie computer. I knew the calories and fat grams in any food anyone could ever name. I always impressed people. My girlfriends would ask me calorie and fat questions all the time, and I liked it. After I got thin, they never asked. I didn't want to tell people anyway because I didn't want them dieting and competing with me."

"I couldn't even lick stamps because I didn't want the calories."

"I have to know the calories and fat of everything before I eat it. I look it up if I don't know and then add extra in case the book is off a little. I never feel comfortable eating anything over 100 calories or one gram of fat, it just seems like too much for me, maybe not for anyone else but for me."

"I only feel comfortable eating 300 calories a day. I don't eat any item of food that has more than two digit numbers and I never want to weigh more than two numbers. Three numbers sounds like too much."

"I know the calories of everything, and when I'm not sure, I won't eat it. I also wipe my fork off with a napkin after every bite so I get rid of a few calories. And I don't trust the dietitian because after I figured up the calories for the day she was off by 10! I can do it better than her."

What the scale says is the most important thing.

"I'm so afraid to get on the scale, but I do it every morning. If I'm down in weight, I feel relieved. I feel so good. If I'm the same weight, I feel O.K., but cautious. If I've gained any weight at all, I feel very depressed and anxious and I tell myself that I should not eat all day or very, very little, or I just blow it and binge, thinking, "What's the use?" I only feel real good when I've lost."

"I got on the scale a couple days ago and saw that I had gained 4 pounds I was so upset I just started drinking water and throwing up over and over until the scale showed that I lost that weight."

"I almost wish someone would secretly tamper with my scale. If it was changed and I thought I had lost weight, I'd feel okay. My whole day is ruined if I get on the scale and I'm heavier, I mean it, my whole day is ruined. Don't ever really trick me or anything though because I'd die if I found out later."

Losing weight is good—gaining weight is bad.

"Losing weight makes me feel safe, like I'm in control. It seems so hard to lose weight that you have to fight to keep it off, so you have to be really careful. Gaining weight makes me panic. I want to gain some weight because I know I need to. I even know I don't look good. I just want it to happen magically because I can't stand to do it."

"A pound today means another tomorrow, if I don't cut back. If I've gained a pound, it means I'm gaining, so I have to stop eating and then I start losing. I don't want to lose, but I can't stand it when I look at the scale and I've gained . Once I reach a certain weight, like 95 pounds or so, I can never go above that weight. I don't know why."

"It doesn't matter what I tell myself, I can never go above what my lowest weight was, so even though I know I said I would stop losing weight at 99 pounds, now that I went below that to 95, I can never go above 95. I just couldn't handle it. Gaining weight is my worst nightmare."

"Losing weight is the one thing I can do well, and I will not gain any back because I fought too hard for this."

You can never be too thin.

A patient of mine, Christy, who weighed 80 pounds, told me she didn't want to come to group.

Christy: I don't think I'll feel comfortable in the group.
Me: You won't want to share your feelings?
Christy: No, I think they'll all be wondering, "What is she doing here? She's not thin enough."

A 53-pound, 33-year-old woman told me, "I don't think I am too thin, but I do want to get better, be in better control. I want to be healthy, but I don't think I have to gain weight to do that; besides I'm not ready for that."

In my own struggle with anorexia, no amount of weight loss was ever enough. I remember thinking that when I weighed 110 pounds. I'd be so happy, that it would be great. Then after I reached 110, I thought I'd be O.K., when I weighed 105 pounds. I could eat whatever I wanted because I'd have some leeway to gain a few pounds. Once I got to 105, I was afraid that if I slacked off I'd just go right up again and wouldn't have that leeway anymore, and besides I could still see fat! I could always see fat on me and places that were too big. I would often think, "If I could just get this fat stomach to go away!" It wasn't till I weighed 79 pounds that I seriously got scared about my problem, but I still didn't want to gain weight.

Being thin and not eating are signs of true willpower and success.

"Because if I'm fat, I am a failure. No matter what else I do, If I don't lose weight, nothing will mean anything to me."

"I felt good and successful if I could make it through the day without eating or with eating very little. I think I needed something to be proud of and successful at and so controlling my weight became it. Other people used to ask me to teach them."

"Not eating is something I'm good at. Everyone always asks me how I have the willpower to do it, to not eat. It was impressive, but now I wish I had the willpower to eat. I try to tell myself that a challenge, a real test of my will, would be for me to eat. Then I think, I'm just trying to find an excuse to eat. It goes around and around like that, a vicious circle, and so far, not eating always wins."

"I always had to do my best, be successful at whatever I did or else I didn't want to do it. Dieting was the same way. I was so good at it."

"It's so hard to be somebody or to feel special, controlling my weight gave me the feeling of success. I could never give that up. If you expect me to give it up, you better have something much better to take its place and I can't imagine what that is. I know how to do this and I don't need anyone's help."

Listening to what young girls are saying, it is easy to see how the desire to lose weight and "Thin Commandment" thinking can take someone from dieting to disordered eating to a diagnosable condition needing professional help. In talking about losing weight, key phrases such as: "It makes me feel special," "I feel in control," "I feel safe," "I feel successful," and "I get attention," provide clues to the underlying issues involved.

4

꙰ ꙰ ꙰

Fit or Fanatic?

Alice never could quite make out, in thinking it over afterward, how it was that they began; all she remembers is that they were running hand in hand, and the Queen went so fast that it was all she could do to keep up with her; and still the Queen kept crying, "Faster! Faster!" but Alice felt she could not go faster, though she had no breath left to say so…

"Are we nearly there?" Alice managed to pant out at last.

"Nearly there?" the Queen repeated. "Why, we passed it ten minutes ago! Faster!" And they ran on for a time in silence, with the wind whistling in Alice's ears, and almost blowing her hair off her head, she fancied.

"Now! Now!" cried the Queen "Faster! Faster!" And they went so fast that at last they seemed to skim through the air, hardly touching the ground with their feet till, suddenly, just as Alice was getting quite exhausted, they stopped, and she found herself sitting on the ground, breathless and giddy.

The Queen propped her up against a tree, and said kindly, "You may rest a little now." Alice looked round her in great surprise. "Why, I do believe we've been under this tree the whole time! Everything's just as it was!"

"Of course it is," said the Queen. "What would you have it?"

Lewis Carroll, *Through the Looking Glass* [14]

Heather, an anorexic college student, was up to running at least 10 miles or more a day on a diet of lettuce and mushrooms. "I really don't feel like I need food," Heather told me, "I know it's crazy, but running is my food." Heather had previously been hospitalized and there were no funds available left for further inpatient treatment so I was struggling to manage this case on an outpatient basis, knowing her life was at risk. I, of course, kept trying to get her to stop running and she kept "trying." Meanwhile, her weight was plummeting. "I don't have a choice," she told me, "There is a voice in my head that says I must run faster and farther, even though I know it's not getting me anywhere I want to go." I read Heather the quote on the previous page taken from *Through The Looking Glass*, and we discussed how, inside her head, she had both Alice and the queen.

Luckily, before Heather died of cardiac arrest or before her parents had to sell their home to pay for another hospitalization, Heather tore her Achilles tendon and, even though she tried to keep running, she was forced to stop. This was the beginning of her recovery. Heather now thanks her injury for saving her life, but she knows that her journey to recovery is not over. She still has a part of herself that thinks like Alice's crazy queen.

The *Alice In Wonderland* mentality is all too common in girls today. Exercise, or working out, is too often approached with a nonsensical, oppressive, compulsive, and even dangerous attitude by the young women who undertake it, while being avoided altogether by those whose bodies could benefit from a more active lifestyle. For females, the fitness craze, with its gym memberships, health spas, and resorts, has more to do with the pursuit of thinness than with the pursuit of fitness. In *Compulsive Exercise and The Eating Disorders*, Alayne Yates discusses this issue and refers to the *Glamour* magazine[15] study of 33,000 women readers that revealed that 95% of the respondents exercised to control their weight, not to improve their health. Therefore, overweight women of all ages are made to feel, as the phrase implies, that "to work out" has nothing to do with play or fun, but is another form of oppression or torture imposed on them in order that they conform to the ideal standard of beauty. A new phrase, "exercise resistance," is now being used to describe the conscious or unconscious apathy or defiance that is emerging in response to pressure to "go for the burn." Parents need to help their daughters turn "working out" back into "having fun through physical activity." They need to put back into their lives, and their daughters' lives, dancing, walks in the park or around the block, trips to the beach, hikes on the weekend, and bike rides. Physical games, such as tennis or softball, can be fun as well. However, even games can be turned into another way to perform, or to be measured, as competitiveness and the desire to score ruin the whole idea of "play" or "fun." As a result, for many of those who do not excel at a particular activity, it may not be fun. For others, winning becomes the only goal instead of simply playing, being active, and having a good time. Our culture is good at promoting competitive sports and the desire to win, and it needs no help in pushing exercise for weight loss. But we have failed at framing fitness activities in a healthy, enjoyable way, one that will motivate young people to engage in and continue them for pleasure. The current poor physical fitness of our youth and adult population testifies to this. Instead of a means to some end, *exercise* and physical activity that add joy, fun, and fitness to our lives need to be our goals.

Another example of goal-oriented thinking and behavior gone awry is the current craze of body composition or body fat testing (See "A Note About Body Composition and the Scale" in this chapter). For example, a gym in my area conducts routine body fat testing for all members. It recently awarded a first place ribbon to 16-year-old Catie, an anorexic patient of mine, for having the lowest body fat of all female gym members. Catie had 9% body fat. Catie also had heart problems, she was not menstruating, and she had recently been discharged from an inpatient eating disorder program. Upon discharge from the hospital, Catie signed up at the gym, where no screening procedures take place. She was exercising against the advice of her doctor and yet she won a fitness award! The paradox here—an outrage and a sad commentary on our society as a whole—is not an isolated occurrence. I have several clients with similar stories. All of this increases resistance to treatment. As Catie's statement to me poignantly describes, "You say I'm not healthy, you say I'm at risk, yet I win the award in my gym for fitness. It's making me crazy. Who can I believe?"

Exercise is a good thing, but, as always, too much of a good thing becomes a bad thing. There are those who exercise for fun or because they just want to be healthy, but according to the clients in my practice, the number of women working out in destructive and obsessive ways is steadily increasing.

Every day I see pale, exhausted, calorie-and protein-starved women who feel they must exercise their skinny, frail bodies in order to "not be fat or get fat," or who boast of attending two, or even three, aerobics classes in one day, or running yet another 10 kilometers. Exercising, for many of them, has become merely a means to achieve a number on a scale, or some other external measurable goal. These girls are far from having the radiant glow of health.

Our cultural fixation on the ideal female figure and appearance, especially thinness, has infiltrated and damaged women's sports, so that elite female athletes are often judged by how they look as much as by how they perform. In this arena, we find the extreme of the "fit or fanatic" spectrum, but we mustn't forget that the extreme indicates the direction or goal towards which all are encouraged to aspire. Ballerinas, skaters, and gymnasts are the most obvious examples. Consider the following scenario. If you had a 16-year-old daughter who watched the 1992 Olympics, she saw female gymnasts whose average age was 16, whose average height was four feet, nine inches, and whose average weight was 83 pounds. In 1976, the year your 16-year-old daughter would have been born, the female gymnasts looked quite different—a year older—6½ inches taller, and 23 pounds heavier than those of today.[16]

In women's gymnastics and figure skating, we no longer expect to see women. We have come to expect little girls. And we expect these girls not only to be very talented, but in order to win, or even be in the running, they must also be very thin, very young, and very pretty. In figure skating, even their costumes, which reportedly can cost as much as $5,000, affect their scores.

In her book "*Little Girls in Pretty Boxes,*" Joan Ryan exposes the truth behind the scenes regarding elite female athletes. Ryan quotes gymnastics trainer Jack Rockwell, "I remember a top American official saying to Mary Lou Retton a year after the (1984) Olympics, 'You know, if I could, I'd take half a point off just because of that fat hanging off of your butt.'" [17] Gymnasts and skaters must not let their bodies grow up and develop female curves, menarche, and postpubescent body fat. In other words, in these sports, to become a woman means your elite career is over. "Because they excel at such a young age, girls in these sports are unlike other elite athletes. They are world champions before they can drive." [18]

Strenuous exercise combined with poor eating can have severe and often unforeseen consequences, for example, delaying puberty. Close to two thirds of female college athletes have irregular or nonexistent periods, a condition known as amenorrhea. With amenorrhea, the rate of bone loss can be alarming. An absence of menstruation means an absence of estrogen, which means bones can't develop properly. This can have a profound effect on a girl's skeletal development, since 48 to 70% of bone mass and 15% of height are achieved during adolescence.[19] A 23-year-old bulimic patient of mine was recently tested for bone density and was told that it matched that of a 65-year-old woman. A 21-year-old amenorrheic anorexic runner I am currently treating tested with a bone density of an 80-year-old woman!

Remember scenario no. 3 from Chapter 1? You were asked, "What kind of limits should you impose on your skeletal-looking daughter regarding visits to the gym or participation on the track team upon discovering that she is no longer menstruating?"

As a parent, you need to step in and say, "Enough!" The trick is to do it in a way that is understanding, yet firm. You may need to establish a weight that must be maintained in order to allow a gym membership or participation in track or other physical activity. Menstruation may need to be a requirement for participation in strenuous physical activity particularly if amenorrhea is combined with restrictive eating or low weight. This may present a real challenge, as amenorrhea is so common and accepted as a part of women's sports that one is hard pressed to find a menstruating female on a track team. And you must always explore what you will lose and what you will gain by forcing your daughter to stop. Sometimes, depending on her age, the most you may be able to do is provide your daughter with the knowledge she needs to make her own decisions regarding this matter.

Having your daughter get a physician's approval to exercise is important, but be sure to tell the doctor about your concerns regarding her eating and any weight loss, because chances are she won't reveal these issues herself. Ask the physician to run more than just routine tests. For example, you may ask for an EKG to check heart function and a bone density test to see if she has begun to lose bone mass or shows bone mineral deficiency. (Runners who are eating properly should have higher bone density scores than nonrunners.) These two tests, not routinely done, are increasingly requested by eating disorder professionals for their patients, particularly those patients who exercise.

Talk to your daughter's coach or the owner of the gym she frequents and discuss your concerns. Provide them with literature. Your daughter may be angry if you "interfere," especially if you speak to others. You need to reassure her that you really don't want to control or embarrass her, but that you do want to make sure she stays healthy and happy. Tell her you need advice, and perhaps even professional help, to know what is best. Most important, consult a professional for help in dealing with this issue. A registered dietitian can talk to your daughter and you about healthy eating for an active body. A therapist can help you decide when you are too invading and when you need to let the decision be your daughter's. Whatever you do, do something. The biggest mistake is to err on the side of believing that these hard-working, disciplined, responsible girls are telling the truth, will not take it too far, are too smart to end up "like that," and, finally, are good girls who will be able to "come around" on their own. This is a common trap. Ask the mother of the late Christy Heinreich, a promising national champion and an Olympic gymnast hopeful, who, at 15 years old, 4 feet, 11 inches tall, and a weight of 90 pounds, was told by a judge that she would never make the Olympic team if she didn't lose weight. In June 1993, Christy's weight had dropped to 52 pounds, and although she herself believed she would get better, and was struggling to do so, in July 1994, at the age of 22 she died of anorexia nervosa.

In Catie's case, I contacted the gym and let them know the dangers of their policies and procedures (especially their body fat contests). I urge any parent in this situation to take my lead. I informed the gym owner that a body fat of 9% was not healthy for a female, and that, in fact, anything below 15% can interfere with menstruation, ovulation, and bone density. I follow up calls by sending literature in the mail and I let gym owners, coaches, dance teachers, and even doctors know that they may be liable if anything happens to young girls like Catie who are using their facilities, or are under their care or supervision.

A NOTE ABOUT
BODY COMPOSITION AND THE SCALE

During the past decade, fitness enthusiasts, coaches, diet centers, and even average dieters have moved away from relying on the scale and have taken up body composition testing.

The body composition test divides body mass into two categories, lean and fat, determining how much a person has of each. How much one weighs is less important, in terms of fitness and health, than how much fat one has. Therefore, when losing weight, it is excess fat that should be the target. This is one reason why scales are misleading and should be thrown away (not to mention the fact that too often they measure self-esteem and self-worth instead of weight). Your daughter may say that she doesn't care what kind of weight she loses, that she's glad to lose at all, and that she needs and relies on her scale. To point out the absurdity of this, I often ask, "Would you chop off your arm to lose weight?" or, "If I drink a soda and then weigh a pound more, did I gain weight?" A five-pound weight loss or gain can be fluid, fat, or muscle, and a scale does not know which is which. A body composition test can tell the difference.

Much to their dismay, dieters who eat too little or exercise too much, lose much more muscle than fat. I have known many zealous dieters who wind up with higher body fat percentages than when they started dieting and even higher than that of people twice their weight. There are other people who, according to height and weight charts, are overweight, and yet are very muscular and very lean. I once tested a 175-pound woman whose body fat was only 17%. Ideal body fat for females is considered to be around 22%.

Body composition testing may have some advantages but is fraught with the same problems as the scale. Young girls and women will dispute or ignore the recommended ideal body fat percentages, just as they do recommended weight. Magazine articles or fitness trainers often encourage lower body fat percentages. One client of mine was recently tested at 12% body fat and was told that if she really worked hard, she could reach 9%! This not only is ridiculous, but it is dangerous. Therefore, although body composition is a more realistic and valuable method to assess health status than is scale weight, the bottom line is that both the scale and the various body composition instruments are ways of using numbers and goals to measure people—and it is this penchant for "measuring" that needs to stop. Why is it so important to know what Jenny's weight or body fat is? Is she eating in a healthy and balanced way, with snacks and desserts included? Is she active and using her body? Is she happy? We must fight against the societal message that now says to young women, "You must be pretty, and thin, and it's not just your weight that counts, it's your body fat too."

IF YOU THINK YOUR
DAUGHTER HAS A PROBLEM WITH EXERCISE,
ASK YOURSELF THESE QUESTIONS:

1. Do you see evidence of aimless and/or excessive physical activity that goes beyond normal exercise or the usual training regimen of others?
2. Do you see evidence of depressed mood and self-deprecating

thoughts or behaviors if she can't exercise (e.g., restricting her eating, crying, or constantly berating herself for being fat)?

3. Does she avoid situations in which she may be observed while eating (e.g., refusing to eat with friends or her teammates or making excuses, such as having to eat before or later than others)?
4. Does she appear preoccupied with the eating and exercise behaviors of other people, such as friends, relatives, or teammates?
5. Do you see any changes in her physical appearance and/or performance that suggest she is run down, weak, and sickly?
6. Is she is able to abstain voluntarily from exercise?
7. Does she exercise even when hurting or injured?
8. Does she miss or avoid social or family activities because she has to exercise?
9. Has the amount of time she spends exercising been increasing steadily?
10. Is she defensive about any suggestion to curb her exercise?

If you can answer "yes" to even one of the listed questions, your daughter may have an eating disorder, exercize addiction, or what has recently been called an activity disorder. You should approach your daughter with your concern and consult a health professional who has expertise in eating disorders. Since she is most likely oriented toward success and accomplishment, your daughter will feel embarrassed about being diagnosed with an eating disorder and will resist the diagnosis and the offer of help. She probably will think and say either that she doesn't have a problem or that she can handle any problem on her own. She even may have tried to correct things herself and failed. Let her know that outside help is almost always necessary and should not be regarded as a failure or lack of effort on her part. Be empathetic but firm and insist that she get help.

Since it is clear that overconcern with weight and shape is partially a result of our cultural idealization of thinness, why, in this climate, where most women are dissatisfied with their bodies, don't all women develop eating disorders? What causes one young girl growing up in this society to develop an obsession with exercize or dieting or a serious eating disorder, while another in the same society does not? What psychological or developmental factors are at play in the cause and development of disordered eating?

5

෴ ෴ ෴

Mothers, Daughters,
and Food

*Anthropological studies show us that no matter what era or group is
examined, women have borne the important responsibility of feeding
others, just as they have had a near-monopoly on child care.*

Margo Maine, *Father Hunger*[20]

*Since I have helped Clara (up until now) maintain a healthy weight,
people assume she doesn't have an eating problem. No one knows the
painful tug of war Clara has lived through … with food and her
desires on one side and me and her healthy weight on the other side.*

Wilma, *mother of an eating disordered daughter*

*Those of us daughters who as children had fulfilled mothers are
fortunate indeed.*

Evelyn Bassoff, *Mothering Ourselves*[21]

With acute attentiveness to their female elders, and particularly to their mothers, little girls today learn that calories are bad, that losing weight is good, and that the female body is an instrument to be used as a source of approval, but that can also be experienced as a source of frustration and pain.

Nine-year-old Annie was in my office last week with her parents for a family therapy session. On the way out, at the end of the session, Annie, who is thin as a rail, eyed my scale. She climbed on and started to cry. "What's the matter?" I asked. "I'm not losing any weight," she replied. Surprised, I said, "Annie, why do you want to lose weight?" Trying to hold back her tears, little 80-pound, nine-year-old Annie replied, "My mom is losing weight and Trisha [Annie's stepmother] is losing weight and I'm not." My heart sank but I was not really shocked. Once again, I was witnessing the evidence that little girls are getting the message loud and clear, "Losing weight is good, gaining weight is bad."

After a session with a chronically dieting, overweight woman, her six-year-old daughter, who was playing in my waiting room, greeted me cheerily and announced, "I'm so happy I had the chicken pox." Startled, I asked her, "Sara, why are you happy about that?" "It meant that I went to bed without dinner," Sara answered. With a mixture of dread and curiosity, I inquired, "Why did that make you happy?" Sara stated matter of factly, as if I should know the answer, "Because it means I didn't eat any calories!"

It's distressing enough that young girls are affected by what their mothers are doing to themselves, but even worse, some mothers not only worry about their own bodies, but become directly obsessed with their daughter's body—heaven forbid she gets fat!

Some of you are mothers, all of you had one. What did you learn about food, eating, and weight from your own mother, and what is your daughter learning from you? How and why do you eat the way you do and how can you prevent your daughter from repeating your mistakes?

Mom was always complaining about her weight and her body and she was always on a diet. She never ate with us; she would fix our food and then go upstairs to eat alone.

Mom never bought good-tasting treats like other moms did, those were all junk food to her, so, of course, it's what I always wanted and would sneak off to get. Only once a year, on my birthday, I could have cake. My brother and I, along with my parents, would eat the whole thing in one night.

I used to watch my mom weigh herself every morning. I learned that it would determine what kind of mood she would be in. I also went to diet doctors with her and would get lectures on staying thin so I would never have to go through the pain of being fat like her.

Food probably has several meanings in a mother's life, as it does in the lives of most women. On television and in magazines women are constantly reminded of their responsibility to feed their family. They are expected to perform this task whether or not their lifestyles are conducive to it. For most moms, this means considering appetites, nutritional needs, and food preferences as well as schedules and finances when planning meals. A large part of a woman's self-esteem seems to derive not only from her ability to feed others, but from being a good nurturer in general.

If you are a woman, the message to nurture others may coincide with the feeling that food is something to give to others but not to yourself. Because of the emphasis placed on women's appearance, you may be among those who view their body as an instrument to be used in the pursuit of approval from others and as a source of personal pride or security, which in reverse can lead to experiencing it as a source of disapproval and psychological pain.

If your body doesn't measure up to the current standards of "painfully thin," you are likely to scrutinize it as something that is not acceptable, always needing improvement, and as an object that must be controlled. Where food may be associated with health and happiness for others, for you it more often becomes associated with fear, fat, deprivation, weakness, failure, or control.

Beyond the nurturing of others, and denial to the self, food may have become a medium through which you communicate many feelings. You may use food to demonstrate love and caring, to get approval, as a way of being creative, as a means of proving how resourceful you are, as a way of distracting from other issues, as a source of comfort, as a means of apology—and there are many more. What has food come to represent in your life and in your messages to your own children?

MESSAGES THAT BACKFIRE

You may be doing or saying things that are sending the wrong message to your daughter. The focus on appearance, even when giving a compliment or being positive, can backfire in many ways. For example, to compliment someone on her weight loss implies that she was not attractive before. Compliments can even reinforce negative behavior. Take, for example, the following statement, which came from a mother who was looking through an old photo album with her daughter.

> You looked so great then, so nice and thin, look how good you looked.

The picture this mother was referring to was taken at a time when, unknown to the mom, her daughter was bulimic. You can imagine the message this daughter received. Even if the daughter had not been bulimic, the praise for appearance can reinforce the notion that external qualities are more important than internal qualities, and that if certain appearances are not kept up, the praise and pride will go away .

> You never want to be fat, like me. I'll do whatever I can to help prevent this from happening to you.

This message is also very damaging because, even if you are worried about and want to help your daughter, the underlying message may be that she is not good enough the way she is. You become her first source of discrimination. If you are concerned about your daughter's weight, it is better to try to improve the whole family's eating habits, to get your daughter to become more active, and to leave your experience of being overweight out of it.

FOOD AS REWARD AND PUNISHMENT

No matter how many sources have said not to do so, food is often used as a punishment and reward and children are taught that certain foods belong in special categories, like "good" and "bad."

> If you are good, I will take you for an ice cream.

> If you don't eat your dinner, you can't have dessert.

This kind of thinking sets the stage for people to restrict, sneak eat, rebel by eating, comfort themselves with, or overly indulge in, the forbidden "bad foods."

How many children have been sent to bed without dessert for not eating their peas or for some other offending behavior? Food is often used as an enticement or reward for being good, doing well, or accomplishing a task. Even when something bad happens, food is used as a reward or consolation for "suffering through it." Using food in this way is very common and will be hard to avoid completely. The degree to which you use food as a reward, and if you use rewards other than food, will make a difference with your daughter.

Sandy, a 38-year-old woman, came to me recently for help with her compulsive eating problem. As Sandy explained, " I have a good life. I like my job. My kids and husband cause me some grief, but for the most part, I have nothing to complain about. I have had therapy for several years regarding my parents, especially my mother, and I know she influenced how I feel about myself. She was mean to me and she was overweight. But I have dealt with her and now it is time to deal with me. Understanding my past has not helped me to deal with my eating and that is why I am here."

I often hear such comments as "I don't want to deal with my parents, they aren't the issue," or "I have dealt with the past, I don't want to discuss it anymore," or "I know that already, I need help now." The problem is that even if these people have an understanding about their past, they have not been able to connect it to what they do with food. They may have to make this link and they need to find an alternative to meeting needs that were not met early on.

Sandy was progressing in her ability to control herself around food but was having problems with bingeing whenever she got really upset. When asked about her thoughts immediately prior to bingeing she could only remember thinking, "Poor me." I asked her to get in touch with her thoughts more clearly immediately before a binge and write them down. Writing helps people clarify what is going on internally when they want to binge. I also asked Sandy, as I do everyone, not to use the word "binge" when describing what it is she wants to do, for example, "I want to eat a lot of forbidden foods," or "I want to eat until I numb myself," or "I want to lose myself in food." Here is a copy of what Sandy brought back to her next session.

The poor me. Thinking about how that association with food began.

I remember so vividly that time when I was probably around three or so and I didn't like what my mother had cooked for dinner. Food was tasteless (or maybe something else had happened) and I was too upset to eat. When I get very, very upset, I don't eat at all, and maybe it was one of those times.

Because I wasn't eating my mother's food, she kept screaming at me. She tried everything but mostly threatened. She even cut a piece of cake and put it up on the hutch behind the table in front of me, and told me if I ate everything, I could have the cake.

I used to throw up a lot when I ate something I didn't like, so this time she threatened to "give it right back to me" if I did it again. That threat was always terrifying. Once she even got a spoon out of the drawer and scooped some of my vomit up and went toward my face with it, but we didn't get further than that.

Anyway, on this particular time, I think I was crying and she was screaming. Even my grandmother and grandfather and aunt came over from next door because they heard it all and tried to convince me to eat. My mother did not let up until very late at night (or it felt like it was late to a child's mind) but it was de*finitely a long period of time.* I felt powerless. If I ate the food, I knew I would throw up, so I sat there. I'm wondering now, what else could I have done. You don't know when you're three years old what other choices there are.

Maybe by not eating I was fighting back. I have always seen this as "poor me." I could do nothing, but was I fighting back by my silence? Maybe there was power in not eating. I let both of us know that day that she could not control me. I would control myself. I did win in the end. She would not rule me. I would rule myself.

Together, Sandy and I processed what this could mean. When Sandy felt "poor me," she always felt driven to binge on sweets. This was her way of symbolically having the cake that her mother put on the hutch, and eating as much cake as she wanted. She began to understand that although bingeing represented a way that she could "eat what she wanted, when she wanted it," she had actually lost touch with what she *really* wanted. Sandy was bingeing on certain foods to assert her right to have them, even if she didn't really want them. Sandy and I agreed that she would purposely begin to add "binge" foods to her daily diet in reasonable amounts. This is scary for people, but done carefully, it can produce excellent results. Although Sandy's is a dramatic example, there are many versions of food being used as reward and punishment that take place.

Ask yourself:

- Are you using certain foods only as rewards or are you allowing yourself and your daughter foods in a balanced way?
- What nonfood rewards do you give yourself?
- What nonfood rewards are you using with your daughter or other family members and what new ones can you start using now?

HUNGER AND FULLNESS SIGNALS

It is amazing how easy it is to disrupt hunger and fullness signals. Dieting alone will do it. You may cause problems in this area by overfeeding or underfeeding your daughter. Often to avoid "spoiling" a child, or to keep her from "getting fat," a mother does not properly respond to her young daughter's true hunger. Mary, a compulsive overeater, explained, "My mother would always criticize the way I cared for Diane. If I fed her when she cried, Mom would tell me I was spoiling her. It was then that I learned that when I was an infant she used to feed me on a schedule that suited her. She told me that even from birth she decided when I should eat and would not feed me any other time, no matter how much I cried."

As far as overfeeding goes, many mothers put too much emphasis on eating, serve too much, demand clean plates, and overeat themselves. Daughters may not have a positive role model or example to follow. Your daughter will learn far more from what you do than from what you say. Don't believe that *telling* her what or when she should eat is enough.

FOOD AS LOVE

Food, early on in the mother–daughter relationship, is connected to love—getting one means having the other. People learn a variety of ways to associate food with being nurtured, cared for, and loved.

Whenever I had a fight with my mom she would want to take me out to lunch the next day, to talk about it. It was harmless on her part, but soon I associated eating with feeling cared about and eventually I used food to feel better about anything that was wrong.

You may give food to those you care about to show your love—baking cookies for the family, making your husband a special dinner, or buying candy for your kids. Your daughter may use food as love if she feels, consciously or unconsciously, that she is not getting it somewhere else. Where emptiness exists in any way, food can mask it and be a substitute filler, at least temporarily. It is important for you to discuss with your daughter what other things can be done to help with feelings of emptiness or lack of love. Be specific with your daughter, discuss these kinds of issues, and help her to separate her food from her feelings.

SWALLOWING FEELINGS/STUFFING ANGER

Stuffing down or swallowing feelings is a metaphor that is useful in understanding how, through eating, a person can distract herself from difficult or painful feelings. If your daughter has learned that certain feelings are unacceptable, she may turn to food to bury them. Many people who use food in this way describe their eating behavior as having a numbing effect on them. Starving is also a way of avoiding feelings or expressing, "I don't have any feelings or needs." This kind of behavior is found in girls who severely restrict their food, and it is too often mistaken for self-sufficiency. Although you may not be able to accept all of your daughter's behaviors, make sure you accept all of her feelings.

FOOD AS ATTENTION AND APPROVAL

The effort that a woman puts into the variety of tasks she handles each day often goes unnoticed. If you are in the position, as most women are, of running your household, you will agree that it is like running a minicorporation. The many responsibilities and duties required of you are often taken for granted or are overlooked. This would cause any woman to feel discounted. On the other hand, food is often one way by which praise can easily be earned. Men who never say a word about the fact that you took your daughter to the doctor, cleaned the house, and did the laundry sometimes will comment on a nice meal. You may make a special meal to show appreciation for your family and to let them know you are paying attention to them, but you may also be doing this because it is you who need the attention. Have you ever gone away for a few days, worrying about how your family was going to feed themselves, only to feel discouraged and displaced if they got along without you? You may need to look for other arenas in which to seek attention, appreciation, and approval.

FEEDING OTHERS AS SUBSTITUTION

Do you find yourself feeding others because you want to eat? "I'll get chocolate ice cream for John because he likes it so much." Are you depriving yourself of certain foods, or of food in general, so that you need to get vicarious satisfaction by feeding others? If you eat and feel guilty about it, your daughter will pick up on it. If you make food for others and don't eat it yourself, what's to prevent your daughter from doing the same?

Is it or or was it easier to share food with your mother/daughter than to share feelings? One mother I know takes her daughter out to dinner to show her she cares about her. Another mother buys food treats to show her daughter love, because it is too painful, for reasons from her own past, to hug her child. You will need to uncover your own feelings and decide which are appropriate to share with your daughter. Let her know that you value her input but are not dependent on it. Listen to her without judging.

If your daughter has a food-related problem, it will not be easy to know what to do, especially if your own mother was not a good role model and did not teach you. How you treat food, your feelings, and your body will probably be the strongest guide for your daughter. As Evelyn Bassoff puts it in *Mothering Ourselves*, "Those of us daughters who as children had fulfilled mothers are fortunate indeed. But those of us who did not are sometimes able to encourage our mothers, no matter what their age, to take new pleasure and have adventures now—for their sake and for ours too."[22]

If you are unsure about where to start, begin by asking yourself if what you are doing to yourself is what you would do with your own daughter, and you will probably be surprised. Would you send her off in the morning with nothing but a cup of coffee? Would you tell her that she will have a bad day if she gets on the scale and has gained a pound? Would you tell her to skip meals in order to fit into a dress she desperately wants to wear? Would you tell her not to have dinner because she wants ice cream instead? Would you tell her to hide chocolate from you so she won't be embarrassed that she eats it? Would you tell her to binge if she's having a bad day? Would you tell her that what she looks like is the most important thing, and that despite what anyone else may tell her, her body, if it meets the proper criteria, is her power, her tool to use to get what she wants and needs in life? Are you telling these things to yourself? I hope not. Instead there are many things you can and should do. For example:

1. Help your daughter turn her focus away from the external qualities of being a female and towards what it means to be female in a more spiritual and worldly sense.
2. Frequently spend time with her talking about mother–daughter issues and what it means to be female.
3. Read together about ancient female traditions and rituals, pass on any you have learned, create some new ones together. It is not too late to start developing family traditions she can pass on to her daughter.
4. Discuss your own mother and your mother's mother and give your daughter a sense of her lineage.
5. Give her examples of respected, powerful women for whom power has nothing to do with beauty and examples of women who were known for what they did rather than how they looked.
6. Help her learn how special her body is for all that it can do for her and for all the functions it was meant to carry out, for example, hugging, dancing, breathing, as well as special female ones such as pregnancy, childbirth, and breast-feeding.

6

ॐ ॐ ॐ

Daddy's Girl

You're the end of my rainbow, my pot of gold, you're Daddy's little girl to have and to hold, you're sugar, you're spice, you're everything nice, 'cause you're Daddy's little girl.

A song my father sang to me when I was a little girl

When a father is unable to help his daughter move out of the maternal orbit, either because he is physically unavailable or not invested emotionally in her, the daughter may turn to food as a substitute ... Anorexia and bulimia nervosa have in common inadequate paternal responses for helping the daughter develop a less symbiotic relationship with her mother. When she must separate on her own, she may take on the pathological coping strategies embedded in eating disorders.

Kathryn Zerbe, *The Body Betrayed*[23]

Freud, the "father" of psychotherapy, put great emphasis on fathering and, in fact, his whole oedipal theory involves the conflict and negotiation that children experience in their relationship with their father. However, fathers are not usually thought of as being as instrumental in child rearing or in influencing their children as are mothers. Literature on fathers and daughters is scarce, particularly in relation to the etiology and treatment of body image disturbance, problems with food, and eating disorders.

If we are to understand and accept that disordered eating is about a struggle within, an attempt to meet certain needs and a longing for love and acceptance, then it is easy to see that the quantity and quality of nurturing from either parent is crucial.

If you are reading this chapter and you are a father, understand that you are one of the most important men in your daughter's life. However, if you are like most fathers, you are not responsible for the day-to-day caretaking of your daughter. You are essentially left out of many decisions regarding her life, and find yourself at a loss for how to connect emotionally with her, since you are probably more comfortable "doing" than "feeling."

It is no wonder that fathers are not prepared to deal with their daughters. Our socialization process for males isolates them from their feelings and teaches them attitudes and skills that are the opposite of and foreign to those learned by their daughters. Boys are brought up to value independence, achievement, self-control, and separation. Girls, on the other hand, are socialized to value relationships, to view popularity as a measure of self-worth, to be more concerned with other's feelings than their own, and, above all else, to connect. To a teenage daughter struggling with her body image, and complaining of being too fat, a well-meaning father may be inclined to say, "Who cares what they think?" or "Get a hold of yourself, honey, it's not that bad." He may also unwittingly apply his values of achievement and control where they don't belong—in the area of weight, body image, and food. A daughter praised by her father for losing weight or running 10 miles will always consider the flip side, "Would he love me if I didn't?"

Fathers often tell me they don't know how to become involved in their daughter's life, particularly after puberty, when she has breasts and is increasingly interested in the opposite sex. Girls at this time are struggling with their sexuality, their changing relationship to males, the transformation of their bodies, the separation from their parents, their quest for an identity, and the cultural standards for females they feel compelled to fulfill. A father can influence his daughter's ideas about what constitutes an attractive and desirable female. Little girls will respond not only to what their fathers say to them, but also to what they hear their fathers say about women in general.

Carla's father, Tony, was always a ladies' man, but *she* was always "Daddy's girl." He loved her mother, but it was clear that his relationship to other women, and to Carla, was different.

My mother was his wife, the mother of his children, but other women seemed to hold his attention—beautiful women, thin women. I know that at an early age I liked the way my father talked about and treated those other women, better than the way he treated my mother. I wanted to be like them. I did everything to please my dad, no one meant more to me. He made me feel special and pretty, and would take me out to dinner and show me off to his friends. My mother, on the other hand, was quiet and hard working and took care of me, but she seemed boring and dull. She was very, very good to me, but his life seemed more exciting, and being with him made me feel special, like something grand was happening.

Carla, in her quest to obtain her father's affection and approval, started dieting at the age of nine. Someone at school had called her "chubby cheeks," and she remembered how her father had said that fat women just aren't attractive. She paid close attention to what he said about all women and how he treated them. It was clear that to get his approval, she would have to remain thin. When Carla went on a diet, both her mother and her father approved. They were proud of her for wanting to eat healthily and take care of her body. "I didn't care about taking care of my body, I wanted to be thin," Carla remembers. Carla got so much praise for her ability to stick to a diet that she continued the diet beyond her original weight-loss goal. She liked not just her new weight, but her ability to lose weight and the praise and attention she got, first for losing weight, and then for being so thin, even too thin. "I was not going to give it up. I was too afraid about what might happen. This was the best thing that had happened to me, a real success of my own. Dieting had become so easy that I had to eat less and less to feel I was accomplishing anything. It didn't take long before my goal was to not eat at all."

Carla's father was resistant when her mother suggested that Carla had an eating disorder and needed therapy. He insisted that his daughter was a good girl and just took things a bit too far. "She'll get over it," he claimed, "All she needs to do is eat. She doesn't need any mumbo jumbo therapist planting seeds in her head. She's not nuts."

When Carla's weight dropped another 10 pounds, he tried to force her to eat. For the first time, they fought openly, and no one realized the irony that in trying to please him, she had manifested a symptom that made him angry, distant, and rejecting of her. She was doing something over which he had no control. Finally, her mother secretly brought Carla to my office and asked that I not call the house because Carla's father would not agree to counseling, would be angry, and would interfere with her getting help. Although I agreed for the short term, I advised them that eventually Carla's father should be told and involved in her treatment. I never insist on inclusion of a family member until I learn more about the family and its members.

Including an angry or hostile parent in the therapy can be counterproductive and sabotage the client, but this is rare. Fathers usually are excluded because everyone is afraid of them, and unwilling to be honest, which is part of the problem to begin with. Additionally, not including the father often reinforces the pairing of the mother and daughter into "us against him or even them," which includes the therapist or anyone who might come between the mother and daughter. This, too, is often part of the problem. Therapists who don't work hard to get fathers involved in their daughter's treatment are exacerbating the problem, as they discriminate against the father, and perpetuate the myth that a father's role is not as important as that of the mother.

I have often heard it said that the best thing a father can do for his daughter is to love her mother. How a girl's mother is treated by her father teaches the girl not only about what it means to be a female, but about what she can expect from men and how to be in a relationship. Additionally, the mother's treatment and well-being will directly affect the role created for the daughter in the family and then carried into the outside world. One must wonder about the often-referred-to enmeshment (overly bonded relationship) between mothers and daughters, especially seen in anorexia nervosa. Could it be that if the mother were getting more nurturing from her husband, she would not need to turn to her child to gratify her emotional needs, thus creating a "parentified" child, so common among anorexics? A mother who knowingly or unknowingly uses her children to vent or soothe her disappointment in her husband, their father, puts the children in an incredible double bind: "Can I be close to one without betraying the other?"

It is true by nature's design that children are more dependent on their mothers from birth, but if the mothers will allow it, and the couple relationship is healthy enough, the fathers can help to provide a nonthreatening transition from this dependency. As a person different and separate from the mother, the father can help his daughter confirm her sense of self and enhance her separation from the mother.

The father's traditional role of being an outside representative is critical in a world where girls need guidance in careers, negotiating the business world, and other pursuits, outside of the home. However, a father's role should not be limited to "outside representative," or public sphere expert—just as a mother can serve as a role model for dealing with a career and the world of business, as well as for home-based pursuits.

Carla was not clear when she came to me that starving herself to 80 pounds had anything to do with her family. Her father's approval, how he treated her mother and other women, how her mother's life seemed dull compared with his, and how she felt successful and accomplished and worldly like her father when she was losing weight were not part of her consciousness. Carla was very defensive in the beginning. Treatment takes time. It is important not to push ideas and explanations on anyone. To Carla, her body, being thin, being in control, and not being weak were what mattered, and most important, she kept reminding me that she just didn't want to get fat. It took several months to sort through those issues, involve her father and mother in treatment, and begin the process of letting go of the very behaviors she thought had sustained her, replacing them with inner strength about who she was, who her parents were, and how to meet her approval needs and desire for success and worldliness in other ways.

Another daddy's girl, Jackie, died of heart failure. I heard about it when I returned from a long-overdue vacation. Even though she wasn't my patient at the time, my secretary knew the news would ruin my trip, and with my husband's approval, reasoned that, since I couldn't do anything anyway, she would send flowers and a card for me and hold the information until I came home. I have since grieved many a night and day and wondered, like most of those who had the opportunity to know and treat her, "What more could I have done, why did this have to happen, how many more have to die?"

I had seen Jackie as one of many professionals whom her family had consulted for treatment over several years, and even though she was not in treatment with me when she died, every life I have touched and every soul who willingly let me enter the sacred space inside themselves will always be dear to me.

When I first saw Jackie, she was 20 years old and very much a daddy's girl. Her father, John, had made the initial call to my office, which is very rare. Of the calls that come into my center, 99.5% are from females. John had heard about me and wanted me to see his daughter, whom he described as suffering from an eating disorder and from compulsive exercise. He explained that they had tried various other approaches, including several hospitalizations and treatment programs, but to no avail. He made the appointment for her and they came together to my office. This too was unusual. I almost never see the fathers on the initial visit, and so far I had heard nothing about Mom.

John was a coach and Jackie was extremely proud of him and wanted him to be equally proud of her. At an early age, she had started training with him and soon adopted the "no pain, no gain" slogan so common among sports enthusiasts. Jackie watched her dad coach and saw how he respected those who suffered but endured anyway, those who never gave up, never quit, and never stopped despite the pain. She also loved the times she spent with him running or training in the gym. Her mother was not interested in these pursuits and Jackie soon came to understand that she held a special place in her father's life and had a role to uphold. Jackie would become, even though John didn't ask her to, the apple of his eye, the dream not only of every father, but of every coach. She would be the player who never tires, never asks anything for herself, sacrifices for the good of the team, maintains allegiance, endures with grace under pressure—the one who lives by the credo of mind over matter and spirit over flesh. Jackie's role grew into an obsession from which she could not escape, one that devoured her.

Jackie had gone from tomboy to female athlete to compulsive exerciser, and by the time I saw her, she was being referred to as "almost psychotic about exercise" by her friends and classmates. At five feet seven inches tall and 85 pounds, her routine, as she described in her journal, was as follows:

4–6:30 A.M.	Morning run (add half an hour to my run in case I ran too slowly for part of it)
6:45–7:45 A.M.	Shower, dress, and eat, but run in place if I can.
School	During the day, run between classes and up stairs, shake my feet while sitting. Try to stand instead of sit. Keep moving at all times. Even leave class if I can be excused and run up and down stairs for 5 or 10 minutes, and then come back to class.

12–2 P.M.	Two-hour workout at gym.
Classes	Same as above.
4–6:30 P.M.	Two-hour run (add half an hour to my run in case I ran too slowly for part of it).
8–10 P.M.	Study but take several breaks to run around building, move legs all the time.
10–11 P.M.	Situps, leg lifts, jumping jacks, running in place.
11–4 A.M.	Sleep.
2–3 A.M.	Jumping jacks in place, sit-ups, leg lifts (when I can't sleep).

Jackie's schedule sounds too rediculous to be true, but it was confirmed by her family and friends. As for her nutritional intake, what I could get Jackie to reveal about her diet was that it consisted mainly of salad and vegetables with a lot of mustard and, once in a while, yogurt.

Jackie eventually agreed to be hospitalized but continued her obsessive-compulsive behaviors, and in that setting was caught exercising in her bed and in the shower and in the middle of the night. She drank water in the shower taped coins to the bottoms of her feet to raise her weight artificially, and sneaked vegetables, including a whole pumpkin one night, and devoured them raw with as much as a jar of mustard. With all of her crazy behaviors, she was also smart, gracious, giving, and filled with spirit, passion, love, and longing. Jackie was a desperate soul asking to be released from herself. Ellen West, the first recorded case study of an anorexic treated sometime around 1914, seemed to be speaking for Jackie and many others when she wrote, "I am in prison and cannot get out. It does no good for the analyst to tell me that I myself place the armed men there, that they are theatrical figments and not real. TO ME THEY ARE VERY REAL."[24]

Jackie's story is tragic and continues to haunt me. Numerous significant details are left out here to respect the family's privacy and to conform to the scope of this book. Jackie's eating disorder and disordered sense of self were complicated and I regret that my description here only scratches the surface of the underlying reasons that led to her fatal battle with anorexia. Aside from her father's influence, Jackie's relationship with her mother, her parent's relationship with each other, the innate, driven personality with which she came into the world, the cultural pressure on her to be thin, her desire to be perfect, even her unique biochemistry, all came into play as causes for her illness. John's role is emphasized here to provide an example and reinforce the message of the significant impact that a father can have on the self-development of a daughter and how exploring the father–daughter relationship is a necessary part of correcting any problems in self-development.

As for what fathers can do, let me return to a statement made earlier, "The best thing a father can do for his daughter is to take good care of her mother." I agree that this is important, but why is it not also said, "The best thing a father can do for his daughter is to take care of himself"? The reason is that we don't expect fathers to know what this means on an emotional level. I have discovered that when the phrase "taking care of yourself" is directed to a woman, people assume it applies to emotions and nurturing, but when it is directed to a man, people assume it has something to do with financial stability and independence.

I encourage fathers to become more involved in their daughter's emotional lives, to learn the value of connecting and sharing, and to work at getting in touch with feelings—starting with their own. For the fathers reading this, you will need help in exploring the unfamiliar area of feelings and needs. Exploring your relationship with your own father—remembering your feelings about him and the disappointments or joys shared with him—can shed light on your current behavior and your relationship with your own children. It may be useful to go to therapy—not just family therapy, which is important, but individual therapy for yourself. If it helps you, justify it by saying that you are doing it for your daughter.

As a father, you can help prevent your daughter from having a body image or dieting problem, or help her recover if she already has one. Begin working on the following things for your daughter *now*.

- Do not make it your daughter's responsibility to reach into your world to connect; make the effort to enter hers.
- Do not focus on your daughter's weight, but on who she is as a person.
- Do not focus on your daughter's disordered eating symptoms, but on her feelings.
- Do not tell her you are disappointed or angry with her, because she will hide more from you.
- Do not reassure her that you know she will pull herself through any problem; this makes her feel that the burden is all on her.
- Do not talk about looks and appearance, but focus on inner qualities. This applies to your daughter *and* all other people.
- Help your daughter learn to identify with women who are interest-

ing, successful, and creative instead of simply being admired for
their looks.

- It's important to do things with your daughter, but spend time *being* with her, not just doing things together. She will value a walk, lounging in the back yard, or just talking in the living room.
- When discussing things with your daughter, be sure to validate her opinion or ideas first, before you offer your own input, even if you think that what she is saying needs to be corrected or is ridiculous.
- When you feel you are absolutely right about something you are trying to impress on your resistant daughter, keep in mind that it is usually better to be loved than to be right.

7

❧ ❧ ❧

Mirror, Mirror on the Wall

I look in the mirror, the reflection I see
Half my weight stares back at me
Where once was a smile
Is now just a frown
Could that monster I see there be me?

Hana

You're so pretty, honey ... if you only lost a little weight.

Hana's mother three years prior to
Hana's hospitalization for anorexia

The larger world never gives girls the message that their bodies are
valuable simply because they are inside them. Until our culture tells
young girls that they are welcome in any shape—that women are
valuable to it with or without the excuse of "beauty"—girls will
continue to starve.

Naomi Wolf, *Hunger* [25]

The term "body image" refers to an individual's perception, feelings, and attitudes toward his or her own body, or how he or she experiences the body psychologically. Your daughter's feelings and attitudes toward her body, her body image, incorporate the interest, caring, respect, and importance that you and others give her body when she is growing up. It is through her body that your daughter first came to know and experience herself as a distinct, separate entity in the world. For your daughter to have a healthy body image, she will need a good sense of body boundaries—feeling separate from but equal to others. She will also need a good role model. Both of these most often start with you, her mother. Dieting, starving, bingeing, and purging may be, among other things, attempts to define and establish boundaries, in a void of other alternatives. As Richard Geist, a psychologist specializing in eating disorders, puts it:

> The anorexic girl peers into the mirror of the mother and perceives not the reflection of her whole body self, but a prismatic image of isolated parts: Her stomach protrudes, her thighs are fat; her birthmark is too noticeable. Only when she allows mother to substitute the latter's "thing creation" does she feel whole and alive, and then only by sacrificing her uniqueness.[26]

The influence of maternal attitudes on the daughter's body image was illustrated in the *Glamour*[27] magazine survey referred to earlier. The survey found that mothers who were critical of their daughters' bodies had daughters who showed a greater use of severe dieting practices, a higher incidence of bulimia, and a poorer body image.

It is true that a daughter learns about her body and its care and meaning primarily from her mother, who, of course, was a daughter herself. Poor mothering is often blamed for the development of body image problems, unhealthy eating habits, and eating disorders. Blaming mothers is easier than trying to understand the psychological factors that have oppressed women in general. But blaming mothers fails to address the male-dominated society in which a woman's appearance is focused on, often to the exclusion of other attributes, and is held up as a means to achieving success and power. After all, even childhood stories such as "Snow White" reinforce the power of beauty. The wicked queen consults the magic mirror on the wall and then plots to kill Snow White simply because she is more beautiful. Is it a woman's fault that she is obliged to conform to a cultural standard that is externally defined, constantly changing, and, for the most part, out of reach?

Our culture breeds an overfocus on and overcontrol of the female body. Females are being exposed to an increasing preference for a lean body type from birth, their mothers having been indoctrinated when they themselves were young. Young girls today are more likely to approach puberty with a negative body image, one often held by their mothers and then passed on to them. What does this mean for a girl who reaches puberty, which automatically produces an increase of 120% in body fat? Puberty should be welcomed by a young girl as a natural and wonderful biological transformation, a female rite of passage, allowing her to conceive and give birth to her own child. Instead, menarche is too often dreaded for the curves it produces, the padding it provides, and the hard body it takes away.

Research in the field of eating disorders has shown that body image dissatisfaction is a better predictor of eating attitudes and behaviors, and dieting pathology, than other variables, such as self-esteem, depression, and social anxiety combined.[28] Furthermore, continued body dissatisfaction is associated with relapse and the poorest patient prognosis.[29]

The body image criteria for Anorexia Nervosa in the *Diagnostic and Statistical Manual of Mental Disorders,* Fourth Edition (DSM-IV),[30] states: "Disturbance in the way in which one's body weight or shape is experienced, undue influence of body weight or shape on self-evaluation, or denial of the seriousness of the current low body weight."

In 1986, when Bulimia Nervosa was first officially recognized, body image disturbance was not even included as a feature. The diagnostic criteria (DSM-IV) now state: "Self evaluation is unduly influenced by body shape and weight."[30]

What constitutes "disturbance," "undue influence," or "denial"? Body image disturbance and overconcern in our society are, unfortunately, the norm, but that does not mean they are healthy. It is not body image dissatisfaction alone that is significant, or that leads to an eating disorder, but rather the importance placed on weight and shape for self-worth, and the measures one is willing to take to manipulate, control, and torture the body to conform to some standard or self-imposed image.

Body image problems involve three main components: perception, attitude, and behavior.

Perception. This involves what your daughter actually sees when looking at herself directly or in the mirror. She may actually see herself as fat even though she is of normal weight or is emaciated. Your daughter's perception of herself may or may not be distorted, but in either case her body is never good enough in her eyes, if she has adopted unrealistic requirements or she needs it to be perfect.

Attitude. Your daughter's attitude toward her body is the meaning she gives to her perception, and reflects the investment of her self-worth in her appearance. It is not your daughter's body itself, but rather the attitude taken toward it, that will cause her to feel and act in certain ways.

Behavior. It is important to understand that such behaviors as fasting, self-induced vomiting, compulsive exercise, and bingeing are, in part, based on perception and attitude. Changing behavior alone will most likely do nothing to change perception or attitude. Forcing your daughter to eat, or to give up sweets, or to gain weight will not work in the long run. I have seen many mothers pressure their daughters into a behavior such as eating a full meal only to find out that they subsequently threw it up. Changing perception and attitude, however, will result in changes in behavior. For example, if your daughter learns to see her body more accurately and to accept it, the need to starve or purge will be diminished.

Body image problems, dieting, and eating disorders are creative behavioral responses to the psychological distress in women's lives in a culture obsessed with thinness.

With the cultural pressure to be thin and the rewards that come with it, any number of underlying problems or developmental deficits, such as low self-esteem, inability to regulate tension, poor impulse control, and sexual abuse, can find expression and release through dieting or disordered eating behaviors. Preventing your daughter from developing an eating disorder or helping her to recover from one involves discovering and resolving her underlying thoughts, feelings, and developmental deficits, as well as dealing with her eating and dieting behaviors. The next chapter, "Diet or Disorder?" will help you to determine if your daughter has progressed from a problem with food or body image to a diagnosable eating disorder.

8

❧ ❧ ❧

Diet or Disorder?

If my daughter uses laxatives, does that mean she has an eating disorder?

Jenny is very overweight, is that an eating disorder?

My daughter only has an eating disorder, she does not have any psychological problems.

The youngest victims, from earliest childhood, learn to starve and vomit from the overwhelmingly powerful message of our culture, which I found no amount of parental love and support strong enough to override. I knew my parents wanted me not to starve because they loved me, but their love contradicted the message of the larger world, which wanted me to starve in order to love me. It is the larger world's messages, young women know, to which they will have to listen if they are to leave their parent's protection. I kept a wetted finger up to the winds of that larger world: Too thin yet? I was asking it. What about now? No? Now?

Naomi Wolf, *Hunger* [31]

When does a diet turn into a disorder? When does thinness become anorexia and overeating become bingeing? How can one tell when the fine line has been crossed, and something must be done?

There is a great deal of misunderstanding in the area of eating disorders. Eating disorders are not just cases of excessive eating or dieting gone out of control. Eating disorders are psychological illnesses involving a disordered sense of self, whose coping mechanism includes a cluster of thoughts, feelings, and behaviors we have come to categorize into one of three main areas of disordered eating: anorexia nervosa, bulimia nervosa, and binge eating. The definitions listed in this chapter will help you to identify whether or not your daughter does have an eating disorder and, if so, which kind. Be careful, however, not to assume that because your daughter doesn't fit all the criteria, she does not have, or more important, is not at risk for developing, an eating disorder. Eating disorders take a long time to develop. You may not even notice the subtle changes until the disorder has fully set in. Even if your daughter hasn't an eating disorder yet, getting help for her early may prevent the development of one.

The following information provides the clinical criteria listed for Anorexia Nervosa, Bulimia Nervosa, and Binge Eating Disorder in the DSM-IV, and examples for each of these diagnoses.

ANOREXIA NERVOSA

DIAGNOSTIC CRITERIA FOR 307.1 ANOREXIA NERVOSA[32]

A. Refusal to maintain body weight at or above a minimally normal weight for age and height (e.g., weight loss leading to maintenance of body weight less than 85% of that expected; or failure to make expected weight gain during period of growth, leading to body weight less than 85% of that expected).

B. Intense fear of gaining weight or becoming fat, even though underweight.

C. Disturbance in the way in which one's body weight or shape is experienced, undue influence of body weight or shape on self-evaluation, or denial of the seriousness of the current low body weight.

D. In postmenarcheal females, amenorrhea, i.e., absence of at least three consecutive menstrual cycles. (A woman is considered to have amenorrhea if her periods occur only following hormone, e.g., estrogen, administration.)

Specify type:

Restricting Type: during the current episode of Anorexia Nervosa, the person has not regularly engaged in binge-eating or purging behavior (i.e., self-induced vomiting or the misuse of laxatives, diuretics, or enemas)

Binge-Eating/Purging Type: during the current episode of Anorexia Nervosa, the person has regularly engaged in binge-eating or purging behavior (i.e., self-induced vomiting or the misuse of laxatives, diuretics, or enemas)

CASE EXAMPLE

Becky, a 16-year-old anorexic, was brought to me by her parents after failing to respond to the treatment they had sought at a university hospital. At five feet five inches tall and 80 pounds, she appeared very emaciated, and worn out, but strongly and stubbornly defiant. She was proud to be anorexic. We talked about "safe" food and scary feelings and what it's like to think of food all day. We talked about what she thought of her body and how she could not really be the judge of it. We talked about the power of anorexia and the fear of losing control. I talked about my recovery and how she could recover too.

I knew it was important to establish rapport with Becky and her parents. They had already experienced treatment failure elsewhere and were skeptical. How Becky felt about me and reacted toward me would say a lot about how her parents would react. She had been so resistant to all help that if she even seemed willing to come back, I had earned points with her parents. The first session went well, with my letting Becky know that I wasn't going to take anything away from her but that I was there to find out what she might want to be different in her life and to help her do this in a healthy way. I also suggested that I was there to help her get her parents off her back.

Becky came willingly to her sessions, and although she continued to lose weight, I felt that progress was being made. Progress is a strange creature when dealing with eating disorders. What is changing on the inside is more important than observable things like weight. Even though Becky wanted to stop losing weight, she could not "allow" herself to eat. She was entrenched in her eating rituals and rules. They had taken over and were now the rulers of her life. It was her desire to stop and her willingness to begin to trust me and let me in on her rules that constituted progress. Progress can be very minimal, just a tiny step, but must be seen and recognized.

Becky kept a meticulous journal recording her intake of food:

Breakfast:	Tea, dry toast
Lunch:	Apple, two rice cakes
Dinner:	Salad (lettuce, tomato slice, one-half carrot, and diet dressing)
Snack:	Swiss Miss chocolate drink with water

One particular turning point in the therapy was the day Becky admitted, "I never, ever, eat anything without throwing up." I'm sure she expected dismay, disappointment, shock, and even anger from me, having been lied to. I simply said, "How hard that must have been for you to come here every week and keep that from me." Becky melted with a sigh of relief that not only was I not angry, but I understood and even felt empathy for her situation. This approach allowed her to further trust me and helped to open the door to her secret world.

Becky was obsessed with a fear of gaining weight, of losing control, of not being perfect, of not being enough. Indeed, her current behaviors seemed far beyond her control, appearing to have a life of their own. If you want to understand your anorexic daughter, you must believe her when she tells you that she thinks she's fat, that she can't stop her behaviors, that she fears losing control.

As is usually the case, Becky would share things with me she could not share with her parents. In order to help you understand what kinds of things your own daughter might be feeling and thinking, I include the following dialogue with Becky, which is composed of excerpts from actual therapy sessions with her.

Individual therapy session with Becky during restricting phase of anorexia

Carolyn: How was your week?
Becky: I gained a pound and it upsets me.

Carolyn: How do you know you gained a pound?

Becky: Because I weighed myself at the gym.

Carolyn: I thought we agreed that you would only weigh yourself here.

Becky: I couldn't take it and I couldn't eat anything. I had to know, I thought I had gained five pounds.

Carolyn: And then after you saw the one pound gain what happened?

Becky: I cut back on my food, because I don't want it to go too fast.

Carolyn: Becky, one pound doesn't even mean anything. It could have been more fluid in your body or weighing at a different time of day, or the gym scale could be different from mine.

(At this point, I weighed her and she was the same weight that she had been last week in my office. We agreed again that she should only weigh in my office. I tried to get her to weigh with her back to the scale, but at this point she wouldn't agree. I then discussed her being upset about the so-called weight gain.)

Carolyn: How did it make you feel, when you thought you had gained weight? What was upsetting?

Becky: I'm afraid of gaining weight. I know I need to but every time I do it's too scary.

Carolyn: Too scary for what?

Becky: It's too hard to give up.

Carolyn: Being thin is more important than anything else, more important than being healthy?

Becky: I want to be healthy, I'm just afraid to eat. I'm afraid to gain weight.

Carolyn: It is scary and hard, I know. You have been in control of it for so long. It's like giving up something special.

Becky: *(pause)* Yeah.

Carolyn: Well, Becky, you are something special. You don't need anorexia for that, you have so much to offer and you need to get better so that you really can be you. Just think of all the things you'd be doing or we'd be talking about if you weren't spending all your time on this.

Becky: I just don't want to eat more, I'm too scared and my stomach hurts.

Carolyn: More than what? How many calories can you feel comfortable with eating in a day?

Becky: Oh, 300? (*kind of laughs*)

Carolyn: Well, that's certainly not enough to be healthy. You could easily eat three times that and not gain weight. What do the calories mean to you?

Becky: Weight gain.

Carolyn: You need calories for many reasons. Calories don't equal weight gain. They are used for all kinds of things. Do you believe me when I say that your body needs more just to stay alive, to grow your nails, bones, to make you walk and to think clearly, to make your heart beat? Remember, Karen Carpenter died because her heart stopped. You're also cold all the time and your periods have stopped. You're cold now, aren't you?

Becky: Uh-huh.

Carolyn: This black hair that has grown on your arm is your body trying to keep you warm. In many ways, your body is trying to protect you from yourself. Your body isn't getting enough fuel so it shuts things down. You know that if your period has stopped, there are other, more subtle things going on, some that you don't recognize yet. It happened to me. Remember, I told you about my hair falling out and that I have to take thyroid pills for the rest of my life. You must ask yourself what price you are willing to pay and it's not worth it.

Becky: I just hate being fat, and when I eat, I look fat, especially my stomach. I feel fat and awful and I hate it. I always just gain it here. (*points to her stomach*)

Carolyn: Show me where you think you are fat.

Becky: Right here, my stomach sticks out.

Carolyn: Okay, I see your stomach. It looks very thin to me. Look at my stomach, I weigh 120 pounds, am I fat?

Becky: No, but it's different on me.

Carolyn: You can't be the judge of that right now. Think of it, at 80 pounds how could you be fat? Do you actually think for a five-feet, five inch person, 80 lbs. is fat?

Becky: Well no, but my stomach sticks out.

Carolyn: Your stomach may feel a little big to you because your body is so thin everywhere else that in comparison your stomach might seem big, especially when you have food in it. But food isn't fat, food is necessary for life! And if you eat and your stomach gets bigger, soon the food will be digested and it will get smaller again. You need to learn that feeling full is not the same thing as feeling fat. You say you want to get better and every time you start to eat you freak out about your stomach. I need you to know that the feeling is not just going to go away. You will have to go through this part, then it gets better, easier, and I'll be here to help you through. Besides, you are the only one who sees that happening to your stomach. And in the long run, is how your stomach looks more important than anything else?

Becky: I just don't feel right. I wish I could just not see it. I'm trying not to look, not to think about it.

Carolyn: What does it mean if your stomach sticks out? What's wrong with that? Why does that bother you so much, I mean, so what?

Becky: Because it means I'm fat. I just can't stand to be fat.

Carolyn: Why not?

Becky: Because.

Carolyn: Becky, if "because" is the only reason, it hardly seems worth it to go through all of this.

Becky: I don't even know any more. I'd like to know.

Carolyn: It's hard to be doing something and realize you don't even know why anymore. I'm going to help you explore that and find out. Meanwhile, since you made up the rules you follow, you can also change the rules. And we will start by making small changes with reassurances that aren't too scary. My idea is that we start with adding some food to your diet and just focus on stopping the weight loss. We won't even discuss weight gain right now. Would you be willing to do that?

Becky: Yes, but how do I know I won't gain weight?

Carolyn: Well, we will start by adding just a little food and a little
            trust. For example, if I tell you that adding a can of tuna
            every day will not cause you to gain weight, you may have
            to trust me and try it so I can prove it to you. Are you willing
            to work something like this out?

Becky: Okay.

Another session with Becky in her binge/purge anorexic phase:

Carolyn: Let me ask you something. What would happen if you
            stopped feeding your dog?

Becky: (*looks down*)

Carolyn: Well? I think it might get tired and anxious and eventually
            even growl and bite people, even those it loved.

Becky: Yeah. (*nervously laughing*)

Carolyn: I kind of think that is happening to you now. Do you believe
            that it wouldn't happen to you?

Becky: Well, I think everybody is exaggerating.

Carolyn: I understand that. But are you sure we are all exaggerating?
            Would you say you don't have a problem?

Becky: No.

Carolyn: Tell me how will it be different for you from all those girls
            you read about? They thought the same thing. You told me
            that when you started this you weighed 125 pounds. At 100
            pounds, you said you didn't want to lose any more weight,
            just maintain it; at 95 pounds, you said the same thing, and
            again at 85 pounds . Now, you weigh only 80 pounds. You
            said you didn't really want to lose any more weight, but look
            what happened. How are you going to stop losing weight?
            You are still losing, and always will if you don't keep down
            any food you've eaten or what you do keep only amounts to
            300 calories a day. Is that still hard for you to believe?

Becky: Yes, I'm afraid I'll gain weight if I eat more than that, so
            whenever I do, I have to throw it up.

Carolyn:	Well, at this point, you could probably eat quite a few more calories and not gain. Your body is desperate for those calories and will use them for vital bodily functions, like keeping you warm, long before you'll put on weight. Anyway, it depends on how much more you eat. Right now I'm concerned that you stop losing. How about that? We will experiment around with what you can eat that will keep you from losing. Okay? But eventually you will need to gain some weight. You are so unhealthy now. You can never be healthy trying to stay at 80 pounds. Remember, it's okay if you want to be thin, but be thin and healthy. You can't be like a skeleton and be healthy. But all I'm asking right now is that we work out a plan whereby you stop losing. Okay?
Becky:	Okay.
Carolyn:	You need to stop the vomiting. Do you think you can do that?
Becky:	I don't know. I get so scared if I overeat.
Carolyn:	I know, but we will go slow with all this and we'll cut back if you start to gain weight and get too scared. Do you think you can do that?
Becky:	I don't know. I want to try, it's just that even if I eat hardly anything, I feel guilty and panicked. I feel like I have to go and get it out. I don't really stop to think about it. I don't feel better, relieved, until it's out. Sometimes I see myself just getting fatter and fatter and completely losing control.
Carolyn:	That's what really scares you isn't it? Losing control.
Becky:	Uh-huh.
Carolyn:	It's like you have to follow little rules to keep you in control and then feel guilty if you break them.
Becky:	I feel in control when I can go without eating, and if I break the control and eat, I must force myself to get rid of it. Losing weight is good and gaining weight is bad. Not eating is good and eating is bad.
Carolyn:	You trained yourself to think like that and it helped you lose weight. But how about when you weigh 79 pounds or 75, 70, 65? Do you see that something has to change for you to stop losing?
Becky:	(*Nods head yes*) I know.

Carolyn: There are a lot of things you are afraid of and this eating
           disorder is your safe place to go to get away from the world,
           to tune out other problems, to feel in control of your life.
           And you don't want me or anyone else to take it away from
           you. It's like your best friend.

Becky: Yes it is.

Carolyn: I won't try to take this away from you. You and I both know
           that I can't do that. I can't make you stop doing this to
           yourself, but I can make you want to stop. I can try to help
           you feel better about yourself. I can help you reach your
           goals in a healthy way instead of a destructive way because
           the truth is that you aren't really happy and this is terrible
           torture you put yourself through. This isn't easy, what you're
           doing, and from experience I know how miserable most of it
           is. You shop, cook for, and feed others but not yourself. You
           obsess over calories, recipes, and menus, but never order
           anything, except maybe a salad. You go to bed thinking
           about food, wake up thinking about food, and often dream
           about food. Am I right?

Becky: Yes, I do think about food and weight all the time. It's scary.
           It also makes me feel worse. I like to cook for my family and
           feed them because if I can't eat, I at least want them to. I
           can't stand it when they waste food. I can never stand that,
           it's like I just have to save it for some reason.

Carolyn: I understand that feeling, but isn't throwing up wasting food?

Becky: Yeah, I guess so, but I feel like I have to be the thinnest I can
           be. Whenever I see someone who is thin I feel threatened
           and I hate that. I feel like I have to work harder and stop
           eating. I have to be thinner than they are. I had a dream
           about that, kind of ... this week.

Carolyn: Oh really, what was it like?

Becky: Well, you know how they have those contests at school
           where people are voted the most popular or the most likely
           to succeed?

Carolyn: Yes, we had those at my high school.

Becky: Well, we were having that at school and there was a category
           for the thinnest and everyone wanted to win it. I was doing
           everything I could. I wanted it so bad. I felt like it was
           something I really had a good chance at.

Carolyn:	Wow, how telling that was! What do you think of it?
Becky:	I know I want to have something, to be special. Lots of people can get good grades or scholarships but I have to do something special, something unique, or I feel like a failure.
Carolyn:	Oh Becky, what pressure to put on yourself. It's not worth it. You are special, nothing like that will make it for you. Being 79 pounds didn't make you really love yourself did it? Did it make other people love you more?
Becky:	No.
Carolyn:	Well, it's the same thing. You don't need to be famous or the best or whatever to be loved and to be happy. Besides, if you do want to do something significant or unique, let's think of something constructive. I'm sure you can do better than anorexia, right?
Becky:	Yeah. (*laughter*)
Carolyn:	Do you want to get better, really?
Becky:	Yes I do but ...
Carolyn:	Do you know what that means?
Becky:	Not really. Yes, gaining weight?
Carolyn:	Well, yes, but it means much more than that. Like I said, I can't make you stop your self-imposed torture and force you to gain weight. Even if I could, the weight itself isn't the cure. Without changing your feelings, you'd just lose it all again, but eating more and gaining weight are an important part of getting better, a very important part. I don't want you to die. Look at yourself. What's really important to work on is in here (*points to Becky's head*).

BULIMIA NERVOSA

DIAGNOSTIC CRITERIA FOR 307.51 BULIMIA NERVOSA[33]

A. Recurrent episodes of binge eating. An episode of binge eating is characterized by both of the following:

(1) Eating, in a discrete period of time (e.g., within any 2-hour

period), an amount of food that is definitely larger than most people would eat during a similar period of time and under similar circumstances.

(2)   A sense of lack of control over eating during the episode (e.g., a feeling that one cannot stop eating or control what or how much one is eating.)

B.   Recurrent inappropriate compensatory behavior in order to prevent weight gain, such as self-induced vomiting, misuse of laxatives, diuretics, enemas, or other medications; fasting; or excessive exercise.

C.   The binge eating and other compensatory behaviors both occur, on the average, at least twice a week for three months.

D.   Self-evaluation is unduly influenced by body shape and weight.

E.   The disturbance does not occur exclusively during episodes of Anorexia Nervosa.

Specify type:

Purging Type: during the current episode of Bulimia Nervosa, the person has regularly engaged in self-induced vomiting or the misuse of laxatives, diuretics, or enemas

Nonpurging Type: during the current episode of Bulimia Nervosa, the person has used other inappropriate compensatory behaviors, such as fasting or excessive exercise, but has not regularly engaged in self-induced vomiting or the misuse of laxatives, diuretics, or enemas

JOURNAL ENTRIES

Every night that I throw-up I can't help but be afraid that my heart might stop or something else happen. I just pray and hope I can stop this throwing up before it kills me. I hate this bulimia and I won't stop. It's hard for me to binge and throw-up now (refrigerator is locked) and I just can't do it anymore. I just can't race through so much food so fast and then throw it up. I don't really want to. There are times that I do but not often. My new pattern is sure leaving me with an awful feeling in the morning. I eat dinner and kind of keep eating (snacking) afterwards to the point where I either feel too full or think (know) I've eaten too much, then I fall asleep (one hour or so) wake up and think I have to throw up. Half of me doesn't want to, the other half does and I always find myself throwing up. I try falling back asleep and at times I ward off throwing up for only an hour or two more but it seems like eventually sometime during the night I always throw up.

I feel crazy when I have a panic attack because someone I'm with is eating totally sugary foods, as though I'm afraid just being near it will somehow allow the food, or the fat, or the calories to attack me. Julie picked me up from class the other day, and she was eating dry sugar cookie mix from a bowl with a huge spoon. I panicked. I shook, perspired, had trouble taking full breaths, and couldn't focus or concentrate with all the thoughts rushing through my head. I wasn't eating it, but I could smell it and see it and heard the sugar crystals crunch as she chewed big mouthfuls of it. Then she started eating a cupcake. I couldn't handle it. She offered me some and I became severely nauseated by the mere thought of her offer. When she dropped me off, I raced into the house to gain control of this incredible binge, failing to recognize at the time that I hadn't binged. I was horrified and sick, saw myself gaining weight through my distorted vision, and immediately took laxatives to rid myself of all that forbidden food I felt inside, even though I hadn't eaten a thing.

After I calmed down, I realized the reality of the situation, and I felt stupid and crazy and like a total failure. Not only do I not need anyone else to abuse me, now that I do it myself, I don't even need to binge to have my purging cycle triggered to an intense degree. What's up with that?

CASE EXAMPLE

The following case example is from a session with Paula, a beautiful, bright bulimic patient, 23 years old, five feet, five inches tall, 120 pounds. Paula was extremely uncomfortable with her weight, always expressing the desire to lose a few pounds. Bulimia nervosa had become, in part, her way of maintaining her weight and her control. Paula became anorexic when she was 19 and when she was 20 years old, she began purging her food and soon after started to binge eat. When she came to see me she had already been hospitalized twice for her eating disorder, malnutrition, and suicidality. Paula had a very troubled past and had developed her eating disorder as a way to cope.

When I first saw Paula, her pattern was to hardly eat at all until she went on a binge, eating up to 5,000 calories in a sitting, and then vomiting and/or taking laxatives to purge herself of the horrible food and guilt. Sometimes she would binge 10 times a day. Her voice was raspy, owing to the constant wash of acid in her throat, and her glands were swollen. In the excerpts, you will see that she is still struggling with parts of herself that exist simultaneously, and battle for control.

Individual therapy with Paula, bulimic, purge type:

Carolyn: Were you able to write your thoughts before a binge this week?

Paula: Yes, only once though.

Carolyn: Well, that's all you committed to. You said you'd try more but only committed to once.

Paula: I know it's funny, what you said about trying is true. It sort of means I don't have to do it.

Carolyn: Yes, you see, that's exactly why I ask my clients to commit to what they can do even if it's small. I want you to commit to something you know you can do, trying is different. So, you wrote once. How did it go, how did you feel?

Paula: Well, I didn't really want to. I felt like it … you … were interfering, and…

Carolyn: Interfering with what?

Paula: You know.

Carolyn: Yes, but I think it's important that you say it.

Paula: Interfering with my throwing up.

Carolyn: With your right to do it?

Paula: Ah, maybe, I'm not sure. It's like I don't want to have to think about you or my problems or bulimia, or anything, when I'm bingeing and throwing up.

Carolyn: Yes, it makes it kind of nice in a way, not having to think about or handle pressure or problems.

Paula: Yeah, it's like I get to block it all out, do what I want, pure release, purely for me. Something sick in me just wants to do that. Isn't that sick?

Carolyn: I wouldn't say sick. I think it's adaptive. But do what? What is it you want?

Paula: Just to keep eating and eating and stuffing my face until I just have to throw up, and not think about anything else.

Carolyn: I got you to think a little, let's see what you wrote.

Paula: (*hands over diary*)

Carolyn: (*hands it back*) No, you read it.

Paula: Do I have to?

Carolyn: Of course not, but I think it would be best if you did.

Paula: (*reads out of diary*) I feel so stuck right now. If I can't just keep eating (snacking) after dinner I feel anxious, deprived and I feel I want to binge.

There is a part of me that is so tired of this stupid eating disorder, yet there's still a part of me that won't let go completely. Why? When will I be able to let go completely? What if I never can? I get so tired of forcing myself to eat, and when I do eat, I watch every bite I take. I hate the fact that it seems I spend every waking minute hating my body, feeling ashamed and too embarrassed to even go outside my house. It frustrates me to know that I will never be "thin enough" and that there's nothing I can do but accept that fact and move on.

Binged:

Two bowls of cereal

One large bag of animal cookies

One quart of ice cream

Two-thirds of frozen cheesecake

Paula: Kind of sad, and like it really wasn't me, isn't me. Well, it is but it isn't. Do you know what I mean?

Carolyn: Yes, I think so. There are two parts of you, one that really wants to give this up and one that is really afraid to do that.

Paula: Yes, that's exactly right. The part of me that's afraid needs

something to take its place. Sometimes I'm afraid of what I
would be without it.

Carolyn: It keeps you from having to face that.

Paula: You think so?

Carolyn: Yes, and I also think it's your way of getting back.

Paula: At who?

Carolyn: Well, I think you'll have to answer that.

Paula: The world (*we both laugh*)

Carolyn: Well, maybe so, and yet I think there may be some specific
           people too. Think about it, you can write about that this
           week. You know actually your bingeing and purging, your
           focus on and obsession with food, keep you from dealing
           with lots of issues in your life where you could really have
           an effect or make a change.

Paula: Oh boy, I really feel that. This is so sick, isn't it?

Carolyn: There you go again, I think it's sad. And I think there was a
           reason why this happened.

Paula: Yeah, me too.

Carolyn: I'd like you to have a dialogue with your two selves that
           we've talked about, the one that wants to give up the binge-
           ing and purging and the one that wants to keep it. It's best if
           you do it before a binge, try that, but commit to at least just
           doing it sometime. Okay?

Paula: Why do you say it that way?

Carolyn: Because it will be hard and I don't want to set you up to fail.

Paula: Well, explain it more.

Carolyn: Well, I want you to have a discussion with your Bulimic Self,
           or with your throwing up or overeating or whatever you
           choose. You talk with it like this, "Hello, Bulimia, this is
           Paula. I want to talk with you." It may say, "Okay, here I am,
           let's talk…" You might say, "I'm upset with you. Why are you
           still here?" You just let it flow. Write whatever comes up. It
           may be hard to get started, but you'll be surprised. Once you
           start it will just come.

Paula: Okay, I can do that. I know how to do that.

Carolyn: Good, then we will go over it next week. You can do it a few
           times if you want. It's pretty powerful.

Paula:	It will be interesting to see what comes up. I want to get rid of this and I want to tell it to go away. It's really not doing anything for me.
Carolyn:	Well, it's doing something.
Paula:	I know, the obvious thing is that I'm afraid that I'll gain weight if I stop throwing up.
Carolyn:	And taking laxatives?
Paula:	I really don't do that anymore.
Carolyn:	You really don't?
Paula:	Oh, only once in awhile.
Carolyn:	How often?
Paula:	Once every two weeks, maybe.
Carolyn:	I wouldn't say that is not doing it anymore, and throwing up? How did you do this week?
Paula:	Well, it's less, only about two times a day now at the most, usually less.
Carolyn:	That's great. I think it's great. How do you feel about it?
Paula:	I think it's good. I feel better.
Carolyn:	I know you're trying and look how far you've come, from 10 times a day to two times a day is big progress.
Paula:	But I just can't seem to give it up altogether, it's so hard. I'm scared about my weight going up and besides I keep telling you I'd really like to lose five pounds.
Carolyn:	Yes I know but you don't need to lose weight, and anyway I guess I need to tell you again that it's important not to have weight loss as a goal right now when we're trying to stop your bulimia. We must first deal with the eating disorder and then we can deal with your weight. Besides, what you're doing is not working. Remember that. If you wanted to lose weight, want to lose weight, you can see that what you're doing isn't working anyway. You've been coming for three months and you are still the same weight. So even by your standards, *what you're doing is not working*. Say that to yourself over and over this week. You are going to have to trust me and eventually your body and allow yourself to get to your natural weight in a healthy, realistic way. Right now, as long as long as you keep up with the bingeing and purg-

ing, you will not be able to repair your metabolism. I have already explained that to you. It is slowing down to conserve calories. Also, by your crazy dieting, you are continually losing muscle, not just fat, and remember it is muscle that burns off most calories in your body. So, you are interfering with your own goal this way because you have to eat less and less just to maintain your weight. I feel like I have to constantly remind you about this. It's as though you don't believe me.

Paula: I know that, I have noticed it. I do, it's just that I don't think about it.

Carolyn: Well, there's a part of you that doesn't want to think about it, that wants to keep doing your eating disorder behaviors, otherwise you would stop doing them. We have to find out why that part of you wants to keep this, that's why I'm suggesting the dialogue with your bulimic self so we can find out more about how and what she thinks.

Paula: Okay. I can do that

Following is a copy of the dialogue Paula brought to our next session. When giving it to me she explained that when she started to write, she became aware of three separate parts of herself—her anorexic self, her bulimic self, and her healthy self—and wrote from all three.

Paula's Eating Disorder Dialogue Among Healthy Self, Bulimic Self, and Anorexic Self

Bulimic Self:

We all know I am the strongest still, no matter how many hospitals, how many groups, how many times we go to therapy. Don't you see that the answer to all your problems is me? With me you can eat what you want, when you want it. You can then just get rid of it. I don't have to count every calorie that passes my lips. If I don't want it inside me, I just throw up. The only thing I have to worry about is pizza because I don't throw up pizza. But then again, there's always laxatives. Think about the weight lifted off your mind when the laxatives kick in. Look at all the foods you can't eat without me. With me you'd be able to eat ice cream, or cookies, or even a candy bar and you wouldn't have to worry about gaining weight. With me you can go to bars and drink a Long Island or a Kamikazi shot and not freak over the calories. I keep us in control, yet free. I allow us to do more while still looking fit and thin.

Why lock us into a rigid little box of rules and guidelines without any room for flexibility in our plan, like Anorexia does? When your world seems to be off track, I come into play and put us on the one track only we control—the bulimic track. Sure, everyone says throwing up and using laxatives isn't being in control, but the reality is, we feel in control, and isn't that exactly what we're seeking? I simply don't see the problem I cause. In my mind, I'm doing you a big favor. You'll thank me come bathing suit season. Just wait.

Healthy Self:

Okay, Bulimia, you've said more than your share. Now it's my turn to respond. I think it's great that there is a part of me so determined to do things her way. I just wish I could help you to see why your way isn't necessarily the best way. Sure, some people can live their whole lives as bulimics, maybe not as severe as you tend to be, but nevertheless bulimic. But is that really how you want to live? Always chained to the bathroom? We watched our dad for 17 years chained to the bathroom and never saw the connection. He used to say our system was just like his, following strict rules and always needing to be near a bathroom. He's 66 years old and still chained up.

Don't you want to break free at 23 and go on to enjoy the world beyond the bathroom? Sure, you allow us to indulge in "delicacies" I normally would turn away from, except maybe a tiny bite or two, and even those few bites aren't enjoyable because we're already concentrating on how to "undo" what we've done. That doesn't put us in control of anything—it puts us at the mercy of our eating disorder. Despite the way our body appeared on the outside, you were tearing it up from the inside. Our stomach, esophagus, throat, and nasal cavities all burned from the constant vomiting. And I don't even want to speculate on the damage being done to our intestines by the laxative abuse. None of that represents control in my opinion.

Learning to eat a variety of foods high in protein and low in fats and in calories that match the amount of calories we burn in a day seems to be the true control we will probably find. But I can't do it alone. I need your effort and commitment as well. Your way may have worked for a while, but we know other, healthier better ways now. For a long time now, about 11 years actually, you have helped me to cope with the stresses of growing up, of being raped, of being stuck in an abusive relationship. But I know new coping skills now that don't hurt as much as you do. You have a lot of strength, which I acknowledge and admire. Let's try to channel that strength into employing our newly learned coping skills, building a strong, healthy body free of the chains of the eating disorder. No one said I have to get rid of you. Just the opposite. Carolyn is hoping I can integrate your strength into me to create an even stronger, much healthier whole. I'm not saying I don't need you; I'm just saying I need you in a new and different way, a healthier way, a way Carolyn is teaching us about and encouraging us to become.

I certainly don't see you as "all bad," Bulimia. I need your determination and your control, but I need it to be expressed in a healthy way. I'm tired of throwing up. I'm tired of the laxatives. I'm tired of always being dehydrated. I'm tired of living my life in the bathroom, sneaking in and out so no one knows or suspects. I'm tired of craving foods I know I'll just throw up if I eat one or two. And I'm no longer proud of the fact that I can throw up so quietly that no one hears. That's a part of your identity that I'd like to leave behind, replacing it with a strength, such as knowing that to eat one or two of our "forbidden foods" won't kill us, and that we can control it without being self-destructive. I need you, Bulimia, you're right; but I need the healthy aspects you can offer, without the destructive ones. That is my goal as the Healthy Self. I hope you'll work with me on this, Bulimia.

Anorexic Self:

Now it's my turn. I'm the Anorexic Self and I disagree with both of you. Why do you want to eat something if all along you know you're going to have to throw it up? Why not recognize the fact that it isn't a safe food for us and not eat it? I want thin legs, really thin legs. And I want my ribs to show, and my shoulder blades and collar bone to show. I want my cheek bones to be pronounced. I want my chest to be about 100 times smaller. I hate that guys look at us and they talk more to our chest than to our eyes. Guys just complicate everything. I want to be unnoticeable to guys. I've told you all along I don't want to go on dates, to be social, to get attention. I just want to get small enough that I can go unnoticed. I want to be flat and "curveless" enough to not be noticed by guys. When guys come on to me, I get scared. We've always been "full-figured" and we were an "early bloomer." Well, I want to go back to before all that happened.

When we were in seventh and eighth grades, we were as safe as we ever could be. We were happier than any other time in our life. We didn't have a big chest, big hips, big legs, a big butt. We were just there, a kid, finally left alone for the first time in years. Is it so wrong for me to want to be like that again? I can do it, you know. I can lose the weight to get back to the way I was. I got down to 98 pounds last year, and I can do that again. I can get to 90 pounds and then I'd be happy. Every time we go to Carolyn's, I see that other, skinny girl in the waiting room, and I want to cry because I want so badly to look like her. I'll do anything to look like her. I can eat salads and that's it, I don't need to eat much because I don't get hungry. I want to lose weight so badly, but the Healthy Self is getting stronger and eating more healthy and trying not to use laxatives. That makes it harder for me. I don't understand why a part of us would agree to not lose weight. Don't you guys realize that our only hope for peace and happiness is to go back to the only time in our life when we weren't hurting? If we get to look like that girl in Carolyn's office, we'll be happier. I just know it. So what if there are things we can't eat. I don't like food anyway. Just leave it up to me and we won't have a problem. We'll be happy again—don't you guys want that?

Healthy Self:

Yes, dear Anorexia, we want to be happy, but not at the expense of our health, and possibly our life. When we were in the hospital being tube fed, we were told repeatedly by the doctors and by Carolyn that if we held on to our goal weight of 90 pounds, we would die. Plain and simple. We would die. We've put our body through too much and it simply couldn't handle it. I don't know about you, but I'd rather figure out a way to live with weighing 115 pounds than to die trying to get to a weight we'll never reach. Whenever we restrict, our whole world turns upside down. Our emotions go haywire, our body barely functions, we become depressed and suicidal, our school work drops until we receive failing marks, we become isolated from all our friends, and we can't even carry on a conversation because our thoughts are so mixed up. And, as our pattern has proved, whenever you take over, we end up in the hospital, having complete memory lapses for whole blocks of time, and getting kicked out of school.

When I was a junior in high school and got kicked out for the third time, they told me I'd never amount to anything because I didn't have it in me to reach my potential. They knew I was smart—my IQ was 148 and my SATs were 1100—but my mind was so obsessed with my anorexia and bulimia that my intelligence wasn't going to get me anywhere in life and those things weren't going to keep me alive. When it came time to apply for college I didn't have any ground to stand on. But over the next two years, I worked hard to be accepted into an extended education program. This was my only chance, my parents paid $1,200 per quarter and I had to get good grades. Finally, four quarters later, I was accepted into the school I wanted. And now, because of my Bulimic Self and you, my Anorexic Self, all my hard work is being jeopardized. I can't let you take this away from me. My goals and dreams rely on my education, and I am more than capable of making those dreams and goals a reality. What good are we going to do anyone when we get our therapy license if we can't even remember our last session with a client? What kind of example will we be setting for the people we are working with if we are 30 pounds underweight ourselves and still chained to the bathroom? We have a life to live today that is free of the past. We don't have to regress to a safer time in our childhood. What we really need to do is grow up and look beyond ourselves and the tiny little box we've given ourselves to live in. The world is ours for the taking, no matter what we weigh. So let's maintain a healthy weight with flexible, reasonable guidelines, and take on the world. We didn't survive the hell of our childhood to imprison ourselves and throw away the key.

You taught me a lot, Anorexia, about myself, my needs, and my pain, and now it's time that I teach you about our world as an adult, and teach you that we can take control of our safety by moving forward instead of backwards. Thank you for all you've taught me and for helping me to cope with the seemingly unbearable circumstances of growing up. But please, give me a chance to learn new ways to protect us from the things that once hurt us. All I ask for is a little time to try it my way, to listen to and grow from what Carolyn teaches us, and to develop me, the Healthy Self, into an even stronger self by integrating your sense of control and Bulimia's determination with my newly learned healthy coping skills. That way, we'll all be safe and, in the end, isn't that what each of us really wants?

BINGE EATING

Binge eaters who do not purge or use other compensatory behaviors, such as fasting, to get weight off, suffer from excessive weight gain and become obese.

In DSM-IV, binge eating is included in the category titled "Eating Disorder Not Otherwise Specified," which lists examples of disordered eating that need treatment but don't meet the criteria for anorexia nervosa or bulimia nervosa.

Many think that binge eating disorder should be a separate diagnostic category and thus it is now also listed in the DSM-IV in a section for proposed diagnoses. The listing includes the diagnostic criteria being considered;

RESEARCH CRITERIA FOR BINGE-EATING DISORDER[34]

A.   Recurrent episodes of binge eating. An episode of binge eating is characterized by both of the following:

1.   Eating, in a discreet period of time (e.g., within any 2-hour period), an amount of food that is definitely larger than most people would eat in a similar period of time under similar circumstances; and

2.   A sense of lack of control over eating during the episode (e.g., a feeling that one cannot stop eating or control what or how much one is eating).

B.   The binge-eating episodes are associated with three (or more) of the following:

1.   Eating much more rapidly than normal

2.   Eating until feeling uncomfortably full

3.   Eating large amounts of food when not feeling physically hungry

4.   Eating alone because of being embarrassed by how much one is eating

5.   Feeling disgusted with oneself, depressed or very guilty after overeating

C.   Marked distress regarding binge eating is present.

D.   The binge eating occurs, on average, at least 2 days a week for 6 months.
     Note: the method of determining frequency differs from that used for Bulimia Nervosa; future research should address whether the preferred method of setting a frequency threshold is counting the number of days on which binges occur or counting the number of episodes of binge eating.

E.   The binge eating is not associated with the regular use of inappropriate compensatory behaviors (e.g. purging, fasting, excessive exercise) and does not occur exclusively during the course of Anorexia Nervosa or Bulimia Nervosa.

JOURNAL ENTRY—JODI

I like to eat when I'm tired because I wouldn't have enough energy to enjoy doing something more active. I'd like some nachos right now, a lot of nachos right now. A lot of nachos with lots of cheese, supernachos with guacamole and jalapenos, plus everything, and then I could go for some toast—cinnamon toast with lots of butter, cinnamon, and sugar. Then I wish we had some cheesecake with crunchy graham cracker crust and creamy filling. Then I would like something with chocolate, such as chocolate ice cream or soft brownies with vanilla ice cream and magic shell or magic shell on coffee ice cream or Swiss almond or oatmeal cookies and vanilla Häagen-dazs with magic shell! Nuked rice cakes, popcorn rice cakes, still warm. Also, I would like a whole bowlful of granola—really good granola with milk. I want granola on ice cream with magic shell! GRUB! Häagen-dazs bar; vanilla with chocolate cover and almonds or coffee toffee crunch. Then I would like toast with butter and spun honey. Yum! Then soft biscuits with butter and spun honey. Yum! Hot, soft biscuits with butter and honey; big ones, crusty on the outside and soft on the inside. Then butter and honey melted together.

Food, different taste combinations, new experiences; old, familiar comforts like pancakes and toast are comforting. The experiments with ice cream are new experiences, breakfast foods seem to be more comforting—toast, cereal, pancakes, etc. They comfort me, a reminder of safety and security, like having breakfast in the comfort of your home before embarking on the rigors of the day. It is a reminder that safety and security are tangibly accessible, symbolized in breakfast foods.

CASE EXAMPLE

Adel, a 16-year-old binge eater, first came to me weighing over 200 pounds. She had gained 60 pounds in the last year. Adel had been on and off diets since she was five years old when her mother had the family doctor prescribe diet pills for her. Adel had a troubled, noncommunicative family. She was always trying to please them but always seemed to fall just short of it. She was constantly turning to food for comfort. She would eat everything in sight one day and try to stop the next, but couldn't. She desperately tried to limit her food intake but was obsessed with the idea of food and eating all day long. Once she had lost weight and maintained it for a year. However, since her parents moved the family out to California, she had experienced a steady increase in weight. Adel was very depressed and suicidal about her failure to control her eating and her weight. Her mother would come to the sessions and complain about Adel's lack of willpower; her father wouldn't come at all. Below is a sample of her answers on an eating behavior inventory she did for me.

Binge eating several times a day
Feeling seriously depressed several times each week
Feeling seriously anxious several times each month
Spending six hours or more daily on symptoms such as bingeing
Spending $50 to $100 per week on binge food, and diet pills
Symptoms have substantially interfered with all areas of life
Current weight 197
Ideal weight 110

Adel felt discouraged, believing she couldn't get over her problem. Her day was filled with thoughts or behaviors regarding eating food and losing weight. She would wake up wanting to diet and then begin bingeing as soon as she ate. Adel spent all her money on food, laxatives, or diet pills, and was so preoccupied with eating and dieting that it interfered with everything else in her life. She thought of herself as a failure and was very dissatisfied with everything. She always felt bad and worthless:

I feel like this is all for a reason. Part of me knows I'll be Okay, another part feels like I'll be miserable till I die. I hate myself and criticize myself. I think of killing myself and feel my family and I would be better off if I were dead. I want to have interests, but outside of my best friends I feel too ugly and fat to get involved. I wake up tired and it takes a lot of effort to do things. I'm always thinking about this problem unless I'm bingeing.

If your daughter is a binge eater, she needs help in establishing a normal and peaceful relationship with food. It is important to take the focus off losing weight and to help her to focus instead on what she is doing with food that she would like to stop doing, or what she seems unable to do around food that she would like to be able to do. Helping binge eaters to try yet another form of dieting will usually not work. Setting weight loss as a goal may even be unrealistic for your daughter. The issue of body size acceptance must be addressed, even if she is determined to lose weight. Accepting herself at present will actually help her to achieve any future goals.

EATING DISORDER NOT OTHERWISE SPECIFIED

There are a variety of forms of disordered eating, other than binge eating, that don't meet the current diagnostic criteria for one of the DSM-IV eating disorders. Your daughter may very well have an eating disorder even though she does not fall neatly into one of the previously described categories. Look over the following list taken from the DSM-IV, for examples of other kinds of disordered eating requiring help.

307.50 EATING DISORDER NOT OTHERWISE SPECIFIED[35]

The Eating Disorder Not Otherwise Specified category is for disorders of eating that do not meet the criteria for any specific eating disorder. Examples include:

1. For females, all of the criteria for Anorexia Nervosa are met except that the individual has regular menses.
2. All of the criteria for Anorexia Nervosa are met except that, despite significant weight loss, the individual's current weight is in the normal range.
3. All of the criteria for Bulimia Nervosa are met except that the binge eating and inappropriate compensatory mechanisms occur at a frequency of less than twice a week or for a duration of less than 3 months.
4. The regular use of inappropriate compensatory behavior by an individual of normal body weight after eating small amounts of food (e.g., self-induced vomiting after the consumption of two cookies).
5. Repeatedly chewing and spitting out, but not swallowing, large amounts of food.
6. Binge-eating disorder: recurrent episodes of binge eating in the absence of the regular use of inappropriate compensatory behaviors characteristic of Bulimia Nervosa.

Anorexia, bulimia, binge eating, and their variations are ways of coping with the world through food and weight. There are numerous overlaps and similarities among the disorders and some people go from anorexia, to bulimia, to binge eating, or the other way around. A good thing to remember in order to differentiate among the disorders is that, more often than not, the binge eater will turn to food to cope whereas the anorexic turns away from it, and the bulimic alternates between those two extremes. If your daughter has an eating disorder, no matter which type, she is using her behaviors around food and weight as a means of coping with her feelings. She has an unnatural relationship with food and her body and is battling, even against herself, in this arena.

From the case examples, you can see that the issues of food and weight have become all encompassing issues for these individuals, often to the exclusion of anything else. And even though they are coming to therapy and expressing a sincere desire to get better or get over their eating disorder, their behaviors often continue, to the dismay not only of those trying to help them, but also of themselves.

Definitions, explanations, and even case examples do not provide you with enough information to tell if your daughter is having a problem. What will you, as a parent, be able to notice, what can you look for and observe in your daughter that will tip you off to the fact that she either has, or is in danger of developing, an eating disorder? The following is a list of questions concerning signs and symptoms that are observable indicators that your own daughter may have a problem.

OVERT BEHAVIORS—WHAT YOU CAN SEE
OR HEAR THAT MAY INDICATE
YOUR DAUGHTER HAS OR IS DEVELOPING
AN EATING DISORDER

1. Does your daughter constantly go on diets and/or make excuses for not eating?
2. Does she exhibit bizarre food rituals or behaviors?
3. Is she preoccupied with food and weight?
4. Does she express herself in all-or-nothing, black-and-white, thinking?
5. Does she avoid social situations, especially if they involve food?
6. Has she started to lose friends and withdraw?
7. Have you found hidden food, laxatives, diuretics, and/or diet pills?

8. Does your daughter go to the bathroom or otherwise disappear after eating?
9. Is she eating a great quantity of food but losing weight or not gaining?
10. Has she started wearing baggy clothing and layers of clothes?
11. Do you notice extreme mood swings in her that have no apparent source?
12. Is food missing from the house with no explanation?
13. Is your daughter spending money with nothing to show for it?
14. Does she fast occasionally with various excuses?
15. Does she get up late at night and have trouble sleeping?
16. Have her face or neck glands become swollen and puffy?
17. Does she have any sign of scars on the back of the hand (due to teeth marks forced vomiting)?
18. Does she seem tired and lack vitality?
19. Does she get depressed and angry for no apparent reason?
20. Do you feel as though you never see her eating?
21. Is she losing weight and is defensive about it?
22. Has your daughter become a vegetarian and/or otherwise avoids specific foods?
23. Is your daughter almost illogical and paranoid about eating certain foods?
24. Does she take showers after meals?
25. Have there been signs of vomiting, although she never said anything about being ill?
26. Are there any signs of enema or laxative use ?
27. Does she seem to feel cold all the time?
28. Is her hair falling out and showing up on her hairbrush or in the shower?
29. Does your daughter obsess over what others eat and does she want to cook for, bake for, and feed others?
30. Is she preoccupied with or does she obsess over pictures of thin people?
31. Does she obsessively weigh herself, panicking at your suggestion of taking the scale away?
32. Does her diet contain an excessive amount of gum, coffee, diet soda, mustard, spices, and other noncalorie items?
33. Has she become a calorie computer?
34. Is she steadily gaining weight?
35. Does she always want and/or use food as a reward?

36. Has she had temper tantrums over food not being "just right"?
37. Have you seen her with bloodshot eyes and burst blood vessels (from vomiting)?
38. Has she had an increased number of cavities and/or a discoloration of the teeth?

The overt behaviors list gives you an idea of things you can look for and things you may not have paid attention to in the past. Even one or two of these behaviors can be the signal of a developing eating disorder. Once you have noticed the behavior, you will need to respond to it. You will have to be careful not to go into battle with your daughter. The way you approach her could make all the difference. Therefore, your understanding of the nature of her discomfort, dissatisfaction, or pain and of the underlying reasons for why she might be starving, bingeing, or purging is important. The more you understand the real issues, the more she will trust you and the better chance you have of helping her. Many times parents ask: "Why is she doing this? What is she thinking? What is going on in her head?" So let us now turn to that issue.

9

❧ ❧ ❧

What's Going on in There?

Eating is symbolically associated with the most deeply felt human experiences, and thus expresses things that are sometimes difficult to articulate in everyday language.[36]

Feeding On Dreams

I don't trust my feelings with people so I just keep it all in and I eat over it. I just get fatter and fatter and fuller and fuller of my own feelings.

Paulette, 36-year-old binge eater

I don't know what's worse: feeling like I am going to explode in my head from not bingeing, or feeling like my stomach is going to explode from bingeing. The second thing is easier because I don't have to talk about it or deal with the way I am feeling. The only thing I think about is how and when I'm going to throw up.

Natalie, 26-year-old bulimic

What is wrong with her? Where did she get these crazy ideas? I used to think she had a great head on her shoulders and now I ask myself, 'What's going on in there'?

Mother of a Bulimic

A mother once called my office when she thought her daughter might be in the bathroom throwing up. Pleading for help, she asked, "What is going on in there?" I realized that I needed to explain not only what was going on in the bathroom but what was going on inside her daughter's head. If your daughter is suffering from an overconcern with her body image, from unhealthy dieting practices, or from anorexia nervosa, bulimia nervosa, or binge eating, she has become a victim of our thin crazed society and a victim of a struggle within herself. Her dilemma goes far beyond one of dieting. For her, the pursuit of thinness becomes the pursuit of something much more. When carried to the extreme, the inner world of someone in this pursuit is so complex and varied, so difficult to understand and treat, that eating disorders warrant consideration as one of the most serious mental health epidemics of our time.

To really understand your daughter, look beyond definitions and further into her inner world. Over the years, several topics have emerged as themes in the lives of young women who develop disordered eating. These themes, which I call "The Real Issues" are listed and described to help provide insight into what might be "going on in there." Always keep in mind that it is from listening to and getting to know your daughter that you will gain a greater understanding of the real reasons that provide the meaning to her disordered eating and/or exercizing habits.

THE REAL ISSUES

1. *Poor Self-Esteem/Self-Worth*
   I'm afraid of myself and of being out of control.
   I'm not very worthy.
   People don't like me.
   I'm no good.
   I can't trust my own judgments or make decisions.

2. *Belief in a Myth*
   I will be happy and successful if I am thin.
   Eating helps me to forget my problems.
   Thinner people are happy.
   Being thin will make me attractive.

3. *Need for Distraction*
   When I'm bingeing or throwing up, I don't think about anything else.

Eating takes my mind off things.
Worrying about my weight keeps me from worrying about other
   things.

4. *Need to Fill up an Emptiness*
    Something is missing in my life.
    I feel empty inside, starving makes it better.
    Eating fills up my emptiness.

5. *Need for Perfection and Black/White Thinking*
    I have to be the best at anything I do.
    I will be the best dieter.
    I will have the best body.
    Black/White Thinking:
       I'm either fat or thin.
       I either binge or starve.
       I'm perfect or a failure.
       If I can't win, I won't try.

6. *Need to Be Special/Unique*
    I get a lot of attention.
    What will I be without this?
    I get to be taken care of, worried about.
    Nobody is like me.
    It is the only special thing I have.

7. *Need to Be in Control*
    My family is too involved in my life.
    I have to be in control of something.
    I'm always in control of everything else, so this is my way not to be.
    The eating disorder behaviors fill unstructured time.
    I'm proud of the willpower it takes.
    This is the one thing no one has control over but me.

8. *Need for Power*
    I base my feelings of self on how others treat me.
    I feel powerless.
    This gives me power over myself and others.
    It's powerful to be able to give up food, like a saint or monk.
    I can really get at my parents this way.

9. *Need for Respect and Admiration*
    Society perpetuates respect and admiration for thinness:
       Gets it through weight loss. (anorexic)

Tries hard to get it through weight loss but can't do it. (bulimic)
Rebels against it. (binge eater)
Everyone respects me when I lose weight.
People admire you if you are thin and/or if you don't eat.

10. *Has Hard Time Expressing Feelings*
Very difficult time with anger, rebellion, resentment.
Symbolically swallows, denies, or rejects feelings.
Can't deal with conflict or confrontation.
Denies feelings or expresses them in destructive ways.
I don't know what I'm feeling, even if I do, I can't express it.

11. *Safe Place to Go—Doesn't Have Coping Skills*
It's a "special world" created to keep all the "bad" out.
If I follow my own imposed rules, I know what to expect, how to "win."

13. *Lack of Trust in Self and Others*
I don't trust myself emotionally.
I never know if someone really likes me.
I don't trust anybody.
I can never make a decision.
It's easier just to follow rules

12. *Terrified of Not Measuring Up*
I can't compete, so this way I take myself out of the running.
What are my good qualities?
I won't have anything if I don't have this.
I'm constantly comparing myself to everyone.
Terrified of being fat. (anorexic)
Terrified of being deprived. (binge eater)
Terrified of being deprived and of being fat. (bulimic)

DEALING WITH THE REAL ISSUES

POOR SELF-ESTEEM/SELF-WORTH

You have you on your side, all I have on mine is me

Ashley Brilliant

Your daughter may feel that she has not found any real meaning in life. She may feel empty and insignificant. She may devalue herself. She may torture her body to conform to some standard she has set, forcing it to be different because it is not good enough. Many times I have asked young girls to tell me the good things about themselves and they draw a blank. How your daughter developed poor self-esteem can be important. Ask yourself if there were early parent messages such as overly praising her accomplishments or looks. Perhaps your daughter has been affected by such comments as "Can't you do anything?" or "You can do better than that." Maybe there was a traumatic event or a series of small events that shattered her self-confidence.

It is important to remember that on the surface your daughter may present a self to others that looks very together and self-confident. In fact, the term "poor self-worth" is more appropriate in many cases than poor self-esteem. Your daughter may actually feel better about herself than do many young girls with poor self-esteem who walk around depressed, with heads hung low, hating themselves. She may have several friends and even be proud of herself for her successes, but has a nagging feeling that whatever she does is not good enough. Even if she has accomplished many things, she may feel that others aren't going to value her unless she does more, so she tries harder to get approval and acceptance, and nothing is ever enough.

Through psychotherapy, your daughter's self-esteem and feelings of self-worth can be explored and enhanced. I believe that if a significant bond is established between the therapist and client, the client's self-esteem increases. To have another human being genuinely care about you is an uplifting, healing experience. People care more for themselves when they feel cared about. You may be saying, "But, I care about my daughter." The problem is that your daughter may be ashamed to let you know how she thinks and feels. She may not want to disappoint you. You may have given her reason to believe that you would be very upset if she told you the truth about her behaviors and thoughts. She may have tried to tell you things but you didn't hear her or didn't take her seriously, or you figured, she could work it out. The self-depreciating self-doubt and the conflict between "I'm worthy" and "I'm not worthy" are expressed in the following journal entries from two clients, neither of whom had told her feelings to her parents.

ஒ ஒ ஒ

Dear Carolyn,

I have been feeling awful lately—for the past month or so, I've been real busy. I work every night that I don't go to school—six days! until 2 or 3 in the morning, then I sleep in and wake up and go to my day classes. In my spare time I eat or sleep or take laxatives. I don't have any time to think and I have this constant feeling that something is going to go wrong or else I've done something wrong. I keep crying and feeling depressed and I don't know what to do. I don't have anyone to talk to. My mom, I have never been able to talk to because she has absolutely no concern for me and she is the problem anyway. I used to talk to my dad, but he hasn't listened for 3 or 4 years. It seems like I can't describe or get out the feelings I have. So there is really no one for me to pour it all out to. I keep thinking I want to kill myself, but something inside me won't let me and then I want to kill that too. I don't even know why I try to tell you all this. I was just hoping you could say something to help me.　—Gretchen

ஒ ஒ ஒ

Dear Carolyn

There has finally come a time when I've thought seriously about some ideas for my future and it is now that I need support from someone (anyone), so that I won't give up (because I would mess it up myself). Now I realize I don't have anyone who really cares about me. It is around 12 A.M. on Monday night and here I sit in my room completely crying my eyes out. Things are awful. As usual, no one knows, cares, or even wonders how I feel so I write it down and send it in the mail thinking something would actually happen because of it. I only wish I had one person who gave a damn about how I feel but my wishes are always too far fetched and impossible. Maybe I just don't even have a clue. I mean, I guess there is no such thing as caring the way I think of it. I want out of here (me) so badly now and I can't make it happen, starving and bingeing and purging don't work either. Every day I wake up and pretend and I can't stand it any longer. If you could help me, Carolyn, I would give my life to you. I am always misunderstood. Can you tell me why I don't think I'm that bad and everyone else does?　—Ellie

ஒ ஒ ஒ

Low self-esteem is often overwhelming and debilitating, causing an inability to make decisions. Young girls and even grown women aren't sure that they can trust their own judgments and are extremely afraid of making the wrong choice, acting as if all decisions are of equal importance. Difficult decisions range anywhere from choosing what pair of pants to wear or what time to eat to which college to attend to whether to stay alive.

You may need help knowing when to take control and make decisions for your daughter and when to foster trust in her ability to make them herself. If she is living life as if everything were right or wrong and cannot tolerate the idea of making a mistake, she needs help in realizing that a wrong decision is not a disaster. Help her to understand that everything is not as crucial as it might seem. You can help to teach her that life is a process of learning, growing, and experiencing. Ask her to go for a walk and look at the ocean or the trees. Remind her through experiences, not just words, about how much is going on in the world that is truly significant and how she might be missing out on it by worrying about the number on the scale or fact that she ate too much last night. Let her know that if she chooses the wrong college she can change. Remind her that she can't possibly know everything in advance and that life is an ever unfolding and changing experience. Reassure her that no one can always make the right or perfect decision and if she decides to change a decision, it will not mean wasted time but rather a learning experience.

BELIEF IN A MYTH

I will be happy and successful if I am thin.

Maria, 40-year-old binge eater and
Sophie, a 9-year-old anorexic

There are many myths involved in the dieting and thinness fantasy. Society may have deluded your daughter into believing the one just quoted here. With all the advertising and the media bombardment, she may believe that dieting or losing weight will solve her problems or that growing up thin will prevent problems. The trouble is that even if she succeeds at the dieting game, she will soon find that she doesn't feel happy or successful about her life but only about her thinness. In spite of this she may continue to diet, thinking that perhaps she just hasn't gotten thin enough, or that at least she is successful at something.

I talk to my clients about what thinness—the struggle to lose weight and disordered eating—does for them. I ask them if they are happier, more successful, better off. "Do more people like you now?" "Do you have more friends?" "Are you making better grades?" These questions most often test the client's reality because the answer is, "No." But there is one thing they usually are getting more of—attention. Whether it is positive or negative, your daughter is probably getting more attention than she ever received, and giving it up is not easy. It's important for you to understand this, even though your daughter may not. But also important is not to use it against her by accusing her of just wanting attention. I guarantee that this tactic will not help and will most likely cause her to hide things from you, to stop communicating, and to think you don't understand. Ask your daughter to consider if what she is doing is worth it. Tell her that ultimately she will have to decide what price she is willing to pay for thinness. Help your daughter find other, more constructive ways to feel successful and accomplished and even to secure the attention she needs and deserves.

NEED FOR DISTRACTION

Bulimic: *Eating will help me forget my problems*
Therapist: *Yes it does, but only for the moment*

Disordered eating can serve as a temporary distraction, but the problems do not go away. They soon resurface along with the added misery caused by the disordered eating itself, "Why did I binge again?" "I am so disgusting and weak." One important point is that when the original problems are addressed and fully resolved, the need to binge, purge, or starve is no longer necessary. However, it is often the case that the underlying problems may be worked on and greatly improved with no reduction in symptoms. Your daughter may change many aspects of her life that contribute to the eating disorder, but still be unable to stop some or all of her symptoms. Do not confuse this to mean she is addicted to the food. It is the behavior that is habitual. This is why behavior therapy and nutrition counseling must be done in conjunction with psychotherapy. Just talking about problems is not enough, an eating disorder professional will also deal with the symptoms.

One is never free of problems. Dealing with underlying issues is a necessary and important factor in reducing disordered eating symptoms, particularly if they are fairly tangible; "I can't deal with my parents," "I push myself too hard all day and this is my release," "My mother controls everything but she can't touch this." Problems will always exist in your daughter's life and she needs to learn how to cope with them in constructive ways.

Simultaneously to working on her underlying problems, your daughter's reaction to pressure and problems by eating, starving, or purging needs to be replaced with a constructive alternative. Finding other things she can do for distraction, relaxation, or catharsis might help: writing, exercise, taking a hot bath, hitting a punching bag, or calling a friend. These techniques will work in varying degrees with your daughter depending on how habitual her behaviors have become, how much she wants to get better, and how extreme the underlying problems are.

FILLING UP AN EMPTINESS

I feel empty a lot of the time and bingeing actually fills that emptiness. I know I'm missing something. I need something and until I find out what it is, until I find a replacement for this (bingeing), I can't give it up. I won't give it up.

Susan, 36-year-old binge eater

Eating fills up a big black hole inside of me.

Paige, 25-year-old bulimic

Your daughter may feel empty inside. Food is a temporary filler at best and eventually the eating disorder leads to feelings of even deeper emptiness. Your daughter will be most reluctant to give up her symptoms until she feels she has something better. Often I ask clients if their method is working; "Is it working and is it worth it? If not, let's try to find something else." The something else may be a career, a boyfriend, a stronger sense of self. You cannot find this for your daughter but you can help her to discover what's missing and help her to find it for herself. Read the following excerpts from the journals of dieting daughters:

> Something is missing here, that's why I am still bulimic and throw up. Will I ever find what it is I am missing? Yes, I'll find it.... Someday. I've found help for my problem with bulimia and that will lead to finding out my underneath problem.

> We talk about my bulimia and what I should do, but lately I haven't done anything. I just haven't felt like doing anything about it. It's as if my bulimia fills a void for me. I have a hunch that I am going to have to do some radical things with my life if I want to get better. I guess it's time for me to let some more people into my life.

> I wish the reason for my eating disorder were as simple as "parents," but mine isn't simple. It stems from the fact that I am not getting in my life something that I need. Maybe I already have it but I won't let myself have it. Why? Because it's not perfect. I am my best friend and yet I am my worst enemy. I want to be good to myself but at the same time I am killing myself.

> I know there is more to life than what I think there is right now, and at least now I am willing to look for it. There is definitely more to life than bingeing and throwing up, there has to be. I feel there is, I truly feel there is. I don't know what, but it's time to start searching.

NEED FOR PERFECTION AND BLACK/WHITE THINKING

> *I always have to be perfect at everything. I have to do the best at everything. I can't stand it. I hate it but I like it. Anyway, at night is when I don't have to do that anymore. It's my time to be not perfect, to get away with something, so then I binge but, of course, get rid of everything afterward.*

I am right or wrong
I am perfect or a failure
I am thin or fat
I starve or binge

Nina, 21-year-old bulimic

Black/white thinking leaves no room for grays. How did your daughter come to adopt this attitude? Was all-or-nothing thinking common in your household? Was this her way of standing out? Whatever the reason, if your daughter has adopted a perfectionistic attitude, her acknowledgment of it is the first step toward getting better. She may not be aware that she behaves as if everything has to be perfect. She may not see herself as a perfectionist, and may actually feel far from being one. However, once all-or-nothing thinking has been pointed out she may recognize it in herself. This is a very powerful awareness. Even if she cannot change her ingrained behaviors with her new awareness, she can begin to see how irrational it is and how impossible a task it is she has set for herself—to be perfect.

Time and again I have seen clients sigh with relief, almost melting at the idea that they don't have to be perfect. Being the best dieter, following the rules perfectly, having the perfect no-fat body, are all extensions of the irrational drive for perfection, and thus imagined safety and self-esteem. When I was anorexic in college and I used to do 205 sit-ups every night, my goal was to do 200 but I did 5 extra just in case I had done a few of them incorrectly! It was as if someone else were watching me and would know. That's how everything seemed. You may find your daughter following self-imposed rules or carrying out rituals like this.

If your daughter has lost weight she is probably very proud of it. Anorexics feel as though they are winning the perfection battle and it spurs them to continue their "achievement" on a destructive course. To your daughter, eating or gaining weight may seem like a failure, a letdown, a weakness. How can she give up what she struggled so hard to achieve?

Bulimics often strive for perfection and are ashamed at not being able to achieve it. They may be closer to being perfect in other areas of their lives but aren't able to do it with food and weight. Sometimes disordered eating is a rebellion against having to be perfect. It is the one area where some individuals allow themselves to splurge or where they reward themselves. An "I deserve this" attitude may cause a binge.

At the end of the day I feel like I deserve a reward. I rode my bike, went surfing, studied. I deserve to have just pleasure and relax. I can do this with food. I start eating and I can't stop but I think, oh well, I'll just throw it up. I feel guilty afterwards but at the time I feel like I deserve this.

Leanne, 22-year-old bulimic

A bulimic trying to be perfect by not eating or eating very little, sets herself up for a binge. It goes like this:

Deny-deny-deny-deny—SNAP—give me-give me-give me

If your daughter tries to achieve weight loss through unrealistic means and by starving herself now, it is very likely that this will lead to stuffing herself later. Even when starving, throwing up, or taking laxatives doesn't work she may be extremely reluctant to give them up because she fears that she will be out of control and will become obese. She may have come to believe that the laxatives or vomiting is the only thing preventing weight gain. It takes a lot of hard work to convince her of the fallacy of her beliefs.

I am really beginning to see how this perfectionism thing has been in my life for a long time. As a kid, when I would compete in sports, I was fine on a team, but in individual competition I would always create an injury or excuse that would keep me from continuing. I did that because I was afraid to lose. Losing alone, because you've blown it, is so much harder mentally, than losing with a team. On a team, there is always somebody else to blame. When I was in sixth grade, I was in a tennis tournament. I was a good player, but at the time I wasn't convinced of that. One quarter of the way through the tournament, I freaked out with nerves, and came down with the excuse, "I am not feeling good," and bailed the tournament. I'll never forget that. I was afraid of losing.

DESIRE TO BE SPECIAL/UNIQUE

Nobody wants to be a plain Jane.

The above quote and the following journal entry is from Carol, an 18-year-old who became anorexic at age 14.

When I first started losing weight everyone came up to me saying "You look great." "How did you do it?" "I wish I had that kind of will power." This was wonderful, I loved it. I felt powerful and special. Countless others that I knew, even close friends had tried without success to lose weight. I had done it. People noticed me! How could I give this up? It wasn't just the weight loss or my new weight which was powerful, it was the unique ability to do it, the process, the passing up of delicious treats, the power to say no to food. I stood out because I could do it. Instead of a certain weight as the goal, losing weight became the goal. The ability to behave like no one else! The envy of everyone. It is also true that I was afraid that if I let up on the behaviors, I would gain the weight back and worse, become normal again. I didn't want to be like everyone else. The behaviors were a part of me now. The behaviors, and following the rules, were the most important things. My eating disorder made me unique, there was no one like me.

NEED TO BE IN CONTROL

There are many things that are impossible to control, for example, my parents' divorce, whether Jim will go out with me, my dad's drinking—but my body I can control.

Eating or not eating is a way for me to control my body. I decide what goes in or out. Even if it is a bad choice, it's my choice.

Lay people attribute the need for control as the most common cause of eating disorders. Frequently, when I tell people I am an eating disorders therapist they ask, "Isn't that all about control?" Indeed, control issues do play a large part in disordered eating behavior. Chances are your daughter is feeling out of control of her life in some way. Life is not turning out the way she wanted or expected and she finds herself feeling as though she has little or nothing to do with the outcome. This is true for all teens and probably contributes to the fact that the highest rate of eating disorders is in the 16–20 year old group. One way your daughter may attempt to gain control of her life is symbolically through her body.

Young girls and women in general are indoctrinated with the notion of asserting control over their bodies. Usually when the pursuit of thinness begins, it is encouraged and approved of; therefore a perfect arena in which to fulfill a psychological need for control. Unfortunately, too often the pursuit of thinness becomes more of a problem than the one it was trying to solve and eventually leaves the individual less in control. If your daughter severely restricts her food, chances are she will eventually binge. After bingeing, she may feel out of control and attempt to regain control by purging the food through vomiting, exercise, or laxatives. Starving sets her up for bingeing, bingeing sets her up for purging, which sets her up for bingeing or starving again. At some point she will be unable to eat without guilt, unable to stop thinking about food, and unable to give up the purging. Sooner or later, the eating disorder will seem to control her, and not the other way around. If your daughter is caught in this cycle, she must be helped to understand that she is not in control—she is out of control. And, when inevitably, family, friends, doctors, and therapists step in, her loss of control will be amplified. She may, in fact, end up with almost no control, with hospitalization or even death being the outcome if the cycle is not stopped.

It is important for you to understand that you can't take disordered eating behavior away from your daughter; you can't make her stop, but you may be able to get her help so she *wants* to stop. Too often a power struggle begins over the disordered eating and weight loss. If your daughter has to fight you, it just entrenches her behaviors as she asserts her right to her own body, "This is my thing," "You can't touch it," "Let me run my own life." The more someone tries to take it away from her or control her, the harder she will hold fast to her position. I'll often just ask my clients, "Is it really control to have to starve yourself to be thin?" "Is it control to take laxatives or vomit?" "Is it control to avoid going to a party because there will be food or to throw food away because you are afraid to eat it?"

Your daughter will need to explore the reasons behind her need for control. In individual, group and family therapy you can explore why and how your daughter developed her strong need to control something and what your part in that might be.

Your family may be too controlling or overprotective or perhaps too chaotic and lenient. In an overprotective family daughters feel too controlled and want to fight back and be in control of something of their own: "My mother could not do anything about my eating. When mom pissed me off I'd say to myself, 'I'm not going to eat all day' because I knew it would make her mad."

The young anorexic, Sara, who said these things felt over controlled. With all good intentions her parents had gone too far. She restricted her food in part as a means to have total complete control over herself and her parents.

Sara first came to me when she was 16 years old. For years, her mother had been controlling her every move, trying to protect her from any harm. This included "bad taste." Sara couldn't wear certain clothes, dangle earrings or the color black, because her mother considered them unladylike. I remember one occasion when Sara came into my office and pulled a black dress out of her shoulder bag to show me.

Sara: See this, my mother won't let me wear it. I love this dress and there is nothing wrong with it. I should be allowed to wear it, don't you think so?

Me: I'm not sure it matters if I do.

Sara: Well, my mom says I can't wear it, so I take it to school and put it on there and just take it off before I come home.

Me: I guess you really are showing her, aren't you?

Sara: You got it, but it's so ridiculous, could you talk to her?

Me: Yes, I think we both should talk to her about this.

My role, in part, in a situation like this, is to get the mother to see that what she is doing isn't working. Parents often become upset if they feel that I am taking sides or telling them how to raise their children. It's important for parents to keep in mind that there are some battles that aren't worth fighting. Not everything has equal weight in terms of importance. It is best to save energy for more important things than what clothes your daughter wears.

I have seen mothers and daughters who have had fist and hair pulling fights over homework! Treatment can be even more complicated as the battle for control extends where it doesn't belong. The same holds true for trying to control disordered eating behaviors. Parents will try ultimatums such as:

"You won't be able to use the car if you don't gain five pounds."
"You are grounded until you gain weight."
"Eat your dinner or you can't go to the movies."
"Lose weight or I won't pay for dance lessons."
"Lose weight if you want new clothes."

Ultimatums and control tactics like those will not work and may even entrench the control issue more deeply. To begin to let go of control in the area of eating, your daughter needs to experience more control in other areas of her life.

In chaotic or lenient families, things are undercontrolled. One or both parents (usually the mother) is weak, or at least overly permissive, even needy and dependent on the child. This situation parentifies the child who feels like she has to be extra strong and resilient in order to take care of her parent(s). Neither parents nor daughter realize this is happening. If this describes your family, your daughter feels a great deal of responsibility with no real power. To provide structure and guidance, she may resort to making rules for herself, setting standards and goals because she feels like she has to. She must have order in her life and she also feels the need to be perfect and in control because her parents, particularly her mother, rely on her.

It isn't always clear *why* but it is always clear *that* the issue of control in eating disorders is an important one. Your daughter will need to find a means to gain a healthy balanced control over her life, and discover what has gotten in the way of her having this to begin with. Your daughter will need to be convinced that, in fact, she is out of control with her symptoms and not in control, as she desperately wants to be.

NEED FOR POWER

Controlling eating behaviors provides a sense of personal power. How powerful you are if you can deny your body food. How powerful you are if all your family is worried about and dotes over you. How powerful if you decide where or what the family is going to eat for dinner. How powerful to be in the hospital and have all your friends and even people you barely know come to visit or send you cards. How powerful to sculpt your body like no one else can. How powerful to be able to eat whatever you want and secretly throw it up so no one knows how you manage to lose or maintain your weight. How powerful to have others coming to you for advice on how to lose weight. How powerful to be different, noticed, a source of conversation.

The truth is that eating disorder symptoms can make one feel powerful, and the individual will not give up those it symptoms for fear of being powerless. Just like the issue of control, the goal of treatment is to help those suffering feel a sense of personal power in other ways. Your daughter needs to know how to gain and channel power into other, constructive uses because eventually the eating disorder power becomes not only not worth it but eventually useless.

I know I did 'it' sometimes to get back at my dad. It would be the only thing that got him really mad, that he could do nothing about.

The power that an eating disorder gives is also the power of having other people notice you, pay attention to you. You have something they don't. You are extremely thin and/or you are needy; you need help. This ties into being special or unique. I once had a 17-year-old bulimic client, Julie, tell me a very revealing story:

Julie: "I'm so mad, I got a ticket this weekend."

Me: "Oh, that's too bad, what happened?"

Julie: Laughing. "Well I was on my way to this party and I was in a hurry on the freeway. I was in my Porsche and that thing goes fast. This policeman stopped me and I started to cry and said, 'Officer, officer, I have bulimia and I couldn't help it."

Me: "And how did he respond?"

Julie: "I guess he didn't really know what it was, he gave me the ticket anyway."

On repeated occasions Julie would come in smiling and giggling while she told me stories of one person after another who she would meet at the spa, school, or mall, and tell how she had bulimia. Julie loved being bulimic and the power and attention it gave her. She had grown up in a household where the parents raised many children together from their previous marriages and she was the only one that they had together. She admits to having been the spoiled, doted-on baby of a very powerful, domineering father and passive mother. As a teenager with all the other siblings gone, she began to miss the specialness she enjoyed as a young child while at the same time resented her father's attempts to maintain control and power over her. Although I do not believe that initially Julie consciously set out to be bulimic, get back at her parents, and regain her power in the family, her disorder did serve this purpose. She would tell me about her father, "This is something he can't do anything about."

Julie loved to tell people about her bulimia, was often late or missed appointments, and laughed, smiled, and giggled when she discussed her problems with me. This lead me to suggest that she enjoyed being bulimic far more than she wanted to get better and that for her, bulimia was something to be used as an excuse for her other irresponsible behaviors: "I can't help it I'm bulimic." In fact, when I asked her about why she binged and purged she said, "Because I'm bulimic," as if that were a given and nothing went any further or needed to.

All my clients are in a battle with themselves over giving up an eating disorder. If I waited for a client to be ready to "give it up" before entering treatment, I wouldn't have any clients. Every client has one foot in the door of wanting to give it up and one foot out, wanting to keep it. The important thing is that at least there are two sides to the battle. The goal of a therapist is to help the client herself want to give it up, not just because she should but because she really wants to, then the rest of the work is much easier. Most clients desperately want to get rid of an eating disorder but their fear prevents them. However, there are a few clients who are not ready to even try to get ready. For example, Julie could only see what bulimia did for her, nothing more. She had in fact previously been hospitalized in an eating disorder unit for four months and on discharge returned to all her previous behaviors, which is why her parents brought her to me. Although it is a rare move on my part, after a few months of getting nowhere with our sessions, I suggested that at this point in time, I could not help her and she dropped out of treatment. I often think of her with sadness because I could not reach her; maybe another therapist did, or will.

NEED FOR RESPECT AND ADMIRATION

In our present day society where thinness is a highly sought-after commodity, those who have it have the respect and admiration of all the millions of those who don't. The anorexic undergoes the ordeal of "dieting" that the rest of those who want to lose weight cannot tolerate. She gains respect and admiration for her ability to win the battle with her body.

It is unfortunate that losing weight receives such admiration from others. If your daughter is anorexic she is envied for ordering salad at the pizza parlor and for saying, "No thanks" when offered ice cream. Her girlfriends wonder and ask, "How do you do it?" Inside she thinks to herself, "How can I not do it?" The kind of respect and admiration bestowed on anorexics is hard to give up and hard to share. Anorexia becomes a precious item or possession, not to be shared with others.

Christy, a 20-year-old anorexic, recounts:

Christy: My girlfriend next door is always asking me to tell her how I do it. That makes me mad. If she really understood she would not want this.

Carolyn: It also makes you mad because this is your thing, right? You don't want anyone else to have it?

Christy: Yes, exactly. Last year, girls in college would follow me around saying, "I'm going to eat what you eat and do what you do." I was angry at them. It felt as if they would take something away from me. I tried desperately to avoid them. One girl living across from me did become anorexic and I was so angry at her for it! I felt so competitive. When we ate together both of us tried to eat less than the other, and consequently neither of us ate much. I wanted her to go get something else, anorexia was mine.

I love that all my friends tell me how great I look since I lost weight. They all want to know how I did it. I never tell them, of course. Now, I feel as though I could never gain the weight back, not anymore, then I will lose all this respect.

Brenda, 16-year-old anorexic

You know it's hard for me in group because of Cathy and Shari (both anorexic). You know the rest of us (bulimics) want to be like them.

Angel, 18-year-old bulimic

If being thin becomes your daughter's source of respect and acceptance, she will be reluctant to give it up. As stated previously, it is not just the thinness, but the willpower—the ability to go through the punishment and the torture to be thin—that is admired. The respect comes not only from others but from your daughter to herself. She admires her own ability to triumph over her body; where giving in would mean the loss of a sense of accomplishment that would feel unbearable. As strange as it seems, to eat might mean to lose respect for herself. If however, she learns to gain acceptance, admiration, and respect through means other than her body or her ability to diet, this particular underlying need for her eating disorder will be resolved. Your daughter will need help in understanding that it is no longer a struggle for her to deny her body its nourishment. The real struggle now is to overcome her need to do so.

EXPRESSING FEELINGS

People with eating disorders don't know what they feel or if they do know have a hard time expressing it.

ಶ ಶ ಶ

Dear Carolyn,

Thank you so very much for all your help. I'm sorry for the way I have been acting lately when I see you. I have been trying to tell you about my fears and feelings, but have been unable to do so. I want to see you and talk to you; yet, when I see you I get nervous, scared and have a hard time controlling my emotions. For the past three weeks I feel like I have gone from a fairly sturdy brick building to one that has cracked and is tumbling down. I feel very childish. I do not feel comfortable putting some of my fears on paper. Hopefully, I will be able to converse with you soon. Please forgive me for the tears and lack of completed sentences. I cannot express my gratitude for all that you have done, and I hope that I have not been too frustrating for you.

Brenda, 23-year-old, Eating Disorder Not Otherwise Specified

My friends were really close and open to me. I knew a lot about how they felt and who they were. I had a good listening ear and had a lot of good advice. Every one came to me with their problems. I could help others, but I had a hard time expressing what I needed. I never did.

Natalie, 19-year-old binge eater

Helping someone learn to identify and express feelings can be a very long and arduous task. My eating disorder clients are masters at denying or ignoring feelings such as inadequacy, shame, fear, neediness, and longing. Even the most physical of feelings, such as fullness or hunger pangs, bursting blood vessels in the eyes, or bleeding gums that are a result of forced vomiting, are often ignored. Clients often talk about their behaviors as substitutes for other ways of expressing their feelings. For example, a client might claim that her eating binges are a way of "swallowing her feelings." Another might say her not eating is a way of "not needing anything or anyone."

Anorexic: I can never be the first person in a crowd to say that I'm hungry or I'm tired, or that I need anything.

Bulimic: I just couldn't deal with any of it, my mom, Bill ... (her alcoholic boyfriend). When I was eating I didn't have to think about any of it to feel anything but the taste of the food or the fullness.

Anorexic: If my mom and I got into a fight I remember thinking, "I'll show her. Today I'll throw my lunch away today; I won't eat all day."

Bulimic: People always say, "You're so strong" and I think, "You don't know me, I have to be the Rock of Gibraltar for everyone." Well, I need someone to take care of me too but it's always me doing it. When I'm eating whatever I want and puking then it's like I'm doing what ever I want. I can then finally let down during that time.

Anorexic: I couldn't talk to them. They wouldn't listen at all, especially my dad. They never do so it's no use. My brother tried to talk to them, to tell them how he felt ... well ... I saw what happened to him and ... well I just know it doesn't do any good. So I do it (throw up) to get back at them to somehow express what I think and feel about them. They can't do anything about it.

Your daughter may or may not recognize that her disordered eating is her way of expressing something else. The goal should be to find out what the something elses are and discover other ways to express them. Have you been able to help your daughter express her feelings, particularly negative ones, or ones that are opposite to yours? Have you reassured her that, "You can be mad at me and disagree with me and it's okay." Communication of feelings is often a problem in families and it is the whole family that needs help with how to communicate with each other.

There are thousands of reasons why a person has become unable to express their feelings. There are thousands of feelings that need to be expressed. It is often a magical experience to be with a person when they are discovering and unfolding their feelings, their personality. However, helping them to experience and express feelings about others or simply about themselves can take a long time, possibly several years. It is necessary that parents be supportive and patient during that time. It's also important to note that just because the feelings start being expressed or fulfilled in other ways, doesn't mean the eating disorder will disappear. For example, a young anorexic girl learns to express her feelings to her father, their communication improves greatly but she continues to restrict her food and doesn't gain weight. Expressing feelings may just be one ingredient in the recovery process. Sometimes many aspects of a person can change while eating behavior stay the same. Behavior modification techniques are necessary to deal directly with the eating behavior itself.

Needs a Safe Place to Go

In a time of trouble, confusion, or danger we'd all like to have a safe place to go, both literally and psychologically. Some people feel safe with another person, some people feel safe when they stay home, some feel safe when they act tough and macho, some feel safe when they take drugs or drink alcohol. Some feel safe when they're working, some only when they're doing something that they are very good at, some when surrounded by friends, and so on, and so on. A safe place can be a place to hide, or a place where everything is under control, familiar and comfortable. One person's safe place may be another's nightmare. Safe places are personal and may not seem safe to anyone looking in. Children from abused homes often run away from foster homes back to the abusing parent because that home is familiar, they know *how* to deal with it, and the unknown is scarier.

Hiding in an eating disorder however dangerous, feels safe to those doing so. It's safe because it is a privately created world where its creator calls the shots and determines what success is: "I am successful if I make it through the day eating only 300 calories;" "I'm successful if I weigh under 90 lbs.;" "I'm successful if I take laxatives after eating;" "I'm successful if I can accomplish a binge in the dark at night without getting caught;" "I'm successful if I can eat and yet not gain weight;" "I'm successful if I get back at my parents this way."

Sometimes eating disorders take precedence over dealing with any other problems. If being thin or in control, is the *most* important thing in the world, more important than school or relationships or health, then one can concentrate on it to the exclusion of all other things. It can be overwhelming to deal with all the other life problems, but while in the throes of an eating disorder they can be put aside. It is also true that parents and others involved begin to expect less. For example: "Let's get her weight up first, then we'll worry about her grades."

As for the bulimics, the safety and comfort of food is often much more appealing than anything else could possibly be. As the perpetual dieter will tell you, food doesn't talk back, food is a friend, food is a treat, food is a comfort. A bulimic will bounce back and forth between the safety of not eating to that of taking laxatives, vomiting, or overexercising to compensate for overeating.

Another issue regarding safety is the idea that by staying thin and childlike, delaying or sabotaging menstruation and/or puberty one can "avoid" sexuality. If relationships with the opposite sex are scary, for such reasons as neglect or sexual abuse, then denial of the body's sexuality is a safer alternative. There is a high incidence of sexual abuse in the lives of people with eating disorders. Wanting control over one's body makes sense if that body has been abused. This issue leads us into the next, having to do with lack of trust.

LACK OF TRUST IN SELF AND OTHERS

I can't seem to make decisions about anything so I just make rules to follow. I don't know how much is too much so it seems easier to try to avoid eating altogether.

Dana, 12-year-old bulimic

I feel as though anything that enters my body, even food, could hurt me.

Cynthia, 35-year-old binge eater

I can't tolerate the feeling of gaining weight, it is like an invasion to my body, a rape, a violation that I must guard against at all costs.

Lisa, 25-year-old bulimic

Intrusive or neglectful caregiving will result in lack of trust in self and others. When trust in others has been violated or trust in one's self undeveloped or destroyed, people create ways to protect themselves and their personal boundaries. Disordered eating patterns are, in part, attempts to resist with the body and to define, establish, or restore a sense of self through body boundaries. Controlling the body, and what goes into and out of it can be an adaptive and defensive reaction to past neglect and abuse.

An anorexic who maintains extremely rigid control over her body may be expressing lack of trust in interpersonal contact. Fear of intrusion or losing control becomes her will to defy her own needs: "I don't need food, I don't need you, I don't need anybody." A binge eater on the other hand may fear people will abandon or neglect her, so she stuffs the fear of emptiness with food. A bulimic with fears of intrusion and abandonment seeks control of what goes in to the point of purging in order to keep things out.

An abused child may internalize an abusive attitude toward herself and or her body. The abuser is not blamed but the body is. It is easier to think, "I am bad" or "My body is bad," rather than, "No one can be trusted."

...I hate my body because it is dirty and ugly and fat. I can never be thin enough. I'm not eating or drinking again. It scares me, it hurts me and I hate it. It sickens me and I cannot forgive it.

Jennifer, 19-year-old anorexic

My body is a useless burden, it will never be good enough, it is not worthy of attention or nurturing.

Betsy, 24-year-old, Eating Disorder Not Otherwise Specified

If your daughter has been abused, she will need help in learning to trust others. She will need reassurance and understanding and support to change at her own pace. She will need to regain trust a step at a time, in order to have a healthy relationship with others and with her own body. If you know or suspect that your daughter has been abused, get professional help immediately.

TERRIFIED OF NOT MEASURING UP

If our will were sufficient to accomplish our desire, many of us would begin to look like our Anorexic sister[37]

It is difficult to measure up to the ideal standards set by our society. This is not just true for thinness but for being a super person at everything. A recent television commercial showed one woman in these various scenes:

Winning a marathon
Cuddling her newborn
Graduating from college
Dressed for success with briefcase on her way to work.
Attending her aerobics class
Dining out with a great looking man

She had a great figure, was thin side, oh, and beautiful of course. Now this is a hard act for anyone to follow. For some people, it may seem easier to demand and get just the *body* to measure up than to try to do it in any other areas. "I can't be a top executive or have a beautiful face but I can force my body to be thin."

Once ingrained in the personality, the idea that thinness equals success, is like being brainwashed. The anorexic is terrified of being fat—and I mean terrified! A mother once told me the horrifying story of finding her daughter in her bedroom with a belt cinched tightly around her waist. The girl was pulling with all her might trying to force her stomach to throw up the food that she had eaten. This girl had welts on her stomach for a week from the belt. She was seized with terror when she could not get rid of her food. Other girls panic at the thought of having dinner at a friend's house and having to eat something "fattening."

My best friend had everything, beauty, money, good grades. I didn't have anything better than her. Now that I'm thinner I have something she really wants but can't have. Thinness is the only thing I have.

Denise, 16-year-old anorexic

The bulimic is terrified of not measuring up but is also terrified of being deprived. Although she would like to, she can't seem to maintain the control of an anorexic, which causes her to have widely fluctuating behaviors of starving, bingeing and purging.

The binge eater, more than anything, is terrified of deprivation and although she would like to "measure up," she more often refuses to even be in the race.

I know I'll never have an attractive body so I don't even try, food is my friend, my comfort, and I'll just be alone with food forever.

April, 19-year-old binge eater

Once you recognize that your daughter is exhibiting any of the kind of thinking or behavior discussed in this chapter, you need to get her, and yourself, help. The following chapter will help you with what you can do to get that help.

10

ᔕ ᔕ ᔕ

If My Daughter Has a
Problem, What Do I Do?

*I wish there were a group I could belong to for parents of children
who overeat. I really needed something like that during all of Clara's
life, to help me not feel lonely and powerless. Maybe I would have
learned ways to avoid hurting her the way I have. When she was
three, her doctor told me to watch her eating habits and to try to keep
her weight in check. But no one told me how to do it.*

Wilma

Mother: I have a daughter who has an eating disorder and I don't
know where to turn. She has always been so responsible that
I never thought something like this would happen. I see her
starving to death before my eyes.

Carolyn: That must be very hard. How old is your daughter?

Mother: She is 32 and doesn't live with me. I don't know how to
convince her to get help. We used to have a great relationship, but she won't listen to me anymore. I don't know what
to do!

If by now you have decided that your daughter has an eating disorder, or that her disordered eating warrants further attention, you will need to do the following: (1) Take her—or, if she is an adult, do your best to convince her to go—to a physician, preferably one who is familiar with eating disorders. (2) Get her help from a licensed therapist, psychiatrist, or dietitian who specializes in eating disorders. A professional will help your daughter explore and understand her perception of herself, her attitude, and her behaviors, and how all of these contribute to her condition. (3) Get help for yourself. A professional will help you to understand the ways in which your daughter is trying to resisting intrusion, feel accepted, and gain control through her body and what part you play in the cause and treatment of her disorder.

You cannot alleviate your daughter's problems with methods that include coercion or control, both of which reinforce the loss of power. You must find a way of relating that will help to establish empowerment rather than taking away the tenuous control that she firmly believes has been achieved through what she is doing to her body.

As a parent, you must always remember not to overfocus on the weight, the food, purging, or other specific behaviors. The relationship between food and weight is important, but the eating disorder behaviors and the underlying psychological issues must be addressed simultaneously. Following are some guidelines drawn from my years of experience, which can be used as a general starting place to begin looking at your own behaviors toward your daughter and your own attitudes toward eating, body image, and weight. Every person is unique and each case entails varying degrees of difficulty, its own nuances, and different characteristics. These guidelines should be discussed with a professional to determine what will work best with your family. The guidelines, like much of this chapter are mostly geared to daughters who are minor children or still living at home. However, much of the information presented here is applicable to adult daughters as well.

GUIDELINES FOR PARENTS

Note: Not all guidelines will be appropriate for your daughter, but use them as a place to begin, discussing them with a professional to tailor them to your situation.

1. Focus on feelings and relationships, not on weight and food.
2. The family should go on with their own lives as normally as possible and not let a dieting daughter disrupt everything. It is helpful, however, if the whole family is on a healthy, balanced eating plan.
3. You will need to work out setting limits and rules in a caring and reasonable but firm and consistent manner. This may come up, for example, when your daughter wants to skip meals or eat alone, or when she gets angry because someone eats her special food.
4. Help the family to show affection and appreciation for each other both verbally and physically. A little unconditional love goes a long way. Underneath obsessive dieting, disordered eating, and body image disturbance is a lack of self-worth.
5. Work on avoiding power struggles and find alternatives to them, an aspect that especially applies to the area of weight; let a professional help with this.
6. Demanding change or berating your daughter for her eating habits will not work.
7. Avoid letting your daughter dictate meal times to the family, force parents or other family members to go out of their way to buy special foods, or restrict food as a means to get her way. However, your daughter must not be overcontrolled either, because the result will be more rebellion. This fine line has to be negotiated.
8. Parents must find alternatives to their current ways of communicating. For example, instead of saying, "Why are you doing this to me?" or "You are ruining our family," it would be better to say, "Would you like to talk now?" or "This is difficult for you and for me, lets discuss it." You will need to find alternatives to yelling, punishing, or other communication blockers.
9. Avoid anger, pleading, demanding, or begging as ways to make your daughter do something or stop doing something. It doesn't work to ask your daughter how you can help her as she probably doesn't know the answer. It doesn't help to be angry; it only makes her and the family feel worse.
10. Generally speaking, it is unwise to have your daughter shop for, cook for, or feed others. For a bingeing daughter, this might be asking too much. For a daughter who restricts her food, by nurturing others, it is easier for her to deny her own need for food. In

some cases, preparing meals may be okay, as long as your daughter eats the same food she serves to the family.

11. Most important, talk to your daughter about all kinds of issues. Often it reaches the point where families are only talking about problems, especially those concerning dieting and weight.

The above guidelines should help you. It is also very likely that reading through them has left you with more questions than answers. In the following section, I answer those questions most commonly asked by parents.

ANSWERS TO QUESTIONS MOST COMMONLY ASKED

1. What should I/my daughter read?

As far as information on dieting goes, there are countless books available. Chapter 12 and Appendix A both provide information on healthy eating and dieting. Appendix C will give you suggestions for further reading that are appropriate for you and your daughter.

As for reading material for eating disorders, only a few books are available that are directed specifically to parents, but other books will be helpful. Find these resources listed in Appendix C. Reading material for your daughter on eating disorders is another story.

In 1978, the first book marketed to the public on eating disorders, *The Golden Cage* by Hilda Bruch, was published, thus beginning the public education on eating disorders. However, educating people can have counterproductive side effects. Books and other media provide ideas about how to go about having an eating disorder, such as, techniques for better purging. Stories about fashion models and television stars with eating disorders or the 58-pound girl who goes on the talk show circuit, normalize and even glamorize these disorders and unwittingly encourage young girls to engage in these behaviors. Many of my clients express the idea that they want to be better anorexics than those girls in the books, thinner with more will power: "I want to be the best anorexic!"

Read all the material you can find to better educate yourself about dieting and eating disorders. However, think twice about getting reading material for your daughter. If you believe she has an eating disorder it is best that you get professional help for her first. I have had too many clients tell me they learned about using laxatives or self-induced vomiting or ipecac (over-the-counter emetic used to induce vomiting in emergencies, such as accidental poisoning) from books, television presentations, or magazine articles on eating disorders. Girls also learn these behaviors from their friends, who have learned from these sources.

I saw that movie "The Best Little Girl in the World" and I realized I could do that too to lose weight.

Kara, 11-year-old anorexic

My mom thought I was having a problem because I was trying to diet to lose weight. I guess she got worried and she bought me Starving for Attention. *I read it and found out a lot of ways to lose weight I'd never thought of, like using laxatives.*

Laura, 31-year-old, Eating Disorder Not Otherwise Specified

My friend and I went to this party and ate so much food. When I complained about all the food I'd eaten, my friend said to come with her to the bathroom, she wanted to show me something. She told me that she did this all the time and then she just threw up. It was so easy for her. At first I thought it was gross, but she said I'd feel much better and I'd never gain weight. She said she read about it. I never ever thought I'd be talking to a therapist about how I can't stop.

Katie, 15-year-old bulimic

Not all of those with bulimic or anorexic behaviors learned them from a book, the media, or a friend. One of my clients ate an ice cream cone on a very hot day, felt sick, threw up, and thought, "Wow! that was easy, what a good idea." And she began vomiting whenever she ate anything she thought might be fattening. Another client told me that she ate and drank too much at a party, felt sick and made herself throw up. It occurred to her that she could do this at other times also. She began vomiting regularly to the point where she is now vomiting up to 10 times a day and feels unable to stop. Until the mid-1980s, my eating disorder clients would express surprise that other people did what they did and that there was actually a name for it. These days, with all the media attention on the subject, it is very rare to find someone who hasn't heard of anorexia and bulimia.

I do think we must continue to educate the public about these disorders and how dangerous they are, but even more important we must focus on what it takes to prevent the disorders in the first place. We must provide young girls with a healthy sense of self, a positive body image, and the knowledge and skills for healthy, effective, weight control.

2. Should I take my daughter to a doctor?

It is wise to take your daughter to a doctor not only if you suspect she has an eating disorder, but even if she just wants to go on a weight loss diet. It is important to assess her health at the beginning of any diet program. If you already are worried about her health as a result of her dieting practices, do not make the common mistake that taking your child to the doctor will uncover and/or solve things. Doctors are not specifically trained to diagnose or treat eating disorders and laboratory tests notoriously miss eating disorder symptoms and thus can be misleading. My mother took me to the doctor when my weight had dropped from 135 to 90 pounds, and yet the result of all my medical tests were fine. I insisted that there was nothing wrong with me and that I would not gain weight. In fact, inside I felt that I was still a little too fat but would never tell the doctor that. He was already suggesting that if I didn't stop losing weight he would have to feed me intravenously. There was no possibility of that! At 18 years old, I was determining my own fate and decided simply that I wouldn't go back! I even gloated over the fact that all my tests were normal, and I remember that he said: "Well, all I can say is that there seems to be nothing wrong with you at this point, but the damage you are doing will show up; sooner or later, it will show up. You will be sorry then."

Unfortunately, for the most part, similar situations occur every day. With all the information on eating disorders and the medical consequences doctors are still more apt to miss the diagnosis if not directly informed or unless the patient is extremely emaciated. Blood tests can remain normal under circumstances of severe food restriction or multiple bingeing and purging episodes. Even if blood values become abnormal, you will not be able to convince your daughter to stop her disordered eating because she may be ruining her health. Remember, for her being thin is probably more important than being healthy.

3. My six-year-old daughter is definitely overweight. Our doctor told me I should control her eating and my friends pressure me. What can I do to help her?

You are in a difficult but not impossible situation. Don't make food decisions based on your desire to help your daughter get thinner. Focus on healthy eating instead of weight-loss eating or dieting. It is your responsibility to provide healthy, nutritious food at regular times, and it is up to your daughter to decide how much to eat, even if she is overweight. Putting your child on a diet will only cause her to feel bad about herself, angry at you, overly dependent, sneaky, and rebellious.

Some kids grow out of a weight problem and others will lose weight when they are ready, not when it is imposed on them. Consult the resource section, Appendix C, for suggestions on reading material that will help you with this problem.

Since genetic factors contribute greatly to an individual's weight, and since interfering and imposing your own agenda can make overeating problems worse, you may have to accept having an overweight child. In trying to help, don't become her first source of discrimination. Instead, help her to develop healthy self-esteem and show her that she can have a happy, successful life.

Here's what you can do:

- Make food plans that apply to the whole family, not just your daughter.
- Establish regular meal and snack times.
- Make meal times pleasant and slowly paced.
- Offer abundant amounts of nutritious foods and modest amounts of sugary and fatty foods.
- Promote an active lifestyle for the whole family.
- Try to establish whether there is some stressor that causes your child to overeat, and then get help for her.

4. Should I insist that my daughter eat meals with the family?

There are many different situations to which this question could apply and each one would call for a different response. Louise, a 16-year-old bulimic, told me that her mom made her eat dinner with the family, so she just decided to throw up everything afterward. On the other hand, often laying down rules about eating is useful, as girls may tend to eat more when dining with the family than if left to eat on their own. I find in most homes these days, families eat at all different times and the typical family dinner time is fading as a traditional family routine. It is a good and healthy goal to get family meal time back but the experience needs to be a pleasurable one, not a time to deal with problems. The important thing to remember is that forcing your daughter to do anything will not be a key to her getting better and may even backfire. If your attempts to arrange family meal times fail, professional help is suggested.

5. How do I find a therapist?

Finding a specialist in eating disorders may be difficult, but it is important. If your daughter is taking dieting too far, then she needs help from someone who can assess the extent of her problem and deal, not just with the underlying psychological issues, but specifically with her disordered eating behaviors and body image.

All too often people come to me after having seen other therapists who believe that if the underlying issues are resolved, the disordered eating will stop. This is not true. If your daughter's therapist is not familiar with eating disorders, you daughter will soon feel that therapy is a waste of time because, "No one understands me nor can they help me," " This person just doesn't get it," "I can't respect or trust this person," "I can get away with anything."

To find an eating disorder therapist, look in the Yellow Pages under eating disorders, or in various other sections where psychological counseling is listed. Local college or university counseling departments will most likely have referral lists of specialists in eating disorders. In Appendix C you will find a list of various eating disorder organizations, which may help you find a trained eating disorder professional in your area.

6. Should I remove the scale?

Yes. There is no reason to have a scale in the house. A number on the scale is never an accurate way to determine health status and it actually interferes with weight-loss or weight-gain goals. Scales can be incredibly misleading. Fluctuation of body fluids on a particular day can make it appear that one has gained a pound when actually the person may be losing weight. And scales do not show regular steady weight loss in the way most people think they do. For example, when dieting, a person can remain at the same weight for six days and on the seventh day show a two-pound drop. From this it may appear that they lost nothing for six days then in one day lost the two pounds. And what if on that seventh day the person had given up and had an ice-cream sundae. Does this mean the ice-cream actually caused the weight loss? Of course not, but this inaccurate assumption is common.

People, especially young people, want to diet for two days and check the scale for results daily if not several times per day. Results of a good diet program sometimes don't show up for a few weeks! This is particularly true for someone who has had a weight problem and been on several previous diets. One woman I treated did not lose weight until five weeks into her program and she ended up losing more than anyone else in her group! However, this woman almost dropped out of the program when three weeks into it she weighed herself and hadn't lost a thing. Without reservation I can say that in my experience, those who do not weigh themselves are more successful at weight loss than those who do.

Weighing is devastating for anorexics and bulimics who have adopted the attitude that what the scale says is the most important thing. No matter how much your daughter complains or pleads or how much she tries to convince you to let her weigh herself, that she can handle it, and that it won't be harmful for her, don't do it—she will sabotage herself every time. She may claim that not weighing makes her worse or that she will simply go find another place to weigh herself. You will not be able to stop her from doing this but you can say that you will not participate in providing a tool that she uses to harm herself. If you feel that getting rid of the scale is a radical move and are unsure about disposing of it, consider the following two examples.

Gretchen a five-feet, eight-inches tall 19-year-old bulimic patient who weighed 130 pounds, was determined to stop her binge and purge eating patterns. Gretchen was not happy with her weight, even though for her height her weight was low; she wanted to lose 10 pounds. It usually does not work to try to convince someone that she doesn't need to lose weight, so I worked with Gretchen initially on stopping the bulimic behavior. This was easier because I could convince her that what she was doing was not working for her as it was not helping her lose the ten pounds, even though she was purging everything she ate. Gretchen was terrified of stopping the purging and feared "getting even fatter," stating, "If I keep my food down, I know I will gain weight because, as it is now, I have to throw it all up just to stay the same." Her comment is a very common one. Purging behaviors initiated for weight loss, only work in the beginning. Most bulimics are of normal weight or slightly overweight. I discussed with Gretchen how many calories I thought she could safely eat without gaining weight and reassured her that we would start her on a lower calorie level than she really needed just to ensure this. My first goal for Gretchen was, "Let's find out how much you can eat and keep without gaining."

We agreed that Gretchen would eat and keep 1,000 calories a day. This is clearly not enough for her age, height, and weight but it was what she was willing to do, and keeping down 1,000 calories is far better than eating and purging 2,000. I asked Gretchen to agree to weigh herself only in my office and then only with her back to the scale because her reliance on the scale would interfere with her progress. She agreed reluctantly.

The following session Gretchen came in crying. "I knew I couldn't do it, you promised and you were wrong! I'm not like everyone else, I'm all screwed up and it's not going to work."

It turned out that Gretchen had eaten and kept 1,000 calories for 3 days and then feeling desperate and fat got on a scale that registered 131½ pounds. In tears, Gretchen said, "I gained, one and a half pounds in three days. Can you image how huge I will be if I continue to do what you say?" I took a deep breath and answered, "This is exactly why I hate scales." I then told her about the garden hose theory: If you take an empty garden hose and weigh it, it weighs a certain amount. If you fill that hose with water and then weigh it again, it will weigh more, yet the hose didn't get any bigger. When a person who has been starving or purging begins to eat again, she fills up her stomach and intestines with food and her whole body becomes more hydrated. Like the hose, she now has additional mass inside, but has not gotten any bigger.

The concept of the garden hose should be explained early on. It is helpful if it is understood and accepted before the issue arises. The analogy helps but it is my word against the scale, which has come to represent a higher authority. This is just one example of why the scale should be considered a tool of destruction that your daughter uses against herself. If you are still not convinced, consider the next example.

Lisa, a 17-year-old, five-feet, six-inches tall, 79-pound anorexic patient was addicted to her scale, weighing herself sometimes ten times a day. If the number was too high she would drink water and make herself vomit until "the scale said the right thing." The right thing, the magic number for Lisa was 79 pounds. I tried at first to get her to weigh herself only three times a day, but to no avail. She would not agree to let me weigh her with her back to the scale and let me be in charge of it so that she wouldn't have to witness the pounds coming on. Lisa could not give up her scale and continued to claim that weighing would help, not hurt. Even though it took months of therapy and a hospital stay for Lisa to finally agree to gain weight up to 90 pounds, she was adamant that she didn't want it, " to go too fast." (Ninety-nine percent of anorexics complain that the weight is coming on too fast, no matter how slowly they gain.) Lisa fought the same one to two pounds week after week. If she gained a pound she would freak out, feel that she needed to slow it down and thus would cut back on her calories and promptly lose that pound.

Lisa continued to "try" to gain the 11 pounds for three months, until I finally began to win her over to the fact that her way wasn't working, that weighing herself was getting in her way and not helping her.

If you still have a hard time getting rid of the scale, you had better ask yourself if you are a scale slave yourself and what you might need to do to let go of it.

7. If I hear my daughter vomiting what should I do?

This depends on whether she is already in treatment. In either case, it is important to understand that you cannot stop her. Pleading, punishing, monitoring, or shaming will only cause her to be more secretive. Uusually the best response is to let her know that you are aware that she is having a hard time and that you are there to talk to her if she needs to. If she's not in treatment you need to approach her about getting help. Tell her she needs it and that you will work with her to find someone with whom she can connect and feel comfortable. If she is in treatment you need to make sure that this is being discussed in her sessions. If your daughter is living with you, you need to be included in her treatment on some level. Discuss this with her therapist.

8. When my daughter asks me if she looks or is fat, what should I say?

Pleading the fifth is the best response. Seriously, you want to figure out a way to let your daughter know that you consider this question irrelevant in a way that doesn't invalidate her need to ask. Here are some possible responses. You will need to choose the one that best applies to your situation. The last response is appropriate only if your daughter is truly very overweight

> No, of course you don't look fat, you may feel fat and I understand that, but feeling fat and being fat are different.

> Please don't ask me that anymore because I feel that there is nothing I can say that makes you feel better.

> It's important how *you* feel about the way you look, not how I feel.

> You aren't fat but you do have fat on your body. Everyone does. If you have more than you want there are several ways to get rid of some of it without hurting yourself.

9. Should I weigh my daughter?

Do not weigh your daughter. If you feel the need to do this there is something wrong and you should seek professional help. Weighing your daughter reinforces the idea that her weight is an important criterion by which to judge her or how she is doing. And keep in mind, the scale is misleading. I have known girls to fluid load, tamper with the scale, and wear several layers of clothes, or put rocks in their pockets, just so they make a certain weight in front of their moms. Clients also try to fool therapists, dietitions, and doctors, but an eating disorder specialist should be trained to catch this. For example, I may choose to have my clients wear an examination gown when I weigh them.

Weight is often irrelevant in terms of progress of recovery. Bulimics can be bingeing and purging daily with no weight loss at all. Although you may be worried about your daughter's weight if it is too low or too high, there are too many reasons why weighing her yourself should not be done.

Let a professional do it. Be sure to read the answer to question 6 about taking away the scale.

10. I found laxatives in my daughter's room, what do I do?

The first question is, what were you doing in her room? This is the first question she will ask you if she is a teenager or older. You will need strong justification for your uninvited entry, especially since you found contraband. Generally, I think daughters need their own private space, but there have been occasions when I have actually told parents that they had a right to enter and search their daughter's bedroom because she was a danger to herself. In these cases, I inform them that they need to make their intentions and rules clear to their daughter to let her know they feel they must do this for her well-being. It is important that finding laxatives, diet pills, diuretics and the like does not lead to punishment; this means she has a problem and needs your help—not discipline. Tell her you will not allow her to use these substances and will continue to take them away if you find them. Let her know you realize that she will get more and hide them better next time, but you still cannot condone it by allowing them in your house. Your goal after finding such items is to express empathy and concern and to get her professional help.

11. I came home early and caught my daughter bingeing, what should I have done?

Refer to question 7 about finding your daughter vomiting.

12. Should I buy special food for my daughter?

Yes, if your daughter wants to be a vegetarian or to eat low-fat and nonfat foods, it's okay to buy her these items. There are only so many battles worth fighting. Your daughter can eat low-fat and even nonfat foods and avoid animal protein and still maintain a healthy diet. Save your criticism and control battles for things she does that are clearly unhealthy. For example, if your daughter eats no protein this is a problem, but vegetarian protein is okay. If your daughter becomes paranoid about fat and stops eating almost everything that contains fat or that she doesn't know the exact fat gram count for, then you have cause to interfere. Also, don't go way out of your way for special foods if your daughter threatens not to eat if you don't get them. Don't let her bribe you by saying that she won't eat. You simply tell her that if she chooses not to eat, that is her decision and with the help of professionals, you will decide what to do about it when you need to. Too often I see mothers scurrying all over town to buy a particular frozen yogurt or nonfat muffin, all because it is food they can get their daughters to eat, and they want to keep them out of the hospital. If this is happening, you require professional help, and perhaps even a treatment program. I have seen too many mothers become slaves to their daughters' food demands in a desperate attempt to keep them from going to a treatment program. Keeping your daughter out of a treatment program should not be your goal. It may just postpone the inevitable and put you in a constant caretaker position that you cannot sustain.

13. How long will treatment take?

I tell parents that two to five years is the expected length of treatment; most literature in the field supports this estimate. Your daughter may need more or less time. There are many factors that affect the length of treatment, for example, how quickly your daughter gets treatment, how long she has been engaging in disordered eating behavior, how supportive the family is, and how much her weight is out of normal range. It is very hard to project length of treatment at the outset. Keep in mind that weight normalization is not an indicator that your daughter is well, whether this means weight loss or weight gain. Also be prepared to feel that not much is happening in treatment, as progress is very slow. Sheila, the mother of Carol, a young bulimic, asked recently, "Why is Carol still vomiting? She has been coming here now for two months and we are not getting anywhere." I pointed out to Sheila that Carol was coming to see me for one session a week, which, in two months equaled a total of eight hours of treatment! I had eight hours of working with Carol, not two months. This helped put things in perspective.

14. My daughter never wants to eat anywhere but at home. What should I do?

You can try to encourage your daughter to eat at places other than home but you can't force her. You can even punish her but what you gain from this will be minimal. Point out that her decision to not eat anywhere but home limits her ability to go places and enjoy life and that you are very sorry she is making that choice. Don't rearrange your schedule or plans to accommodate her but make sure that she has food to eat if you are going out. If your daughter is too young to leave at home alone, she can bring her "special" food to the restaurant, or to a friend's house for dinner, or camping. If she feels awkward doing this, point out that it is her choice. This phase may pass or she may need to go into a treatment program.

15. Other people want to discuss my daughter's weight or illness with me, and I find I need to talk about it but this infuriates her, what should I do?

You have the right to a place where you can vent and get things off your chest. Your daughter also deserves privacy. Therefore, you need to find a compromise with your daughter on what you are allowed to say when people ask about her. Examples: "My daughter and I have an agreement not to talk about this issue," or "She is getting help for her problem so I stay out of it." As for your needs, tell your daughter that you need someone to talk to and there are one or two people you are going to confide in and she will need to accept that. If reasonable, let her have some say in who those people are, particularly if they are relatives. Do not let your daughter convince you to keep things from your spouse, unless you believe it will cause violence or some disastrous result. If this is the case, go for consultation with a therapist immediately as there is a much bigger problem than the eating disorder!

16. My daughter sometimes binges on all of the food in the house, costing us money we don't have. I don't know how to handle this.

It's not fair for you to suffer unnecessarily. Your daughter needs to be responsible for her actions even if she does have an eating disorder. Within reason and depending on her age, you may want to hold her financially accountable for food on which she binges, although this would not be the first course of action. She does have an illness, and at first you need to be supportive, get her help, and not make the loss of food more important than she is. However, if she continues to binge out of control and it is hurting you financially, you can have her add funds to the grocery budget (if she is old enough). You can also tell her you will supply only a certain amount of food for her but when that is gone she will have to buy more. Don't be angry. Make sure your daughter knows your actions are not meant as punishment but as a means of putting controls on a situation that is out of control and as a protection for the rest of the family.

Labeling food sometimes helps: "tommorrow's dinner," "Shawn's lunch," or "please save." An action as simple as this helped bulimics to keep from bingeing.

It probably won't work to lock up the food in the house, although I have had parents try this strategy at their daughters' request. If your daughter really wants to binge she will find a way. One bulimic who had asked her parents to lock the refrigerator took food from the house during the day and hid it in the trunk of her car for night binges.

17. My daughter spends all of her money on food, the gym, diet pills, and laxatives then asks for money that I don't want to give her. But I know she can't help it.

Supplying your daughter with money to use for self-destructive purposes is not recommended. You surely wouldn't do so if you knew she used it for drugs. However, don't expect her behaviors to change because you are not giving her money. She will find ways to get her diet pills or whatever, but at least you won't be helping to supply them. If there are other things you want to pay for, there are ways to make sure the money is spent on them. You can go shopping with her; you can ask for receipts; you can write checks directly for certain places; and so on. I know of several parents who, in order to provide fuel for their daughter's car have given her a gasoline company credit card to use instead of money. Some girls even found a way around this by purchasing food items along with the gas at the service station. Another approach is to admit that you cannot prevent her from purchasing or even stealing certain items. Make it clear that you will give her only a certain amount of money and if she uses it up on laxatives and the like, then that is the choice she makes. Be aware that any confrontation can cause much anger and terrible quarrels can ensue. Again, professional help is advised.

18. My daughter refuses to see a therapist and is getting worse every week. How can I make her go? If she won't go, what else can I do?

Depending on your daughter's age you may or may not be able to force her to go for help. And depending on your daughter's problem she may or may not need to go. If she is overweight and does not want help, don't force her. If you suspect that she is bulimic or anorexic, and she refuses to acknowledge it or accept therapy, you may set some goals with her and tell her that if she can meet those goals you will not insist on therapy or other professional help. This will give her the opportunity to prove that she is not out of control and can do these things without outside help.

Some example goals:

No more weight loss.
Must gain five pounds in one month.
Must eat at least three dinners at home during the week.
Blood tests must show no indication of diet pills or diuretics.
Must skip two days of exercise per week.

If your daughter cannot meet the agreed-upon goals, or if she won't even agree to goals, you may have to force the therapy issue. You may be surprised; some girls are relieved that their parents are taking control. Do your research ahead of time to find someone with expertise, who is highly recommended, and even have a session with the therapist yourself to see whether your daughter might relate to the person. Tell your daughter that she has to go to the therapist at least three times and if she still hates it, you will find someone else. Don't let her get away with trying to bargain with you, claiming she will get better on her own. You may actually have to "bribe" her into seeing the therapist. Don't offer to give her anything for going but don't allow her certain privileges if she won't. For example, take away use of the car, money, gym membership, privacy, or special foods. Let her know you don't know what else to do to protect her, and that if she were seeing someone professionally, you could lighten up on her because at least you would know she was getting help and would know if she were in danger.

If your daughter is over 18 years old and living at home, you may have to resort to asking her to live elsewhere else if she won't go to therapy and continues on the same path. Tell her that if she chooses to keep her eating disorder, you cannot stop her, but that you will not watch her destroy herself in your house. This is probably the hardest stance to take, but I have seen families destroyed because of one member with an eating disorder who "ruled the house." Note that in 16 years of private practice, however, I have suggested only three times that parents might need to ask their daughter to leave the house. Some people don't ever recover from eating disorders and/or never agree to seek help or take their problem seriously. If your daughter won't go for treatment, seek professional help for yourself so you can figure out whether you have exhausted all of your options. A last resort is to have an intervention with your daughter. This is described next.

19. I have heard of interventions for drug and alcohol users, is there something similar for eating disorders?

First, let me define intervention in this context. An intervention is an attempt by significant others, with guidance from a professional, to intervene in a loved one's life for the purpose of convincing the person that (1) he or she is in denial of the problem or at least of the seriousness of it, and (2) he or she needs outside help for the problem, usually in the form of attending a treatment center.

Yes, interventions are done for eating disorders. There is very little information on the subject and I know of only two people beside myself who have done this kind of intervention. Most interventionists are known for their work with drug addicts, and alcoholics. This does not mean that an experienced eating disorder therapist or a drug and alcohol interventionist could not do an intervention for someone with an eating disorder. However, carrying it out is tricky, risky, and complicated. You must have full trust in the competence of the person in charge. As I write this, I am planning an intervention at the request of a mother who described her 90-pound daughter on the phone in this way: "She is ruining my whole life. I know she is sick but she has spent all my money, used up my credit-card limits, won't get a job, won't eat a thing, depends on me for everything, has no insurance, is in and out of medical hospitals due to her anorexia, and won't agree to get psychological help. She is in denial and I am about to lose my sanity and lose my house because of the financial debt she is causing me." When I asked her daughter's age, I learned that she was 32 years old and lived in her own apartment. This sounded like a case of the mom needing to let go. Her daughter might not get better, but I never assume that someone is beyond help until I have tried. After sympathizing, I explained how interventions work and told her to get back to me about whether or not she was going to go through with the first meeting. I also asked this mom to think about why she was willing to do this for a daughter who apparently didn't want help and why she wasn't willing to let go. The next morning she called me to say that my question had made her think. She said, "I thought about why I wanted to do this and the answer is that she is my daughter and that is enough." This is very sad indeed. I cannot tell someone to let go or give up. I may try to make them really think about their actions and limitations. I may ask how far they are willing to go. But everyone has limits and must make up his or her own mind regarding this most personal decision.

20. My daughter has an eating disorder. Will she have it forever?

Although it may take time, I like to work from the premise that all my patients are capable of becoming fully recovered. I run a clinic with many recovered staff members. I have countless former patients as examples that full recovery is possible. I don't believe that, once an individual is a bulimic, binge eater, or anorexic, that person is always one, as in the case of alcoholism. When the underlying issues are resolved and the person no longer needs the disordered eating behavior, full recovery *can* take place and a natural relationship with food can be regained. This does not mean that everyone *will* recover. Some people give up too soon, some truly don't want to recover or are too afraid to give up their eating disorder, and others are so damaged that there will never be enough time to cure all the wounds to the point where the eating disorder is no longer serving a purpose. However, every patient who walks through my door is viewed as having the potential for full recovery. If I was able to recover, they can as well.

21. I don't think my daughter is telling her therapist the truth. How should I handle this?

You can ask your daughter if she is discussing certain things; believe it or not, sometimes this simple question may help her to bring it up in the session. You can also share your concerns in front of her in a joint session. If there hasn't been such a session, ask for one. If the therapist tells you that joint sessions are not a good idea or your daughter refuses them, you may need to hold out for a while. You may need to find a therapist for yourself, preferably with the understanding that the therapists will be consulting with each other. However, I have often seen young girls dictate treatment and refuse to allow parental involvement, only to continue dysfunctional, clearly inappropriate behaviors within the family that remained unknown to the therapist, such as leaving vomit in the toilet or bingeing all night and keeping others awake. Family issues must be dealt with, no matter the daughter's age, if she lives at home. At some point, family therapy will be necessary, even if it takes place with someone other than your daughter's therapist.

22. I am overweight myself and want to go to Weight Watchers. Should I hide this from my daughter?

After reading this far, are you sure you want to? Be sure to read Chapter 12, "So You Want to Go on a Diet," before you make a final decision. Your daughter will be more likely to do what you do, not what you say.

If you do decide, despite my warnings, to go on a diet program, please choose one that offers a balanced food plan that you can continue for life. Do not hide your dieting from your daughter, but don't make a big deal of it, and don't discuss your weight, how much you've lost, or any other such issues. Get the scale out of your house and weigh elsewhere if you must. Keep your program to yourself and do not seek feedback from your daughter. And do not ask for feedback from someone else in the presence of your daughter.

Remember, you are a role model for your daughter, so don't do anything you would not want her to do. Exceptions to this rule exist. For example, you may go on a diet of 1,400 calories, whereas your anorexic daughter may need at least twice this amount. This will be very hard for her to accept. If your daughter *is* anorexic, I suggest you do not enter any formal weight loss program until she is doing fairly well with her eating plan. Ask a professional for advice on this. However, there is no need to wait to eat a healthier, lower fat diet (20 to 30%), and to add exercise to your day.

23. If I think my daughter has a problem, should I start with a dietitian or a therapist?

As long as the person is trained in eating disorders, it really shouldn't matter. A good eating disorder dietitian will know if and when to make a referral to a therapist, and vice versa. Generally, I believe that if the problem is one of being overweight, you can safely go with a dietitian first; if your daughter has anorexic or bulimic tendencies, I suggest you first seek an eating disorder therapist.

24. Would it help my daughter to attend Overeaters Anonymous meetings?

Overeaters Anonymous (OA) is based on the 12-step recovery model originally designed for alcoholism, and promotes the idea that eating disorders are addictions. Some people, particularly those with binge-eating problems, who consider themselves compulsive overeaters, have benefited from OA meetings. Generally, my experience is that anorexics do not do well with this approach, and bulimics are varied in their responses. I also find that teenagers with eating disorders benefit less than do adults from 12-step groups. Anyone with a diagnosable eating disorder should use this approach only in conjunction with psychotherapy.

If you feel that OA might be helpful to your daughter, tell her about available groups and let her decide. Keep in mind that besides the groups for overeaters, there are specific groups just for anorexics and bulimics. Information about Overeaters Anonymous is provided in the resource section in Appendix C.

25. My daughter has asked for liposuction and I think it will really improve her body image and self esteem. I want to give her this as a gift. How should I approach it?

Refuse to participate in any such idea! No matter how much you think plastic surgery will improve your daughter's self-image or raise her self-esteem, this decision must be hers alone, when she is 18 years old or over and capable of paying for it. Consider how you would feel if your daughter had complications under anesthesia that led to partial paralysis of her face. This actually happened to someone I know. Furthermore, consider 19-year-old Natalie, who burst into tears when describing the nose job her father had given her for her 16th birthday. "Even he thought I was so ugly that he wanted me to have plastic surgery." Consider Tara, who wept as she shared her mother's comment with me: "How about if I pay for you to go to my plastic surgeon? He said it would be easy to get rid of that double chin of yours, and if it makes you feel better, it's worth it." This same mother offered to buy more liposuction for Tara, if Tara would "get over her bulimia." Tara's mother loved her very much, and she was only trying to help, but this kind of help is terribly misguided. The sooner we get back to making looks less important than selves, personality more important than appearance, and health more important than slenderness, the safer, happier, and saner we all will be.

26. I pay for my daughter to go to Nutri-System, but when I find candy and cookie wrappers in her car or room, or even when I realize she is not sticking to the diet, I get upset and don't know what to do.

First of all, stop paying for Nutri-System and, if appropriate, find your daughter a dietitian to work with. If your daughter is over 18 years old, especially if she is not living with you, you may not be able to stop her from going to Nutri-System and paying for it herself. So be it, but don't contribute to it. Second, no matter what diet she is on, or who she is seeing for help, it is her body, her diet, and her success or failure. Of course, you will be upset if you are paying for the dietitian or therapist and you think she is not using the money well. If you are unhappy with your daughter's progress, you need to go to the professional and get some feedback and reassurance that your daughter's sessions are not being wasted. A good and respectable professional will not keep your daughter in treatment if it is futile to do so. Problems of disordered eating require long-term treatment. Telling your daughter you are unhappy with her progress may cause her to drop out. Making her feel guilty about money will only shame her more, and cause her to hide from you more than she already does. Threatening to take professional help away if she doesn't do better may result in a response you do not want, such as, "Fine, take the sessions away. You are the one who thinks I have a problem anyway. I don't care if I go." *Do not make treatment a reward or punishment, but rather an inevitable course of action for an illness.*

11

ও ও ও

Packaged Meals and
Promised Deals

*"A man has his clothes made to fit him; a woman makes herself to fit
her clothes."*

Edgar Watson Howe

*"I've lost over 100 pounds and I still weigh the same, … it was the
same 20 pounds a year for five years."*

Frustrated Dieter

*"Desire to have things done quickly prevents their being done
thoroughly."*

Confucius

There is a huge weight-loss industry beckoning your daughter even as
you read these words, offering packaged deals and promises it can't keep.
Easy, affordable solutions are promoted but with no guarantee or proof of
success. And we keep buying them, to the tune of $33 billion in 1990
alone. [38] Recent studies cited in Diane Epstein and Kathleen Thompson's
book, *Feeding on Dreams,* indicate that:

- Four out of five people who sign up for weight-loss programs will not stay long enough to lose any significant amount of weight.
- Of those who do lose weight, only one out of 10 keeps the weight off for two years.[39]

Even though there is abundant information to indicate that diets don't work, your daughter, like many diet industry victims, may fall prey to the glitzy advertising and diet campaign promises that bombard us every day. Even if your daughter knows that 98% of the people gain the weight back, she, like countless others who defy logic, may agree to start a diet program with the idea, "I just need an easy way to do it," or "This will help me get started and then I'll learn to keep it off the right way," or "This time it is going to be different," or "I am going to be among the 2% who succeed." Can you imagine buying suntan lotion that failed to work 98% of the time, or clothes that 98% of the time didn't fit a week later, or a birth control method that failed 98% of the time? Nonsense. But the diet industry is built not on logic but on hope. Dieting involves our emotions, our dreams, our fantasies. Dieting is like buying a lottery ticket, given the promise, a long shot seems worth trying.

It is important to know something about the various diets and weight-loss programs to which your daughter is exposed. What follows is a summary of the most popular diet programs, or diet plans published as books. The information was compiled by me and my staff and clients through reading the diet book or brochures and other literature on the program, reading books that evaluate the programs, making direct phone inquiries, and personally interviewing friends, relatives, clients, or diet program personnel.

OPTIFAST (OR OTHER LIQUID FASTING PROGRAMS)

Most of these programs are based on a modified fast of about 400 to 500 calories of liquid protein per day for approximately three to six months. After the initial period one is weaned off the supplement drink and food is reintroduced. Unfortunately, most people don't stay long enough to go through this phase. There is always an initial medical exam and some kind of weekly monitoring. Sometimes there is counseling. Usually these programs claim to include behavior modification, nutrition education, exercise information, and emotional support—but all this usually takes place in a group setting once a week!

Fee: Approximately $400–$500 per month.

Pros: If it is based in a hospital, it may be covered by insurance.

Cons: This is probably the most destructive form of dieting. Not only does it not work in the long run, but it makes people fatter, sets them up for bingeing, postpones having to deal with food, and is medically risky.

NUTRI-SYSTEM

Nutri-System is basically a packaged food program where individuals sign up, pay an initial fee, and then come in and buy food for the week. Anyone can sign up by just filling out a health screen. Under certain conditions, such as admission of an eating disorder or diabetes, a doctor's note is required. With a doctor's approval, Nutri-System will accept individuals as young as 14 years old. Doctor approval can be a simple note, which—at least in some locations—Nutri-System feels no particular obligation to verify.

A weight goal and calorie level are established by the program counselor assigned. But beware: One mother described taking her daughter in to lose 10 pounds, whereupon the counselor told her she really needed to lose 20. At the expected two pounds per week, this would take her 10 weeks and not the five weeks for which she was prepared—meaning five more weeks for Nutri-System food sales.

In addition to the packaged foods, the program includes group education classes, workbook assignments, weigh-ins, and food journal monitoring—all run by Nutri-System "counselors." The goal is to be less and less dependent on the packaged food as the program progresses and the weight comes off. The maintenance phase is when customers are supposed to learn how to eat normally to maintain their weight loss.

A client of mine called Nutri-System to see what she could find out and here is what she was told:

Fee: At Nutri-System you have several programs from which to select.

    1. Premier Program
       $499
       Special, $399 + $48 per month

2. Full Program
    $299 + $48 per month
    Lose all the weight you want plus 1 year maintenance
3. If you have just a few pounds to lose, there is a three week program at $19 a week.

Additional food costs: You can buy a food card for $149, which averages food at $49 per week, or_buy the food as you go for $69 per week.

Nutri-System food is freeze dried. A typical menu of packaged food for the day is cereal, soup and crackers, beef and potatoes, a cookie, and popcorn. And you could buy this on your own for half of the price of $69 per week. Since you are required to go shopping for additional items, such as vegetables, fruit, milk, and drinks, you might as well also buy the other food at the market. And then, why would you use the Nutri-System?

My client was told that if she chose to participate in the premier program, she would be participating in the Johnson & Johnson Health Management Resolutions Program. (What that is exactly wasn't explained.) I later found out that the Premier Program meant that you could come back and pay only $49 to reenter Nutri-System at any time, for the rest of your life. Would you sign up for anything else where the seller admitted that the product probably wouldn't work, but that you could keep coming back and trying to make it work whenever you wanted?

For the first six weeks, the information you provide is fed into a computer. The computer sends back information about your health profile. Although you do see a "counselor," you may not have the same counselor every time you go; it depends on who is scheduled to work at that time. In other words, you are not assigned a person with whom you will work consistently and so there is not the opportunity to build rapport or trust, and no one person to get to know your special needs or circumstances.

Weekly: Weigh-in, receive new activity and behavioral plans book along with pamphlets on various topics such as cholesterol; general weight loss; and exercise.

Counselor Training: Unfortunately, there is no requirement that "counselors" hired by Nutri-System have a degree in nutrition or counseling. In fact, bulimic clients still in treatment with me have been hired for these positions! When I called Nutri-System, I was told that counselors are trained by for two weeks and that they take a few classes covering the sales process and weight-loss program. What I have read elsewhere is that for Nutri-

System, which is considered one of the best programs, "Nutritional counselors are required to have only nine hours' worth of nutrition courses in college. Behavioral counselors must have had the same amount of course work in psychology, social work, or some other related courses."[40] However, since 1991 a cross-training policy allows nutrition counselors to be behavioral counselors and vice versa. Now where's the logic in that?

Pros: It is easy to follow because the food choices are all decided for you, packaged, and ready to go. All you have to do is eat according to your food plan until the maintenance phase.

Cons: Although there are problems with this approach in general, it's the maintenance phase that's the real problem. This is not a plan people stick to for life. Most people don't even stay around for maintenance where the real changing begins; once the weight is lost, they don't want to keep paying for the program. I refer to these kinds of plans as "postponing the inevitable." Inevitably, one must learn to deal with food realistically, shop, cook, and basically make peace with food in order to deal with food for life.

My staff's comments about phone inquiries:

I had a hard time getting any facts about total costs and success rates.

It seemed like they were more interested in selling different programs, not what the program included. I felt like I was speaking with a kid who was just there to answer the phones, and it turned out she was one of their trained counselors. It seemed that basically they hire anyone who can sell the program.

JENNY CRAIG

This program is based on the same concepts as Nutri-System. A member of my staff found the following information. During the first call, she was told that Jenny Craig was having a special—*Lose all the weight you want for $1.00 per pound.* We called back later. It turned out that they were having the same or a very similar special every week we called. Furthermore, the Jenny Craig people are still periodically calling my staff member at home to ask why she hasn't come in yet.

Food: Packaged, frozen food averages $10 per day and you start off eating it seven days per week—three meals, three snacks. The diet is composed of 60% carbohydrate, 20% protein, 20% fat.

You may choose your own foods based on your lifestyle and likes and dislikes.

The meals "encourage" smaller portions—meaning that they provide very small portions.

You still need to purchase your own fresh fruits and vegetables. When you reach half your goal weight, you switch to five days of Jenny Craig food and two days of store-bought. Eventually, you are weaned from the Jenny Craig food. That is, you are not weaned from the food plan, just from the Jenny Craig food. They still have you follow a plan.

Their motto, "It's not just taking it off, but keeping it off."

Sounds good, but the results are yet to be backed up with statistics.

Counselor training: The Jenny Craig representative on the phone glossed over the training question, stating that the counselors are there basically to motivate, help with menu planning, and give nutritional guidance. They are not registered dietitians. However, she did add that the menus and meals are prepared by a registered dietitian at headquarters. You can request to see the same counselor every week or change if the two of you are not compatible, but there is no guarantee that a suitable arrangement can be worked out.

As is typical of all of the packaged food programs, the qualifications most sought after by the organization when hiring counselors are the person's having lost weight on the program herself and sales ability. At Jenny Craig, the counselors' take-home pay is correlated to food sales.

The staff member doing research for me asked if she could get some information pamphlets to show her doctor. She was told that Jenny Craig has each person complete a health questionnaire. She was then assured that it would be a good idea to get started with the program right away and then take her menu plan to her doctor to be reviewed. The Jenny Craig "counselor" emphasized the importance of getting started at once.

Pros and cons: See the listing under Nutri-System.

My staff members' comments:

This was high pressure. The counselor stated at least four times that Jenny Craig is an excellent program, one of the best available, and that it could not hurt anyone. She was anxious to get my name and phone number, and repeatedly asked me to come in for my free consultation so that they could explain the program in greater detail. When I asked about any additional fees, she said that there are some additional fees for tools I would need in my program and I would be told what they were during my consultation.

DIET CENTER

This program does not rely on packaged meals, but as in other programs, clients go to the center for monitoring, weigh-ins, and the like. They are asked to come daily, but if this is not possible, or at least three times per week. Clients are given a food plan to follow and they buy their food and make their own meals according to the Diet Center guidelines. The plan is low in carbohydrates and very low in calories. Clients are given several dieting tips, such as drinking hot water with lemon juice in the morning, and not shopping when hungry.

There are several phases in the Diet Center program, the first being the "conditioning phase," which is designed to prepare you to diet by dictating kinds of foods to eat rather than restricting calories. In this phase, only two carbohydrates are allowed each day. The next phase is the "reducing phase," where calories are limited to 950–1200 per day and foods not on the list are strictly forbidden. The "stabilization phase" and the "maintenance phase" are designed to help with the transition from a reducing diet to everyday eating.

Upon calling the local Diet Center, my staff member was told the following.

Fee: The first 10 weeks cost $500, followed by one week free—in total, an 11-week program. There is a $50 registration fee for the first time at a Diet Center. If you sign up for a second 10 weeks there is a discount, though she was not told how much.

Diet: For the first two days you are on the conditioning diet, which means eating at least six to seven times a day, but fruit and protein only.

The program promotes a high protein diet because they say it cleans the system of impurities and rids the body of water. You must have fruit first, then protein.

After this initial phase, a fat test is given and a computerized report is issued listing what you should have in your diet. The computer tells you how much dairy, fat, protein, carbohydrates, fruits, and vegetables you may have.

Every three or four weeks or at each 10-pound weight loss, the fat test is readministered.

You take supplemental vitamins, including vitamin B, which they claim controls blood sugar and gives you energy.

The Diet Center does have some prepackaged foods, but the counselor with whom we spoke stated that they prefer people to eat their own food, as they lose weight faster. (We all wondered what was meant by that comment.)

Training: In a phone conversation we were told that counselors attend a seminar at headquarters. There is a registered dietitian and a medical staff, but only at seminar headquarters. The counselor at the on-site location weighs you and discusses your eating habits. If there are questions, then the counselor calls headquarters.

Pros: People choose this program because it seems easy. Even without packaged meals, there is not much to think about when everything is specifically spelled out. Weight loss happens rapidly because the number of calories allowed is so low and the program is very strict.

Cons: Calories are too low and the program is too rigid, making this plan hard to stick with. Also, the many diet rules and food restrictions make it too difficult for people to comply with it, for example, no caffeine, eight glasses of water per day, hot water with lemon juice in the morning, for the first week protein and fruit only, and going to the Diet Center three to five days per week.

Comments from my staff member:

Basically, it felt to me that you are paying for a computer to pick your diet and for someone to weigh you every week. Also, if I could eat only fruit and protein every day, even for a week, I know I'd lose weight and why would I need to go to them?

WEIGHT WATCHERS

The Weight Watchers plan is based on sound nutritional principles and was originally promoted as a balanced diet using all of the food groups, similar to what the American Dietetic Association endorses. However, now that Weight Watchers has literally "sold out" to Heinz, the tune has changed to a push toward packaged foods and the use of their "Personal Cuisine" program, which is their answer to Nutri-System and Jenny Craig.

The program is based on attending meetings, having group support, weighing in, keeping food journals, and following the meal plan. Basic nutrition and weight loss principles are taught.

Weight Watchers does not claim to do counseling or medical monitoring. Clients are told to get their doctor's approval.

I called Weight Watchers' number and received the following information:

Fee: Free registration until April 15 (2 weeks away)
    Regular registration fee after this date = $17
    Weekly fee = $13

They offered me a prepayment plan via telephone with my charge card and I was told I could buy 10 weeks for $107.25

Since there are different programs from which to choose, the fee can be misleading. And don't forget the $70 to $80 dollars per week of food expenses.

I was also told that if I did not lose 10 pounds in five weeks, I would get two weeks free. This was said me despite the fact that I was not asked my weight at this point or how much I wanted to lose. In fact, anorexic clients of mine have signed up for Weight Watchers and were accepted. The condition was that they not lose weight but learn to eat right.

Weekly:

- Attend weekly meeting
- Get weighed
- Hear success stories
- Group support

Training: A meeting leader can be anyone who has lost 10 pounds on the program and goes through company training.

Food: There are now three food plans. I was told that the program is flexible and that I could switch at any time to a different program.

Program Choices:

- *Fat and Fiber*
  Monitor fat and fiber
  Learn to monitor fat without giving up foods you love

- *Structured program controlling more than fat and fiber.*
  Select from six food groups
- *Personal Cuisine*
  Prepackaged food that is low fat, low sodium
  Includes breakfast, lunch, dinner, and dessert

Pros: Weight Watchers used to be one of the most reasonable programs, even with all of its monitoring and weighing of both the food and the clients. Clients have told me that it is run more like a support group than a lecture class. It is probably the least expensive of the packaged programs. The original plan promoted good, balanced shopping, cooking, and eating right from the beginning, and came closer than most programs (but still doesn't quite hit the mark) to the kind of normal eating that a person would have to do for the rest of her life in order to be successful.

Cons: Weight Watchers has gone overboard in what they try to provide. It is too bad that they decided to join the competition and offer the "postponing the inevitable" packaged food plans. The program was more reasonable and realistic prior to this change.

Again, there is the problem of lack of training for the "counselors." Success in Weight Watchers is the only criterion for counseling others, which makes it sound a little like the 12-step model or the Overeaters Anonymous approach. The importance of this aspect really depends on who is going for help. Kelly, a 13-year-old girl, signed up for Weight Watchers with her mother. Unfortunately, Kelly, who was five feet, five inches tall, and weighed 126 pounds, was told by the counselor, with her mother present as a witness, that she should weigh between 109 and 113 pounds. Kelly is now an anorexic patient of mine, who keeps using this counselor's comments to prove I am misleading her when I tell her that 109 pounds is not a realistic weight for her. She continues to try to use the Weight Watchers' counselor's words to persuade me to agree to 109 pounds as her goal weight. She even brought me her Weight Watchers' card on which the counselor had written that weight.

LINDORA MEDICAL/WEIGHT LOSS

The Lindora program is often joked about because of the injections patients receive, which, at one time, although no longer, came from the urine of pregnant women. It may sound crazy, but I have known many women—

and girls—who went on this diet program, often mothers and daughters together.

Upon calling the clinic I discovered the following:

The clinic makes a big deal out of being a medically supervised program.

Clients need to visit the clinic daily.

Clients receive an exam, including having blood drawn, by either a doctor or a nurse practitioner, who then okays their using the program's menu.

Diet: High-protein, low-carbohydrate diet, and clients use their own food.

- Supplement with protein drink (used on "protein" days).
- For the first three to four days, you receive a protein supplement only—to get your body into a "ketosis state."
- You buy vitamins to go along with the diet.
- You see a nurse every day and receive a "vitamin" shot.

When asked about the rate of weight loss, they said, "We like to see you lose three pounds per week, but individuals vary." Such careful wording sidesteps the fact that there are no guarantees. It's not important what you'd like to see, but what you do see—not just initially either, but over the long term—that is important.

Initial consultation: No fee and no obligation.

Once you decide to go on the program, you meet with a consultant who explains the program in detail, including protein supplements and vitamins. The program consultant also conducts a body analysis. (This person sells you the program and gets you started.)

You meet with a registered nurse or a licensed vocational nurse daily or at least three times a week.

Fee: They would not discuss cost, stating that the program consultant would be better equipped to do so.

Since the program is so strict and involves daily visits, I asked how long one can expect to be on the program. They stated that the time on the program was a maximum of eight weeks, but agreed that this could be extended if more weight loss were needed.

Pros: A physical exam by a doctor or nurse practitioner is provided, which is more than most programs offer.

Cons: This is a low calorie, low carbohydrate, high protein diet that is not healthy to follow for an extended period of time. "Ketosis" occurs with the absence of carbohydrates and ketosis is considered to be unhealthy. Also, the diet is too strict to maintain.

PRITIKIN

The Pritikin program has been around since the late 1970s and was popular throughout the 1980s. The Pritikin program is still available, and Nathan Pritikin did pioneer work to promote healthy, low-fat eating. The Pritikin program was initially formulated to foster good health, as well as weight loss. It was designed to lower blood cholesterol and help prevent artery blockage. Pritikin discovered the dangers of fat and cholesterol in the diet that we hear so much about today. The program consists of approximately 80 percent complex carbohydrates, 10 percent protein, and 10 percent fat. Emphasizing a menu of grains, beans, vegetables, and fruits, Pritikin stressed the value of a low-fat and low-protein diet in combating heart disease, and ultimately resulting in the loss of weight.

The Pritikin meal plan guidelines are listed in *The Pritikin Permanent Weight Loss Manual:*[41]

1. Eat two or more kinds of whole grain daily (pasta, bread, cereal, etc.).
2. Eat two or more servings of raw vegetables and two or more servings of cooked vegetables daily.
3. Eat one piece of citrus fruit and three or four servings of fresh fruit a day.
4. Do not use sugar or honey of any kind. Sweeten with fruit or fruit juice.
5. Limit protein intake to 24 ounces per week of low-fat, low-cholesterol meat, fish, shellfish, or fowl, with a maximum of four ounces (uncooked) per day. Drink up to 16 ounces of skim milk on vegetarian days and 8 ounces on days when protein allotment is eaten.
6. Eight ounces of cooked beans or peas may be substituted for meat on vegetarian days, otherwise avoid these.
7. For weight loss, increase vegetables in the diet and decrease grains.

Upon calling the Pritikin center here in Los Angeles, my staff was informed that Pritikin has two programs, an outpatient program and an inpatient program.

Inpatient: This program is called, "Live In." The live-in stay can be for one, two or three weeks, depending on the need.

Fee: $4,000 per week with a $500 discount special, which was quoted as good for the next two sessions. Of this cost, $545 can be considered medical expense for insurance purposes.

Outpatient: The client comes in three times a week from 5:30 to 8:30 P.M. The program consists of one and a half hours of exercise, one hour of lecture and an evening meal.

Fee: $1,134 for a four-week program. $589 can be considered medical expenses for insurance purposes.

With both programs, the client receives a physical exam and an evaluation by a physician. The client is placed on an exercise program and receives comprehensive health education.

The staff member at Pritikin stressed that the Pritikin program is a way of life. She said that they want to teach the client to keep weight off permanently, but that it must be done safely and so they do not promote rapid weight loss. Pritikin feels that with proper education and an integrated exercise program, the client will be successful at achieving a permanent loss of weight. The Pritikin representative asked my staff member what she was looking for and whether she had any medical problems. My staff member explained that she had asthma and was just starting out slowly with exercise and that she wanted to lose weight. Although individual trainers are not provided, clients meet with an instructor who, after determining the heart-rate range according to age, stamina, and treadmill results, designs an individualized program. They said they realize that everyone's needs are different and therefore the exercise program is tailored to the particular client.

Comments from my staff members:

The basic components of their program are education on proper eating and exercise, with the ability to practice this while at Pritikin in order to establish these habits for life. When I told her that I needed to talk with my doctor about various weight-loss programs, she offered to send me brochures on both programs and gave me her direct extension to call if I needed any further assistance. She said that she would be checking in with me to see how I was doing.

She was not a hard-core salesperson. She seemed more interested in what would be best for me.

Pros: This program promotes fairly sound principles when compared with your daughter's, or even your own, diet. Who can argue with the promotion of regular exercise and the eating of quality low-fat protein, fresh fruits, vegetables, and grains? If your daughter is overweight, this approach may not be as discouraging as others given that the low percentage of fat in the diet, which automatically reduces the calories, means that a fairly abundant amount of food is allowed. This program is also good in terms of educating anorexics who eventually come to view all food as "fattening." I have been able to use Pritikin principles to get anorexics to start eating foods that they had previously eliminated because they believed, erroneously, that they are fattening. The Pritikin program encourages personal responsibility from the beginning and includes a minicourse on nutrition and how one's body uses food. Bulimics can benefit for the same reasons as anorexics, however, black/white thinking is likely to set in when they "break a rule." following "Cons".

Cons: The problem with Pritikin is that the food guidelines are very strict. It is hard to live in a world where all our food is measured, where there is no sugar, where four fruits must be eaten every day, and where most of the foods we are accustomed to eating have more fat than the Pritikin daily allowance. I promote low-fat, low-sugar eating, but the Pritikin diet is far too strict and is unnecessary for anyone without a serious health problem. Furthermore, the attack it makes on dietary fat and, to a lesser degree on protein, may serve to increase your daughter's paranoia about eating protein foods and anything containing fat. Black/white, all-or-nothing thinking too often comes into play when one is trying to follow a program like this and then goes beyond the guidelines. If your daughter eats a candy bar, she should not be reinforced to feel guilty about it or made to feel she will gain weight. The concept of balance should, as always, be invoked. Strict programs do not make for a balanced approach. However, the Pritikin program counselors might not be as hard core in their own perspective as the guidelines seem to suggest. If your daughter is overweight and there is a Pritikin in your area, it might be a good move to explore this option and find out about the staff involved and their philosophy. If you daughter is anorexic, you will need to work with a dietitian and/or her therapist, The Pritikin books have been helpful in some cases, but leave it up to the therapist to decide. The book *Beyond Pritikin* is an important resource for either anorexics or bulimics, as it highlights the limitations and long-term consequences of a diet too low in fat, and points out the need for essential fatty acids in the diet.

FIT FOR LIFE

This diet comes from Harvey and Marilyn Diamond's book, *Fit For Life*.[42] The information that follows comes from that book and other material about this type of food plan and from interviews with clients and friends who have tried the program. The diet is basically a food-combining approach. The motto of the program is, " It's not what you eat, but when and how that counts." The Diamonds are "nutritionists" whose interest is in debunking what they consider myths about weight loss and the importance of such things as milk and protein in the diet. They believe that if you eat foods in the right combination and in accordance with your natural digestive cycles, there is no need for calorie counting and portion control. The idea is based on the assumption that if one eats in accordance with certain natural laws of digestion, weight control won't be a problem. "Safe and permanent weight reduction is directly related to the amount of vital energy you have at your disposal and to the efficient use of this energy to eliminate waste (excess weight) from your body. The key to this system is that it works with your body to free up energy. With this new energy pool, your body goes to work automatically to shed any burden of excess weight."[43]

The diet principles are fairly easy. There are other concepts, such as eliminating dairy products, caffeine, and sugar, but the main tenets of the program are these:

1. Eat as much as you want, but only fruit or fruit juices until noon.
2. Never eat protein and starch together.

Pros: A big plus is *Fit for Life's* simplicity and the lack of calorie counting. How easy it is to eat as much as you want as long as you eat fruit until noon and never combine protein and starch at a meal. The pros stop here.

Cons: How long could one continue to eat like this even if the principles were sound? I have no indication that they are and there is no scientific proof. The prospect of eating only fruit in the morning looks bleak after a few days. Furthermore, so many foods are completely and forever out:

sandwiches, tacos, hamburgers (even chicken or turkey burgers). And why can't I have grilled fish and rice, or a chicken breast and baked potato, or a poached egg (or egg whites) and toast? Weight loss does usually happen, at least early on, with this approach because the foods eaten are controlled. Protein or starch eaten only with vegetables automatically reduces calories. But how much fish and broccoli or chicken and salad, or fruit for breakfast can we consume?

Last, how the above-mentioned "energy pool" acquired from improved digestion gets rid of excess weight is not sufficiently explained. It may be true that digestion is better if foods aren't combined, but the effect this has on weight loss is unsubstantiated.

THE FAT-COUNTING DIETS

There are many variations of this basic diet technique. Restricting fat is probably the most popular diet method currently in use. What began with Pritikin has become an obsession in this country. The newer versions of low-fat dieting try to promote a more realistic amount of fat than the 10 % allowed by Pritikin, but less than the 30% that has typically been recommended by the American Heart Association. However, it is those people who follow these diets who have gone to extremes, eating far less fat than the diets recommend. If less fat is good, no fat is better. To summarize the various versions of restricted-fat diets, they all encourage people to determine their calorie level and then eat approximately 20% of those calories as fat. The easiest way to keep the fat intake within the 20% level is to find out how many grams of fat constitute the 20% and then restrict your diet to that many grams of fat.

Example: If your daughter is on a 1,500-calorie diet, then 20% of 1,500 is 300 calories. Therefore, only 300 calories of her diet should come from fat. Now, she can stop here and try to figure out how many fat calories are in the food she eats, but counting grams is usually easier. Most products label their fat in grams. To figure out how many grams of fat are in 300 calories, simply divide 300 by 9, because fat equals 9 calories per gram. In this example, your daughter's fat allowance is 33.3 grams a day.

Fat-counting diets will teach your daughter how to determine how much fat she should eat, and how to count and limit her grams of fat. This will either help her in her math skills or she will avoid eating anything with fat so that she doesn't have to figure all this out. Seriously, this knowledge is valuable, and you should know how to do it as well. See Appendix A for further information. (*Note:* If your daughter is not already obsessed with limiting her intake of fat, don't introduce her to counting fat grams without first getting professional advice. A little knowledge can be dangerous.)

Pros: Knowing the quality and contents of the food we eat is important. Educating yourself and switching to a low-fat diet, as long as you eat a balance of foods, is a healthy way to lose weight. It is easier than counting calories and tends to help people not feel deprived, at least in terms of the quantity of food they can eat.

Cons: Basically, low-fat eating is a good approach. However, all fat has become the tangible enemy, with eradication as the goal. It is not a low-fat, but a no-fat, diet that is often, and wrongly, sought. All the focus on fat has caused an obsession with getting and keeping the fat out of everything. Instead of limiting fat, most girls strive to eliminate it. This means that, among other things:

- They won't eat any animal protein.
- They think a pat of butter, a drop of oil, a piece of avocado, or a bite of pizza will make them fat.
- They would rather starve than eat food with fat in it.
- They will eat only nonfat dairy products, even if they are on vacation and nonfat products aren't available.
- They won't eat at restaurants or at friends' houses because the meal may contain hidden fat.

One 17-year-old dieter told me that even though the pasta sauce at a restaurant was listed as nonfat, she inquired further and discovered that a teaspoon of oil had been added to the water in which the pasta was cooked in order to prevent its sticking, and so she refused to eat it.

In trying to make a point to a patient who was overly obsessed with fat, I told her that even grapefruit has fat in it and that, in fact, all food has at least minute traces of fat. To my dismay, she said, "Oh no, you mean I can't eat that either." Don't underestimate or take lightly the indoctrination and propaganda to which your daughter is exposed in this area.

One other potential problem with focusing on fat intake is that other principles are often neglected altogether. For example, Jenny came to my office one day and announced how proud she was that she had eaten no fat for the last three days. However, one look at her food journal revealed a serious flaw in the no-fat approach. One of her fat-free days looked like this:

Breakfast: Shredded wheat and nonfat milk
Snack: Jelly beans (one large bag) and eight fat-free cookies
Lunch: Nonfat frozen yogurt
Snack: Three large fat-free rice cakes, cappuccino with nonfat milk, three packs of Life Savers
Dinner: Green salad (carrots, green beans, and tomatoes), fat-free dressing
Snack: Fat-free frozen yogurt, nonfat chocolate cake, a half box of red licorice (watching a movie)

Eating no fat is not healthy. A certain amount of fat is necessary (see Appendix A, Nutrition Guide) and eating only low-fat foods is not enough. It is important for your daughter to understand that what she does eat is just as important as what she doesn't eat.

THE ROTATION DIET

This diet is based on a three-week plan that varies the daily intake of calories in a rotating manner. For women, the rotation amount is 600, 900, and 1,200 calories per day. A person who has more weight to lose begins the rotation again after a maintenance or rest period. The idea behind this plan is to avoid lowering the metabolic rate as happens when following a strict 1,200-calorie (or less) plan. The author of the *Rotation Diet* book, Dr. Martin Katahn, says that instead of training bodies to get along with less food, rotation dieters "are increasing their ability to eat after the diet without regaining weight."[44]

Upon reading the book, one finds the usual principles, such as drinking a lot of water, eating less fat, and eliminating sugar and caffeine. All of these diets seem very similar on close inspection.

Pros: Keeping a healthy metabolism is a good thing and three weeks of dieting sounds easy enough. Furthermore, Dr. Katahn has written other books on the subject of dieting and seems to have done his homework in the area of dieting and metabolism. In his book, he includes research supporting his program. His information on exercise, weight loss, and metabolism offers a realistic and healthy approach.

Cons: Again, here we have the basic strict low-calorie plan, even if it only lasts three weeks. The concept is good, but if your daughter ascribes to this idea, her rotation calorie levels had better be higher. Furthermore, although the maintenance or rest period offers a break from the rotation phase, it is more than a rest from dieting. Maintenance is another phase of the diet that also must be followed. If one goes back to one's original eating habits, all lost weight will be regained. So, like most other weight-loss books, the book's cover makes the plan look a lot simpler than the inside details reveal.

THE FIT OR FAT TARGET DIET AND OTHER FIT OR FAT BOOKS

In 1977, Covert Bailey published *Fit or Fat,*[45] the first successful consumer book on why diets don't work, and what does, with an emphasis on the difference between being overweight and overly fat. This book describes the important difference between losing fat and losing muscle on a weight-loss program and details how losing fat is best accomplished. One of Bailey's basic tenets is that fit people use fat efficiently and fat people store fat efficiently, and in the area of weight control, what is important is getting fit, not dieting.

Bailey's books offer an easy-to-read, easy-to-understand explanation of exercise and dieting physiology, along with what to do and not to do to lose weight. In addition to *Fit or Fat*, there are *The Fit or Fat Target Diet,*[46] *The Fit or Fat Target Diet Recipes* (coauthored by Lee Bishop),[47] *The Fit or Fat Woman* (coauthored by Lee Bishop),[48] and *The New Fit or Fat* published in 1991.[49] The approach to weight loss in these books focuses on fitness, including a healthy body fat percentage as the goal, rather than a weight goal. *The Fit or Fat Target Diet* offers sensible, balanced eating strategies and easy ways to incorporate a healthy, nondeprivation-oriented food plan into your life. The concept of a bull's eye target is used, with the bull's eye representing the most nutritious food items from each of four food groups: meat, milk, breads and cereals, and fruits and vegetables. A series of concentric circles represents the most to least nutritious items. Thus, the outside ring represents such food items as, butter, table sugar, and pepperoni, while the bull's eye and first ring contain such foods as nonfat yogurt, water-packed tuna, and shredded wheat. A system for using the target is cleverly devised and spelled out. This program is not overly burdensome or restrictive. Even if the available charts are not used, this book and Fit or Fat Target Recipes are informative and usable and well worth reading. *The Fit or Fat Woman* adds to Covert's other books by addressing special topics for women, including eating disorders, depression, hormones, premenstrual syndrome, osteoporosis, and body image.

ENTER THE ZONE DIET

Dr. Barry Sears, author of *Enter the Zone*,[50] believes that humans are getting fatter because they have been sold a bill of goods with the idea that eating less fat and more carbohydrates, particularly grains and pasta, is the way to a slim body. Instead, Dr. Sears feels that people should eat a balance of protein, fat, and carbohydrate that keeps them in "the zone." According to Sears, "the zone" is a real metabolic state in which the body works at peak efficiency, and one that can be reached by everyone, and maintained indefinitely.

The principle, as described in Dr. Sears' book, is basically that it is the ratio of protein, fat, and carbohydrate in your meals that is the key to permanent weight loss and good health. It is eating excess carbohydrate, not fat, that makes you fat because the body responds to excess carbohydrates by turning them into fat.

Pros: Dr. Sears discusses many sound nutrition principles in his book and explains how Americans have reduced their intake of protein and fat far too much, putting them out of balance hormonally, particularly with regard to insulin. He states that increased insulin levels resulting from excess carbohydrate intake tell the body to store fat and they interfere with the burning of fat already stored. Dr. Sears also says that too much carbohydrate means too much insulin, and too much insulin means you are out of the zone. His plea for fat and protein phobia to end is a welcome addition to the numerous diet protocols.

Dr. Sears explains how to get the proper balance of protein, carbohydrate, and fat, which varies according to the individual. For example, if you are an active person with a lean body mass of 95 pounds, Dr. Sears recommends 95 grams of protein per day, or 1 gram of protein per pound of lean body mass. Next, for every seven grams of protein you eat, you need to eat 9 grams of carbohydrate and 1 1/2 grams of fat. Fats slow the entry rate of carbohydrates into the system, which is the main goal of what Sears refers to as a hormonally based diet. The book describes a system whereby the right amount of protein, carbohydrate, and fatty foods are put into blocks with recommendations for how many blocks of each will meet different individuals' needs.

Cons: The problem with the zone diet is that Sears, like many overzealous advocates, overstates his case. To make a point, Dr. Sears claims that eating sugar is better than eating carrots (hormonally speaking, of course), since carrots have a higher glycemic index and supposedly raise blood sugar, and thus insulin levels, faster. Making this kind of statement is not a healthy approach to any eating plan. Furthermore, this plan, like any other, can be cumbersome if followed too strictly. Assuring that you are getting the right blocks for every snack and meal should not become another oppressive dietary regimen. Last, Sears does not cite any research, although he talks about it. The reason for this is that there are too many studies to cite! When my staff member phoned the main office to reach Sears, she left a message and as yet (2 weeks later) has received no response.

HOW DO YOU CHOOSE?

There are countless other diet programs, plans, and books on the market. The very best plan is an individual one designed for the unique individual that your daughter is. Overall, in helping your daughter to select a diet, whether by joining a program, following a plan from a book, going to a professional for help, or creating a plan of her own, the following questions should be answered with a "yes." (Remember, it is not a good idea to go on a diet with her, unless this means simply that the entire household is switching to healthier eating habits.)

ANSWER "YES" A HEALTHY DIETING PLAN/PROGRAM

1. Does the plan follow and teach the principles of sound nutrition for good health?
2. Does your doctor approve of the plan?
3. Has the diet been successful for large numbers of other people or people like your daughter, and can you get statistics?

4. Will individual health problems be taken into account?
5. Is it a fairly easy plan to follow without undue preparation or time requirements?
6. Does the plan provide for long-term changes and maintenance of weight goal from the beginning?
7. Is this a diet that will not lower metabolic rate if followed too long?
8. Is this a diet that results primarily in fat loss?
9. Does this diet provide for adequate intake of nutrients for both physical health and psychological well-being?
10. Does the plan afford enough individual flexibility: Is it realistic?
11. Is the plan one that your daughter can follow for life?

The nutrition guide in Appendix A will give you important, useful information on food, eating, and dieting that will help you in devising a nutrition plan for your daughter and your family. The next chapter is written for your daughter. It is important that you read it yourself, and if your daughter is old enough, you can give it to her to read. Remember, even if your daughter is very young, dieting is ultimately her own choice. You can present material, supply nutritious foods, and offer guidance, but she will be the only one who can accept a plan and make it work for her. Your job, helping her to live a healthy life is a formidable one.

12

ↂ ↂ ↂ

So You Want
to Go on a Diet

I did not die from dieting, but I did lose my hair, my ability to have children, my thyroid function (so my metabolism shut down), and all the good times I should have had in college. All I wanted was to lose weight, then all I wanted was to lose another 5 pounds, then another, then another, until I lost not only weight but also perspective. At 79 pounds I still thought I was and actually saw myself as fat.

I have been recovered now from anorexia nervosa for over 20 years and I have gotten back much of what I lost. I now treat others who are still struggling, still dying to be thin. Many are not as lucky as I. I am alive, but others who are just like you have died. I would be lying if I didn't admit that I do not want to be fat, I do not want to lose control, but my perspective is back and therefore, I will no longer do anything that is harmful or self-destructive to reach or maintain those goals. There is a healthy way. The book this chapter came from was written to help parents protect their daughters from becoming one of society's diet victims. This chapter was written especially to you, in hopes that it my help to protect you from yourself.

Carolyn Costin

If you have been given this to read, someone who loves you is very concerned about you—your feelings and behaviors involving your body image, weight, and food. They are worried that your eating habits and attitudes are unhealthy and/or disordered. Please read these pages all the way through even though some parts may not apply to you. Do your best to accept what is written here as true, even if it's difficult to admit. Perhaps none of what is presented here will apply to you. In that case you should reassure the person who gave this to you that there is nothing to worry about. Most important, discuss how you feel about these issues with someone you trust. If you know you need help, and want to get better, now is a good time to start.

As a female in this society, chances are that you are concerned about your weight and have dieted in the past or are dieting now. It is very likely that you are overly concerned with your weight, perhaps even obsessed to the point that it is interfering with your life. Or perhaps it is others who think so. Whatever the case, if you want to diet and lose weight, you may need help to do it in a healthy way. If you are obsessed with your diet or your body, then concentrate on making it a healthy obsession. If you want control, use your willpower and control to achieve healthy goals. Get a sense of pride from being able to create a diet that styles a *healthy* body, not a disordered, fanatic, unhealthy one. Take it from me, I have done it both ways.

While pursuing a weight goal, you need to remember to like yourself and to value yourself more than you do any diet program or number on the scale. This means allowing yourself to be less than perfect. You won't gain weight, your diet isn't blown, your willpower isn't shot, and people aren't going to like you less if you put cream cheese on your bagel, eat a cookie, or skip your exercise. You won't fall apart and be fat if you break "the rules." Be flexible and balanced. There is balance in following rules or guidelines—and having the freedom to break them. To do this will involve making peace with food and with yourself. You must learn to see your worth in things other than how you look and what you weigh. Being thin is not important enough to starve yourself, live in misery, or harm yourself in any way. Being healthy and happy is what's important. How you feel about your whole self, not just the way you look, ultimately will determine whether you can find a balance that gets and/or keeps you out of destructive patterns and ensures a successful, happy life.

You may have forgotten how to listen to, or you may ignore, your body signals. You need to learn that eating when you're hungry is a good thing and that being full is not the same thing as being fat. Fullness after a meal is normal, not bad, and not a signal that you have eaten too much.

You must accept that your body needs calories just to survive. You don't have to do anything to earn your food. Approximately 80% of your daily caloric requirement is used to heat your body, pump your blood, and perform other life-sustaining bodily functions. You must eat properly to grow hair, nails, and skin, maintain your menstruation and ovulation, and have healthy organs and bones. You must eat to live and eat healthy to live healthy.

The reality of dieting, or of using any unhealthy or even "short-term" method to lose weight, such as going on fad diets, starving, taking laxatives, vomiting, or doing excessive exercise, is that in order to keep the weight off, you must continue these behaviors, which in time can cause serious damage and even death. Eventually, you may even need to go into a hospital or treatment program where the environment is controlled enough to stop you from bingeing, starving, or purging. If you don't want to do damage and don't want to be sick, sooner or later you have to deal with the real world. You must rethink your goals to include the ability to deal with pizza, salad dressing, parties, Thanksgiving, and your refrigerator without compulsion or fear. Your main goal should be to reach your other goals while staying healthy.

You first must decide whether you at least have some interest in pursuing a healthy diet and in trying new ideas and techniques. Chances are that what you are currently doing is not worth it. You only have to be willing to try. I know that you cannot commit to anything new until you learn more about it. You will not use new methods to control your weight until you feel safe giving up the old ones. No one can make you give them up. If you are willing to seek and accept help, you will find newer, better ways that will be worth it. For the time being, just think of putting your old behaviors up on a shelf. Rather than using them automatically, you can bring them down and use them if you need them, but it is your choice. If you are suffering from disordered eating, or a full fledged eating disorder, you can recover, but will need help to do so. It will be a long process, there will be times when you are afraid, lost, feel out of control, and resistant. Don't do this alone. Find someone to help you go through it, someone who will help to keep you on track when you feel like you can't go on. It will also help to keep a journal. It will be useful in the process of learning about yourself, sharing things with others, organizing your thoughts on paper, and responding to questions and challenges.

Food can be or has become your greatest pleasure and your worst pain, your friend and your enemy. Food has taken on new meanings, representing both comfort and pain. To get started on the path toward well-being, it will be important for you to realize, and to believe, that dieting does not work. You should never do anything to lose weight that you aren't prepared to do for the rest of your life. To go *on* a diet means you can go *off* it. You need a plan that will help you reach your goals, one that is healthy, and one that you can do for life.

The following guidelines will help you to achieve a slim, healthy body permanently.

1. Setting a Goal Weight

It's hard to know what an appropriate weight goal is. Various sources such as the Metropolitan Life Insurance Weight Tables provide ideal weight ranges but are controversial as to their validity, with some thinking they are too lenient and people should weigh less than the tables suggest. In September 1995, The New England Journal of Medicine published a study indicating that lower mortality rates are associated with women who are leaner than the current tables "allow." However, one flaw of the study is that most of the women surveyed reported their weight by telephone! Besides, there is no doubt that how one becomes thin certainly makes a difference. If thinner is better does starving oneself to get thin count?

There are formulas that have been devised to determine goal weight. One formula commonly used by health professionals is to "allow" 100 hundred pounds for 5 feet and five pounds for every inch after that. For example, if you are 5 feet 4 inches tall, a healthy weight goal would be 120 pounds.

Another formula is the Body Mass Index, or BMI, which is your weight in kilograms divided by the square of your height in meters.

Example:
If you are 120 pounds and 5 feet, 5 inches tall, your BMI=20.
Weight: 120 pounds = 54.43 kilograms
Height: 5'5" = 1.65 x meters which when squared = 2.725801
54.43 divided by 2.725801=20.
The body mass index in this example is 20.

Guidelines for body mass index suggest that if you are age 19 or older and your BMI is equal to or greater than 27, treatment intervention is needed to deal with the excess weight. A BMI between 25 and 27 may be a problem for some individuals, but a health professional should be consulted. A low BMI score is also indicative of a problem. Anything below 18 may even indicate a need for hospitalization due to malnutrition. Healthy BMIs have also been established for children and adolescents,[51] but standardized formulas should never be relied on exclusively.

Both of these formulas are criticized for not taking into account lean versus fat body mass. Another method of establishing goal weight, *body composition testing*, measures lean and fat. A healthy total body weight is established based on guidelines that recommend a body-fat level of approximately 22% as the ideal for females and a body-fat level of approximately 15% as the ideal for males. This method "allows" for higher weights if the body fat is low. Whatever method is used, it is imperative to understand that all standardized formulas are difficult to apply to individuals. If you are far above the proposed goal, you may think and even know that it is too low for you and may realize that in order to reach it you would have to starve or otherwise harm yourself. You may give up altogether. On the other hand you may say, "The weight goal is too high, I want to be thinner," and ignore the goal.

The bottom line for determining a goal weight is health and lifestyle. Keep in mind that a healthy weight is one that facilitates a healthy functioning system of hormones, organs, blood, muscles, and so on. It is not a number but a range that allows you to eat without severely restricting, starving, or avoiding social situations where there is food. Even if you want to be thin, you need to eat enough to stay healthy and happy. You need only know what is best for you, not how you compare with some standard table or someone else.

2. STOP WEIGHING YOURSELF

Although this is one of the most difficult things I could ask you to do, stop weighing yourself and get rid of your scale. Reliance on the scale will result in your being fooled, tricked, and misled. Consider the fact that in my sixteen years of helping clients with weight control and eating disorders, I have found that those who don't weigh are the most successful. You need to learn other measures to evaluate how well you are doing. You won't need a scale to tell you if you are bingeing, starving, or otherwise straying from a healthy eating plan. Scale weight is misleading and cannot be trusted. Although weight changes daily owing to fluid shifts in the body, if the scale registers a one pound gain, people frequently react as though their program is not effective, they become depressed and often give up. I have seen many individuals who are on very good eating regimens become distraught if the scale doesn't show the loss in weight that they expect. Even if you are on a healthy weight-loss plan you should never weigh yourself. You will need to find other ways to determine whether what you are doing is or is not working. It takes time for healthy, permanent weight loss.

If you are anorexic, even if you have agreed to gain some weight, the scale will sabotage your efforts. You will desperately want to lose any weight you gain even though you need the weight gain to be healthy. You will always have to torture yourself unless you give up the idea that you must weigh whatever unrealistic amount it is that you have set for yourself. It's okay if you want to be thin. But it's not okay to starve yourself. You need to learn to be happy with your weight gain as a sign that you are getting better, getting healthy, getting in control, and out of the grips of this awful prison where you have kept yourself.

3. Preplanning Meals and Snacks

Come up with an eating plan with which you can feel comfortable according to your preferences and your lifestyle. This is not a plan that you must be rigid about or stay with forever. It is only a guideline to get you started toward healthier eating. Perhaps you have been starving during the day and overeating when you get home or at night. Perhaps you try to resist food constantly until you can resist no more, then you give in to your compelling "urge" to eat and thus go overboard, which causes weight gain or interferes with weight loss. In another scenario you restrict your food and then eat *the wrong things*, things you feel guilty about and thus feel the need to get rid of, so you throw up, take laxatives, and so on, only to feel more guilty and you must now starve again. You can see why it might help to initially plan meals and snacks. Your attentiveness to your hunger and fullness signals might be faulty at this point, or you aren't listening to them. Planning helps you to feel safe and comfortable so that you won't make emotional spur-of-the-moment choices that you later regret. Ignore your compulsive, fearful thoughts and commit yourself to some kind of plan, including between-meal snacks.

4. How Much Should I Eat?

Think of your food as fuel. It provides the energy your body needs to carry out all of its functions. Your body uses a certain amount of fuel for normal functioning and it needs even more for any exercise or extra activities you might do.

Simple facts:

- When the food you eat equals the amount your body uses, you will not gain or lose weight—even if you are on a diet of 50 percent fat!
- If you eat more than your body needs, the extra fuel will be stored as fat. The good news is that, your body needs a lot of food.
- If you eat less than your body needs, your metabolism will slow down to conserve fuel and the difference will be made up from sources within your body—your fat stores, your muscle tissue, and in some cases even your bones.

There are Recommended Dietary Allowances (RDAs) for different age groups. The RDAs are established by the National Academy of Sciences in Washington, D.C. The RDAs are listed in ranges. For example, ages 19 to 24 call for a caloric need ranging from 1600 to 2400. Individual caloric needs are based on a variety of circumstances, including physical activity. See Appendix B in this book, Recommended Dietary Allowances for more information.

The RDAs are not set for weight loss but only give you a general idea of what is considered a healthy amount of calories for different age groups. You may be surprised. In India, one of the poorest countries in the world, the very poorest women eat 1400 calories a day. I would not recommend any one eat 1400 calories per day—it is not enough. Eating too little slows down your metabolism and is counterproductive.

General food selection guidelines:

- Eat 4 servings of fruits and vegetables daily.
- Eat 4 servings of grains daily.
- Drink 2 cups of milk daily, for children and adults, or 4 cups of milk daily, for teens.
- Eat 4 to 5 ounces of protein (meat, nuts, fish, beans), for teens and adults, or 2 to 3 ounces of protein, for children.

For further information on food selection and quantity, consult Ellyn Satter's book, *How to Get Your Kid To Eat ... But Not Too Much.*[52]

5. WHAT IF I AM OVEREATING?

First, overeating is hard to define. Are you bingeing large amounts of food and feel that it is out of your control? Do you eat constantly, even when not hungry? Are you trying to restrict your food and therefore consider yourself overeating if you exceed your self-imposed limit? These are important questions to answer. If the last applies to you, you are not overeating. If one or both of the first two apply and you seem unable to stop, you will need to consider the several reasons why you might be eating to cope with other feelings. Look at the list below to get an idea. Make your own list using any of these that apply to you and adding others that you come up with for yourself.

- Need to express myself
- Need to fill up an emptiness
- Need to be heard
- Need to rebel or escape
- Need for entertainment or fun
- Need for distraction from my problems or pain
- Need for attention or for a relationship

Take time with this exercise. After you make your own list, write about how you use food to deal with your unmet needs. You can overcome overeating and should find an experienced professional with whom to work. Following are tips for what you can begin doing right away.

- Structure your meals and snacks, at least until you feel more in control.
- Focus first on the quality of food you eat and deal with quantity later. For now, start by eating good, wholesome foods, as much as you want, at your planned meals and snack times.

6. WHEN SHOULD I EAT?

There are no hard and fast rules about when to eat. Even trying to eat, "only when you are hungry" can become restrictive and abnormal. I often point out to my clients that if I have a chocolate bar in the afternoon or a bowl of ice cream in my bubble bath at night, I may not be eating from hunger cues! There can be other reasons to eat besides hunger and they are perfectly normal.

As far as three meals a day versus grazing all day or eating snacks between meals, it is an individual choice. However, it seems best to spread your eating throughout the day instead of having two or three large meals. Eating throughout the day gives you more energy, and your body can digest and use the calories more efficiently. Additionally, it seems to be less threatening to those who need to gain weight to eat smaller amounts several times during the day, especially in the beginning. Whatever you do, don't save up your calories for the evening by eating little or nothing during the day. Research evidence suggests that if you skip meals during the day and eat only at night, your body will eventually "learn" to turn more of that evening meal into fat for storage since it will not be fed again until the next evening. Your body needs fuel all day to function effectively. Your brain needs the glucose from the food to work at its best. Glucose can only be stored for about four hours! So listen to your body and eat throughout the day.

Furthermore, it's important to start your body off in the morning by eating. Eating actually raises your metabolism. This is especially important in the morning when you have been essentially fasting during sleep. In case you don't remember from health class, the word "breakfast" derived from breaking the fast. Giving your body food in the morning is like putting paper on smoldering coals and igniting the flames.

7. DON'T LABEL FOOD "GOOD" OR "BAD"

Eliminate any idea that there are good foods and bad foods. Most likely, you have decided that certain foods are bad foods, fattening foods, or binge foods. When you eat these foods, you may engage in irrational disordered eating behaviors. For example, "I had a cookie" becomes, "I might as well eat the whole bag." Labeling certain foods as "bad" can become an excuse to eat uncontrollably and then get rid of what's been eaten by purging. You might be avoiding your own so called "bad foods" to the point where you create an increased desire and obsession for them. This is reminiscent of a famous experiment in which psychologists observed children's behavior when playing with toys. Before leaving children in a room with several toys, the psychologist would say to the child, "You can play with any toy in here, except the green truck." Once the psychologist was outside and observing through a one way window, what toy do you think attracted the child? The answer, of course, is the green truck. Think of this when you tell yourself, "I can eat any food, but the bad foods." Can you see how you may be setting yourself up?

There are no bad foods, but there are bad eating habits. There are no fattening foods, only fattening eating habits. Ice cream isn't a bad or fattening food, but eating ice cream all day long is a bad and probably a fattening eating habit. If you binge on certain foods such as doughnuts, cereal, ice cream, chocolate, or chips, you need to learn how to integrate these foods into your life in a balanced way. If you always binge when you have ice cream, avoiding ice cream isn't the answer—learning how to eat ice cream appropriately is. Learning to incorporate your so called bad foods into your diet may seem difficult at first and you may need help. Start slowly with one or two foods at a time. If eating a certain food always causes you to binge and purge, then substitute something similar for that trigger food, for example, frozen yogurt for ice cream or graham crackers for cookies. Keep in mind that the goal is to be able to deal with all food so that food decisions can be made based on preference and not fear. Sometimes, it's hard to decide when to push yourself to eat a certain trigger food and when to avoid certain foods altogether for the moment. You will probably need a therapist or dietitian to help you work this out. If you are still living at home and under your parents' care, ask for support in finding someone to help you. If they gave you this chapter to read, they already think you need help.

8. What Else Should I Do?

- Start a journal. Write in it daily or more often.
- Write down your list of "binge", "trigger", or "scary" foods. These are the foods you will try to introduce into your daily normal eat-

ing. Try to pick a food a week to add to your diet even if you add it in small amounts.

- Make a list of the times and situations where you find it most diffi-cult to overcome the urge to eat inappropriately, binge, throw up, take laxatives, and so on. For example, teens often say that they have a big problem around 3 or 4 P.M., when they come home from school. Many people say their problem arises at night.
- Make a list of things you can do during your difficult times to help you with your eating. You may choose to do something else to occupy your time or to find a friend to be with. It may help to select one particularly difficult time per week to focus on, depend-ing upon how serious your problem is.
- Whenever you feel like bingeing or purging, describe in your jour-nal all of the things you are feeling and why bingeing or purging is something you want to do.
- Do not expect to conquer all of this at once. Most likely your prob-lem with your weight, body image, or food has been developing for years and it will take time for you to readjust.

9. What Should I Eat?

First of all, remember that *any* food is okay and you can eat whatever you want. But try to listen to and respond to your body's signals. Naturally thin people usually eat what they want when they're hungry. Fat people are usually the ones who go on diets, which means following externally im-posed rules. Some people avoid certain foods for health reasons, such as sugar or beef or high-fat foods. I challenge you to consider your motives if you are one of these people. Being a vegetarian, eating low-fat foods, or abstaining from sugar is fine, as long as it's not because you are terrified that eating them will make you fat and as long as what you do eat is healthy. Some of the vegetarian, no-fat, no-sugar diets people are eating are the unhealthiest, least nutritious diets I have seen. Furthermore, telling yourself you can't eat certain foods, is a setup for craving them and think-ing of them as rewards, or as foods to eat on the sly. You need to incorpo-rate them into your eating in a way that works for you. If you *really* want a candy bar, have a candy bar, enjoy it, and don't feel guilty about it. You will learn how often you can have a candy bar and not gain weight. Eating candy bars all day long is not appropriate either. But if you did this, you wouldn't really be listening to your body, would you? With a healthy attitude toward food, allowing foods in moderation, you won't have a constant desire for candy bars all the time. If you still decide that you want to give up certain foods, that is your choice, but don't force it on yourself or it won't work.

You might be thinking that you will find it difficult to bring back certain "forbidden" foods to your diet. You might be thinking you will get fat if you eat those foods. Actually, the beauty of it is that you can eat that way and not gain weight. I do, my clients do, you can as well. If you eat regularly, you'll maintain a healthy metabolism. If you eat properly and exercise moderately, you will increase your metabolism and thus the calories burned. If you eat enough, you will satisfy yourself and won't have the urge to binge. If you commit to giving up erroneous weight-loss methods such as fad diets and purging your food, you won't be tempted to overeat with the excuse, " I can just get rid of it."

Even if you are overweight and trying to lose weight, you need a lifestyle pattern for eating that includes all foods in moderation. If eating certain foods makes you think that you've blown it, and thus you might as well eat the whole box, eat all day, or eat five more servings, chances are you will continue to eat in a self-destructive way. You must get rid of the all-or-nothing attitude. If your car has a flat tire, do you decide, "Oh I've blown it; I might as well punch holes in my other three tires"? Of course, you don't, so why would you respond to blowing your diet by wanting to create even more damage to repair?

All or nothing thinking has to go. When someone says, "I'll go on a diet tomorrow," I can bet that person is not going to be successful. Healthy eating does not start and stop like that. Does saying, "I will start tomorrow" mean you want to keep doing something today? Whatever it is, the point is that dieting isn't about giving things up, it is about fitting them in appropriately.

Obviously, some ways of eating are better and more nutritious. However, there are many myths about eating, dieting, and losing weight. You will feel and look better if you fuel your body through a *well-balanced* diet. Unfortunately, many people really don't know what a well-balanced diet is. Be open minded—what follows may go against all that you have been telling yourself, as well as what others have been telling you.

10. What Are the Nutritional Components of a Well-Balanced Diet?

Food can be broken down into three main categories: proteins, fats, and carbohydrates. Proteins and carbohydrates contain four calories per gram, while fat contains over twice that amount, or nine calories per gram. Popular weight loss diets vary as to the use of these three sources of energy, but a safe and healthy diet for life needs to provide the proper balance to maintain good health. Generally speaking approximately 15 to 20% of your diet should come from protein, 50 to 60% from carbohydrate and 15 to 25% from fat. The following information provides a definition and summary of the importance of these three food groups in your diet. For more detailed information on nutrition, consult the Nutrition Guide in Appendix A and the Resources in Appendix C in this book or find a good book on nutrition at your local bookstore.

Protein

You should receive approximately 15 to 20% of your daily intake from protein sources.

Animal sources (complete proteins)	meat, fish, poultry
	dairy (milk, cheese, yogurt)
	eggs, organ meats
Plant sources (incomplete proteins)	legumes (beans, peas, lentils)
	grains
	nuts, seeds

Protein foods are the building blocks of the body. Adequate protein, on a daily basis, is necessary for the growth and repair of muscles, hair, skin, teeth, and organs. One of the biggest problems with female dieters is that they avoid protein, believing it to be too high in calories and fat. This not only is an unhealthy perception but also is untrue. Four ounces of tuna contain 120 calories and approximately one gram of fat. This is fewer calories and less fat than in most bagels! Protein is vital and, if anything, when cutting back on calories, the percentage of protein in your diet should increase. If you want to be a vegetarian, you need to choose your protein sources wisely, so that they complement each other, giving you the necessary amino acids or building blocks for your complete protein requirements. If you want to cut back on animal foods but are still going to eat some meat (don't confuse meat to mean just beef) and dairy products, you don't have to worry as much about protein combining. However, if you are completely vegetarian you need to be more concerned. A good rule of thumb is to make sure you eat more than one vegetarian category of protein at the same meal—for example, beans and rice, tahini or hummus and pita bread, tortillas and beans, or nut butter on whole wheat bread. If you haven't eaten these things or don't even know what some of them are, you are not doing your homework and are not practicing healthy vegetarianism.

Fat

Fats are the body's main source of stored energy and used as fuel for rest, low level exercise, or long-term physical effort. Consumable fat can be obvious, as in butter or olive oil, or disguised, as in beef and baked goods. The thought that all fats are bad for your health is a misconception. It is important to be aware of and limit the amount of fat in your diet , but it is also vital not to cut out fat entirely. Don't become fat phobic! The nonfat or no-fat mentality is dangerous. According to various health professionals your daily diet should consist of somewhere between 15 and 25% fat. A good way to think about it is that to shoot for 20% is appropriate and to go lower or higher sometimes is no big deal.

Fat is essential for normal bodily functions. In fact, you need to eat a certain amount of fat to retain your body's ability to burn fat. Fat acts to protect and cushion all your major organs. Subcutaneous fat, a layer under your skin, preserves body heat by acting as an insulator against the cold. Fats carry the fat-soluble vitamins A, D, E, and K, that nourish your bones, teeth, hair, and skin.

Part of the reason that fat has acquired a bad reputation is that, at nine calories a gram, it contains over twice as many calories as protein or carbohydrate. Therefore, consistently eating too many high-fat foods will automatically result in a larger number of calories being consumed than if you were eating lower-fat foods. However, if the calories you eat equal the calories your body uses up, the amount of fat makes no difference with regard to gaining or losing weight.

The key is eating the right kind of dietary fat. The other reason that fat has a bad reputation is that unlike food in general there *are* "good" and "bad" fats. Dietary fats are either saturated or unsaturated. Saturated fats are the type to avoid. They metabolize slowly, raise blood cholesterol, clog the arteries, and contribute to heart disease. Foods high in saturated fats are butter, beef, cheese, lard, and ice cream. The most nutritionally desirable fats are the unsaturated fats, which help to eliminate excess cholesterol in the body and lower blood cholesterol levels. These fats stay liquid at room temperature and are found primarily in vegetable, nut and seed sources. There are two types of unsaturated fats, monounsaturated and polyunsaturated. Monounsaturated fats are the most desirable and are the main component of avocados, and canola and olive oils. Polyunsaturated fats are the next best and are found in corn, sunflower, soybean, safflower and cottonseed oils, as well as fish oils (omega-3 fatty acids).

It is critical that fats are part of your eating plan. If you need to lose weight or simply want to maintain your weight in a healthy way, cut back on fat and make healthy changes, not radical ones. Have a little salad dressing, use some olive oil in your cooking, and consume some foods, such as animal protein or baked goods, that contain fat. You are going to feel deprived and depressed if you deny yourself all forms of fat. Life without fat is not only boring but also is a wasted effort—so allow it. Remember, there are no fattening foods, only fattening eating habits.

To determine how much fat to eat, it is easier to count grams than figure out percentages. Most packaged food items now indicate the number of fat grams per serving and there are several books on the market that list grams of fat in foods. To find out how many grams of fat you need per day, figure out what 25% of your calorie level is.

For example, if you eat approximately 2000 calories, 25% of that number is 500. Therefore you need 500 calories from fat. To find out how many grams of fat this is, take 500 calories from fat and divide by 10 calories per gram. (I use 10 instead of 9 as it is easier to do mentally). Therefore, if you are eating 2000 calories a day, you can consume approximately 50 grams of fat. (To be exact, using 9 cals/gm, the number is 55.6 grams of fat.)

If you eat 1500 calories, you can eat 37.5 grams of fat. Now that you understand the logic, there is a *very* easy formula to follow to obtain the same results. Simply multiply your daily caloric intake by 0.025 to determine how many grams of fat constitute your 25%. For example, if you eat 2000 calories a day, multiply that number by 0.025 and you will have calculated that you can eat approximately 50 grams of fat.

Whatever you do, don't get stuck on the above formula. It is a guideline and not a hard-and-fast rule. There may be days when you eat more fat and others when you eat less. Balance is the key.

Carbohydrate

Carbohydrate foods should make up approximately 50 to 60% of your diet. In fact, your body needs a minimum of 400 calories of carbohydrate daily to maintain of your brain and nerve tissue. Carbohydrates are your best source of energy and are necessary for your muscles to burn fat. Carbohydrates comprise sugars, starches, and fiber (the indigestible fibrous material found in certain foods).

Basically, dietary carbohydrates can be broken down into two categories, either simple or complex. Simple carbohydrates (sugars) are found in table sugar, honey, natural fruit sugars and molasses, and in sugary and white flour food products. Examples are candy, soda, doughnuts, cake, cookies, fruit juice, and alcohol. Complex carbohydrates are found in starchy foods such as beans and grains, and in vegetables and fruits.

When carbohydrates are broken down, glucose (blood sugar) is the resulting product. Simple carbohydrates have only one or two molecules of glucose linked together; thus, they break down quickly in the body, causing a rapid increase in blood sugar. Complex carbohydrates consist of several links, which delay digestion and provide for a slower, longer release of energy and a longer delay in the return of hunger.

Many people believe that starches are fattening. This idea is completely false. Starches are low in fat and in their unprocessed form are high in fiber. Fiber absorbs water, produces bulk for fullness, and passes through your system without being absorbed, thus fiber adds no calories. High fiber foods, in addition to being low in fat, can actually lower the amount of fats in the blood. Too much starch is not appropriate either; again, balance is always the key.

A diet of good, filling, low-fat, high-fiber foods that provide adequate protein and consistent long-term energy is your goal.

Don't follow fad diet advice about what healthy eating is. You need to make a commitment to yourself in the area of sound nutrition principles. What nutrition goal will you work on this week? Write one down in your journal and commit yourself to achieving it, however small it might be. You will notice that if you say, "I'll try to do this," it leaves you plenty of room *not* to. Besides eating 4 servings of fruits and vegetables daily, you should eat 4 to 6 servings of complex carbohydrates—rice, cereal, bread, potato, pasta.

11. What Is a Healthy Attitude Toward Weight Loss?

Don't allow yourself to be caught up in the diet industry propaganda promoting the "diet mentality." For a quick check on where you stand, just ask yourself which side of the following list developed by Diana Lipson, R.D., represents your current thinking.

"Diet Mentality" versus "Balanced Eating"

Focus on weight loss	vs.	Making choices for better health
Any weight loss will do, the faster the better	vs.	Gradual lifestyle changes.
Self-acceptance is only achieved after weight loss	vs.	Begin now to self-accept and nurture
Goal weight is the measure of success	vs.	Find some success every day
No pain, no gain	vs.	Being active for fun and enjoyment
Food is the enemy and deprivation the goal	vs.	Food is a welcomed friend and healer
Should I have it? Do I need it?	vs.	Do I want it? Am I really hungry?
I must have it all or nothing at all	vs.	I can have it in moderation
There is a certain way to do it, try for perfection	vs.	Flexibility, "go with the flow"
Follow rules, there are no choices	vs.	There are choices—You decide what/when to eat
Responding to psychological hunger and fullness	vs.	Responding to physical cues
Going on a diet to lose weight	vs.	Eating like this for the rest of my life

RECOMMENDED READING

Breaking Free From Compulsive Eating, by Geneen Roth

Feeding On Dreams, by Diane Epstein and Kathleen Thompson

Intuitive Eating, by Evelyn Tribole

Living Binge Free, by Jane Latimer

Making Peace with Food, by Susan Kano

The New Fit or Fat, The Fit or Fat Target Diet, or any of Covert Bailey's books.

13

❧ ❧ ❧

Dear Mom
and Other Letters

This chapter was written by the people this book is about.[*] Over the years, I have been the recipient of hundreds of letters, some were never meant to be sent, others reached their destinations, with me as a stopping place in between. These letters are written by daughters to parents, parents to daughters, and, in some cases, from parents or daughters to me. They speak for themselves.

❧ ❧ ❧

Dear Mom and Dad,

From the day I was born you have given me all and more of yourselves to make me happy, And because of that I am so sorry I have failed you in so many ways. You mean the world to me and I respect and look up to both of you in more ways than you will ever know. I wish I had half the strength that you have, but I feel like I have no strength. I hate it so much when we fight, and I hate when I am impatient and yell at you. I'm fighting a constant battle in my head and I don't know what against. I want to be perfect, but it seems like everything I do takes me in the opposite direction. I feel like I am constantly trying to please myself. I feel like I'm trying to

---

[*]Names and other identifying characteristics have been changed to protect the confidentiality of the writers.

get rid of my headache by banging my head against a wall. I wish I didn't have to worry about how I was going to wake up in the morning and feel because of something I have eaten. To be honest, I don't even like food anymore. It's easy for me to skip a meal or throw it up. I like the feeling of not being full inside. I don't know why I eat the outside of everything, I guess to make me feel less guilty. I wish I could feel the way I did when I was skinny. To get there is like running down a hall to a door that keeps getting further, and I'm so tired of running. The main purpose of this letter is to ask you guys for one more chance to show you I can do something and complete it. I want to get better, and I don't care if I get fat, I just want to feel better inside. I know that you have thought I did this for attention because you said that, but believe me, the last thing I want is attention on me. I don't like the feeling of everyone's watching me at all. And if I could have it any way, I wish you would never have found out, only because I want you to be happy and not have to worry. I love you so much, and I want to grow up and find love like you have with each other and have children of my own. I hate to know that I am the cause of problems in this family, that tears me up inside. I know I have a problem, and I have had it for a while. I hope I can talk to someone who understands, who has been there, because I feel so lonely and strange inside. I'm afraid that is how I come off to other people. I know I am always talking about dreams, things I want to do or be. And I hope that someday I can. I don't say these as lies. I want more than anything for you to be happy with me and me to be with myself. I love you so much, Mom and Dad. Please believe in me that I can get better.

Love, always your daughter and friend,
Forever, Amelia

ॐ ॐ ॐ

"God grant me the serenity to accept the things I cannot change,
the courage to change the things I can,
and the wisdom to know the difference."

Dear Mom and Dad (letter no. 1 from Kathy,)

I don't really know where I should begin. I know that you have a lot of questions and I don't know if I'll be able to answer them all in this letter, but I hope it helps you understand. I know that you're both angry and frustrated, but so am I. I feel like I'm at my wits end. A long time ago, you both said that you were educating your-selves on bulimia and anorexia and I feel like all you have educated yourselves on was the surface of the disease. I'm angry because I have asked for so many things that have been ignored. I asked for respect, respect for my privacy. That means if I don't want to tell you everything that's going on in my life, I don't want to be bad-gered, please let me be. When I went into the hospital, I wanted to do it alone. I did not want the pressure of explaining the daily tasks and breakthroughs to you both. This was not meant to be mean, but I knew that the hospital would be difficult. When I did talk to you while I was in the hospital, it only upset me ... the digs about Roger, the questions about if I had finally found the root of the problem....

I did continue keeping in touch but I really felt that there were certain things that I wanted to do on my own. When I wanted to tell you things but specifically asked you not to give me your opinion, you never listened to my request. So I de-cided to take some time out alone ... and you didn't even respect that request. I know that you feel that I've hurt you both terribly by cutting you off without an explanation, but I gave you the best explanation in the beginning that I could. The more you ignored my request of no contact, the more I wanted to be left alone.

I am facing a lot of hardship right now. No, I am not lying dead in the street, but there are times when I feel like I might not make it at all. This last week has been especially hard. I know that emotionally it has been rough for the both of you ... but again I cannot handle hearing Mom having an emotional breakdown ... I'm in therapy because I can't handle things in my life. I only wish you would do the same for yourself. I can't make you better or happy, and I certainly can't handle being one of the people who has the power to make or break you.

I love you both very much. I had a great childhood. I was provided with only the best you could give, with love as a bonus. However, there are things that have been difficult for me as well. You both are not to blame for my eating disorder, but I did not arrive at this point alone. There are reasons for everything, and all I'm asking for is to have an open mind to explore these things. I would like to see you both and talk to you. I want Carolyn to be present because I've been talking to you both for 27 years and that hasn't worked so I'm trying something new. Please be patient, that's all I can ask for.

Kathy

◈ ◈ ◈

Dear Mom and Dad (letter no. 2 from Kathy, one year later),

There is so much I want to say to you both, the first being that I'm so sorry.

I can't believe it's been a year since this whole fiasco started. I've done a lot of thinking and a lot of growing and you both have done the same. I want to take this time to apologize for putting you both through hell. It's not easy watching your child try to kill herself and be expected to "give her space." There is no book on how to raise children, how to be fair, or what to do when this happens to you. I love you both so much. I never did anything to intentionally hurt you, and when I did hurt you, I was lashing out (it felt good at that moment), but after my temper tantrum was over, I felt lower than low.

I cherish you both so much. The thought of your being hurt or sick or in any kind of trouble makes me crazy. I want you both to know that you are great parents. I am lucky to be your daughter. I know that I pushed the limit on many things. . . . It was almost like a test to see how far I could push you . . . to see what it would take for you to stop loving me. The joke was on me because you both were there holding on stronger than ever. I guess I expected you to give up on me like I gave up on myself.

I don't know why I have anorexia/bulimia or if I'll ever really be cured. I do know that I have a lot to be thankful for and a lot to want to live for. I am so sorry for the hurtful way I treated you and the contempt that I had. It wasn't contempt for you that was coming out, it was contempt for myself. I just wasn't grown up enough or strong enough to admit to myself or to you that I was frustrated with who I was as a person.

As I said before, we've come a long way, I hope that we will continue to grow together. There's so much more to experience together as a family and I can't think of anything more exciting than to get to know you better, two incredible people with two pretty incredible kids.

I love you both so very much.

Kathy

 କ କ କ

Dear Dad,

How could you have known that I trained myself to feel guilty if I ate. I trained myself to pass up food, to say No, to go without. The training became ingrained, like brainwashing. To drink a regular soda was like poison. I could not do it, and being forced to eat something that didn't fit in with my idea of "good" food or "safe" food was extremely upsetting. I remember many sad situations now where I put you and Mom through so much pain and grief about this. I remember that summer I lived with you and worked at your friend's novelty shop. I came home one evening and you had made dinner for me: steak, potatoes, green beans, salad. Instead of being grateful, I was in a panic. You had never made dinner for me before and I was touched, but panicked at the thought of having to eat it. I cannot explain this rationally. Of course, one dinner would not have made a difference in my weight or the way I looked. Of course, I was being ridiculous. The feelings, however, were so powerful that I got angry, "thinking you were trying to fatten me up," and then I went to the bedroom and cried. When you came in, I was still sobbing. We had a few soft words, and I can't remember now what they were, but I remember feeling a little better, but so guilty. I was guilty for doing this to you and to Mom but I couldn't stop. The thought of eating that food was worse than anything else I could imagine. Oh how I wish there had been someone back then who knew or realized what I was going through and could have helped us both.

Carolyn

ल्ल ल्ल ल्ल

Dear Carolyn,

Casey is fat again. . . . Her shorts that were loose . . . are so tight that they're almost indecent. When I see her filling out like this, it scares me to death. She is already heavier than I was at her age.

Casey wasn't always inclined to overeat. But her great aunt started the habit of "special treats" when she was very young. Casey learned early on that she could have all the doughnuts, yogurts, cookies, etc., at her house.

I actually think writing to you helps. I'm writing because Casey has passed from "chubby" to fat. She went down for a few days, but now she is absolutely bulging. Her face is round and full. Her senior pictures are to be taken in two and a half weeks and we'll have to put out $350 for a stranger. I have enclosed a typical picture of her from the summer of her sophomore year. I know all of this says "looks, looks, looks." But since it's something she's already experienced, it does have a heavy bearing on how she feels now.

I'm wondering if letting her heal, grow on the inside before she worked on her weight, is creating a negative cycle. She feels bad, and eats, and then feels worse. Why can't she get help in both areas? She said she doesn't know how to lose weight without always feeling starved. I told her to ask you.

She is back to eating huge amounts of food at a sitting. She heaps her plate full (just like her great aunt) and then takes bites from the serving bowl. Then she goes back for "seconds." I bought her larger shorts so her size 6's wouldn't continue to haunt her.

The family gatherings are like a convention for fat ladies. I love them all, but I see them suffer from high blood pressure, diabetes, gall bladder problems, and arthritis, and go through stomach stapling and suction procedures. I was once very fat and I overcame it. I know it can be done.

We do need your help,
Wilma

∂∂ ∂∂ ∂∂

Dear Carolyn,

I wish there was a group I could belong to for parents of children who want to overeat. I really needed this all of Clara's life, so that I didn't feel so lonely and helpless. Maybe I would have learned ways to avoid hurting her the way I have. I was told by her doctor, when she was three, to watch her eating habits and help her keep her weight in check. But no one told me how to. Family and friends would ridicule me when I would monitor desserts and junk food. I needed help and support . . . and guidelines . . . all these years.

If there are support groups for alcohol and drugs, cancer, etc., then why not support groups for parents of overeating children? I see chubby and fat students at school, and they are all usually loners, or they seek negative attention. Parents have shared with me their helpless feelings toward their child's condition.

We need training, counseling, and opportunities to share our fears and frustrations. None of my friends have overeating children so they don't have sympathetic ears. Since I have helped Clara (up until now) maintain a healthy weight, people assume she does not have an eating problem. No one knows the painful tug of war Clara has lived through . . . with food, Grandma, and her desires on one side and me and her healthy weight on the other side.

Can a parent self-help group be formed? I need that much more than reliving my own past again. Hank's and my problems are working out. I think they are related to mid-life crises and not to Clara.

I honestly don't know what I should have done differently. I know other parents must feel the same.

Thank you for listening,
Marion

ઐ ઐ ઐ

To Whom It May Concern,

When my wife told me that she suspected our older daughter was anorexic, I was unimpressed. I had only a vague knowledge of anorexia or bulimia, and this just seemed to be one more crazy thing to cope with during a lifetime of coping with problems, stretching back to the moment she was born.

The endless concern and pressure over the years had created so many defense mechanisms that it was almost impossible for me to identify how I really felt. I loved this child so much, and could find no rational reason for her behavior. Despite the fact that my wife and I were concerned, caring people, I felt betrayed in so many ways that I came to think of myself as uncaring and consciously tried to divorce myself from the whole family process. I was so overloaded that I just wanted to get through the day with a minimum of required decisions or actions.

Faced with the inescapable evidence of her sickness (i.e., her appearance) as clear proof of anorexia nervosa, I felt angry. Because I loved her, I needed a scapegoat and blamed my wife and her. At that point, I was more concerned with me than with anyone else. The counseling process for her treatment was often painful, highly emotional, and depressing. The rewards came slowly, and then only after highly structured agreements that frequently challenged the foundations of my attitudes and beliefs as a parent.

I was often overwhelmed by the insights the counselor offered during many stormy meetings. Without her total commitment (which I felt was greater than mine), my daughter's recovery would never have been effected. After more than two and a half years of treatment, my daughter is healthy again.

Was it worth it? For my daughter's sake, the answer is an unqualified "Yes." She has made a marvelous recovery and her growth has been very satisfying. The alternative would have been devastating.

I've changed in certain ways. Facing the truth hurt. I've learned, not always *successfully, to recognize her more as an individual—different than me, her mother, or her sister. However, the recognition has a cost. The cost is a feeling of distance, knowing that the confrontations changed us in ways that can't be recaptured. I think I had to let her go before I was ready. I hope some day that the pain of this premature separation heals and we can come together again.*

A father

 familiar

To Whom It May Concern.

      Scared! I was so scared. My child was trying to kill herself. She was literally starving herself to death and I could not prevent it or help her.

      I remember the evening I finally caught her throwing up. I said "caught" because I had been carefully watching her to find out if she was making herself throw up to lose weight. She had become so skinny over the past months that I could count her ribs when she wore a bathing suit and still she complained that her legs or stomach or thighs or arms, etc., were too fat. My husband insisted, when I pointed this out, that she "looked terrific—just like all the other California girls." I knew this wasn't true, but I could not make him believe me. But then, we had been having problems almost since the day she was born.

      For me, becoming a mother had meant living with a new feeling; not the euphoric happiness I'd read about and been expecting, but fear—24 hours a day—fear of not being able to do it right. Obviously, I had not even started it out right. Up until Sara, everything I did, I did well. In fact, better than most. I believed in doing things right and doing them the best you can. So when Sara didn't even weigh five pounds at birth and had to remain in the hospital after I left, I took it very personally. I had intended to breastfeed, but the milk started drying up while she was in the hospital, even though I used a pump and went to the hospital each day to feed her. When she came home, there just wasn't enough milk for her, and she had to have supplemental bottles. This was the beginning of a feeling of failure and inadequacy on my part when it came to dealing with Sara. On the other hand, my husband felt only joy with Sara, and wonder at her perfection.

      Sara, for her part, came equipped with a monumental ego that demanded instant gratification. I had never experienced living with anyone who screamed at me or demanded my constant attention, and I had not been expecting a baby who cried all the time. Sara did not have colic and was not sick, but she was awake and alert and bored, and, as one pediatrician put it when she was three months old, "She's a bitch and you need tranquilizers." To keep her from screaming, I got in the habit of either jumping up and immediately responding to her first cry, or anticipating it and having ready whatever it was that I thought she would want. However, when I anticipated incorrectly, or didn't respond quickly enough and she truly launched into one of her tantrums, my reaction was totally opposite. Once she made the demand, my reaction was not to allow her to "push me around," and she had to learn that she could not scream every time she didn't get what she wanted. I didn't allow her to have whatever it was she was screaming about. I think now that it was a feeling of rejection because she didn't accept what I offered her that caused me to "punish" her by not giving her what she wanted in the first place. We continued that pattern for 16 years, up to the time we went into counseling.

I could finally show my husband proof of what I had been telling him for months! I was terrified at the thought of losing Sara, and, at the same time, I felt helpless. When my husband had to accept the fact that she was throwing up to lose weight, I thought that now I would have help in dealing with this situation, but his reaction was anger (which, I believe, masked his fear). He threatened to put her in the hospital. I told Sara I would call the doctor in the morning. She wildly promised she would never do it again; she would have promised anything then because she was frightened at being caught and afraid we were going to put her in the hospital.

The next day, I called our children's' doctor and told him about her throwing up and asked if he could recommend someone to deal with this. Anorexia and bulimia were very new words in my vocabulary. I had heard about these disorders and had read a little about them, but really didn't know much. I did know that when I saw Sara losing weight, pushing food around on her plate, constantly talking about food, there was something wrong and had started trying to find out what it was. I had come across "anorexia" and "bulimia nervosa" in the library, newspapers, etc., and read as much as I could find. Our doctor could not recommend anyone; he knew very little about the disease, and less about the treatment, counselors, etc. So my fear grew, and the feeling of being helpless grew with it. Then I got angry. No nebulous "craziness" was going to take Sara away—not as long as I could fight!

Two days later, I had an appointment to have my nails done, and I kept the appointment. By that time, I felt hopeless and so drained that I can only believe something much larger than anything in this world led me to keep that appointment. As

I was sitting there telling the manicurist what was happening with Sara, she told me about an article in the local newspaper she had read concerning a recovered anorexic who now counseled people with this problem! I couldn't believe it. I found out who the person was and called the next day. I explained the problem, made an appointment for the next day, and went home to tell Sara there was someone for her to talk to. I think she was truly relieved and grateful, she certainly didn't argue against going.

When we walked into the therapist's office, I immediately knew she would be able to work with Sara. She looked and acted like someone Sara could identify with—relaxed, "laid back," and thin. She spoke softly in contrast to Sara's own stridency and my authoritativeness. Of course, that first day Sara was downcast, didn't look directly at anyone, and was very quiet.

The counseling process was so slow ... at first. At first, the therapist dealt with Sara, then with all of us as a family, and finally with my husband and me. My husband and I had many problems between us—some stemming from his child-hood, some from Sara's birth, and my problems with her, which also affected us, to name just a couple. I was sure that my brand of motherhood was right. My husband had so many problems of his own left over from his childhood that I knew I was better balanced and, therefore, had to be a better parent.

How hard it was to learn that my behavior with Sara was a major cause of her problem. That sentence looks so innocent. The word "hard" doesn't come close to expressing my feelings when I finally had to admit to myself, to the therapist, and to my husband that if I didn't change some of my behavior patterns, Sara would die. Me! I loved her more than anything in the world, but no one knew it. She certainly didn't know it, and probably still doesn't. No, that isn't true. She knows I love her, but she is just as sure that I don't like her. And she is probably right that I didn't like her, and maybe sometimes I still don't. She is not "my" kind of person. I wouldn't pick someone like her for a friend. I don't understand her thinking, the things she does, why she dresses as she does, what she likes or doesn't like. We appear to be very opposite, but actually there are many things about us that are similar.

Sometimes I believe that Sara does things consciously to be different from me, and then when she isn't thinking about it, the similarities unconsciously slip through. Because I don't understand her or like her choices, I constantly criticize her, her friends, her clothes, the things she does, etc. It didn't occur to me that what I called giving her values, showing her what was "right," teaching her clothes coordination, etc., was so belittling to her, so undermining to her whole being that she began to feel like a nonbeing. She felt she had no "control" over her own life. She believed every decision of hers had to be Okayed by me or she wouldn't be permitted to make that decision. And we had reached such a difficult point in our lives together that it seemed to her that I had to approve of everything she wore, the friends she chose, the places she went, the things she did, or she wasn't allowed those choices. She needed my acceptance and I never gave her that.

How much of this was truly the way it was and how much was in Sara's head is not relevant. What is relevant is that this is how she perceived her life and how she felt. Maybe everything she felt was true, maybe none of it. Most likely, a lot less than everything and a lot more than none. My husband agreed almost wholly with Sara that I tried to control everyone and everything. Certainly, he believed he was controlled by me. The strange thing is that our other daughter does not feel this at all. And I, too, never believed that I tried to control. I tried only to do what I thought mothers were supposed to do: guide, teach, show by example. So imagine my devastation to finally have to reach the conclusion that I could no longer hide from, that I had been the main cause of Sara's feelings of being totally controlled and, therefore, the cause of her fighting back with the only weapon she could control, her eating habits. I was the cause of my daughter's trying to kill herself! But, of course, she wasn't trying to kill herself; she was only trying to escape what had become for her unbearable domination, and her loss of weight was a silent scream for help.

Without the therapist's gentle, oh so gentle, handling throughout this learning period, we could never have accomplished anything. She cared so much and became so involved with us that many times it was the thought of letting her down that forced me to "act" the way she had taught me was the only way to get through to Sara. By changing my responses to Sara and my pattern of behavior in almost everything else in our lives, Sara began to be able to allow her therapist to help her. The therapist has a wonderful line she used with me that really helped, "Sara doesn't have to clean house as long as she's guarding the fort." She finally got through to me that only by allowing Sara to be herself and not have to be on guard against outside influences (me!) would she be able to turn inward and deal with her own problems.

After many, many months, Sara reached a turning point in the battle and was able to eat a little, to gain a half pound and not go crazy, to buy a pair of slacks in size three instead of one and know she was not "fat." Naturally, the competition and struggle for control between Sara and me were not her only problem. Now we are dealing with the others: to help her become a fully happy, total human being. There have been many signs of growth, and many steps backward that bring pain and anguish and the feeling that nothing has been or ever will be accomplished. But I know that isn't true. The therapist helps me see the signs of growth and keeps us all on the right path. And she cares so much that we have to.

A mom

Note: Sara is fully recovered now, her mother and she are the best of friends, she maintains a good relationship with her father, her other sister did have her own rebellious stage, and her parents have found that they like themselves and are happier when they are not married to each other and thus are divorced.

ভ ভ ভ

Dearest Arielle,

You are now in your seventh year . . . and have from the beginning been a dream come true for me. Since you were born, I have felt deeply honored to be your mother. You are a great child and a great friend to me already, even though my job is still to function as a parent. I want to write about the kind of hopes I have for you that are specifically related to your gender as female.

You have come to this life at an interesting time and place for female potential. Our culture has many material advantages and opportunities to be grateful for, but is void in one of the most critical areas for women. I notice this void in my counseling work with women, in my friends, in all my family members and have felt it deep within myself. There seems to be a longing, a mad searching, a desperation for something that we do not seem to have a name for. Addictions are abound, all kinds of compulsions, strange behaviors toward ourselves and each other are common, all symptoms that something is deeply wrong. What is it?

We do not have in this culture a real tribe with real means of connection to one another . . . a real tribe with rites of passages throughout life, giving deep meaning to all of our transitions—even death. A real tribe with mentors from the Wise Ones and traditions that feed our inner life instead of our external/material life. And for women, a tribe to provide a way of being in our bodies is lost now—a way of connecting with our female development, sexuality, menses, and menopause that is buried in thousands and thousands of years of ancient tradition. Now I know that these traditions are buried in our psyches, not lost completely. I hear women thinking, "There must be more to being a woman than to spend all my energy trying to look great and please others." "There must be more to life than this." "There must be more to sex than this." "There must be more to growing old than this." Some of us run, in our searching, the other way, gaining weight, starving ourselves till we're half dead.

All of us, I believe, remember. We remember. I believe we remember that thousands and thousands of years ago women were connected in circle. Thousands of years ago there was a female face to God too. Women were revered for those unique qualities the anima brings to this world NOT limited to narrow standards of external beauty for value. A woman's power lies in the center of her pelvic bowl where a flame lives. An ancient fire interconnecting women of all cultures throughout time.

I want you, Arielle, to know about this. And you won't find it in our tribe's mentoring, which mostly comes through the media. The media is deeply contaminating. I will guide you toward women's circles, mentors besides myself (since mothers are limited in what they teach their own daughters). We need other wise women to raise our daughters! I will guide you to different kinds of singing. The kind that echoes so deeply within our soul life we weep amidst it. I will guide you to nature, to silence, to drumming, to ceremonies that your heart may be touched, your spirit might taste again and find its path. I also welcome your sexuality as a part of who you are. I will do my best in my own uncertain way to welcome you as a sexual being, in hopes that your life as a woman is full of wonderful and powerful experiences.

And eventually, my sweet child, you will be on your own. There will come a time when I won't be able to guide you anymore. Your spirit will fly and my voice will weaken. As long as you listen to your heart, you will find your way. It will be your turn to guide the young ones in your life who will pass the traditions on to theirs, and to theirs and onward, back home to reconnection to that unspeakable beauty of the great Feminine.

> Thank you for coming to me.
> I love you with all my heart.
> Francie

⤙ ⤙ ⤙

Appendix A

ॐ ॐ ॐ

NUTRITION GUIDE

Sources: There were many sources used to compile this nutrition guide, gathered over the years, but three are of specific importance because of the detailed information they provide.

1. *Understanding Nutrition,* Eleanor Noss Whitney and Sharon Rady Rolfes, 7th ed., West Publishing Co., St. Paul, MN 1996
2. *Encyclopedia of Food Values,* Corinne Netzer, Dell Publishing, New York, NY 1992
3. *Nutrition Made Simple,* Robert Crayon, M. Evans & Co., New York, NY 1994

This appendix provides a minicourse on nutrition. A basic knowledge of nutrition can help you understand the healthy aspects of weight control and may answer questions or clear up misunderstandings you or your daughter may have.

In general you need to understand calories and the macronutrients, protein, fat and carbohydrate, and the functions these have in a healthy diet.

CALORIES

A good way to describe calories is to call them the energy units found in all foods. Like the fuel that makes your car run, calories provide energy units that make your body run. Calories make life possible, but too many can weigh the body down with excess muscle and stored fat.

How many calories do you need to maintain your healthy body weight?

This is a difficult question to answer. There are many people who claim to gain weight on very little food, and others who eat all day without ever gaining an ounce. Individuals are unique and their caloric needs are influenced by a number of factors including:

1. *Age:* After around the age of thirty or thirty-five, caloric needs generally begin to decrease.

2. *Sex:* Men, have more muscle and usually need more calories than women.

3. *Activity level:* Physically active people burn more calories than inactive people, both during physical exertion and at rest.

4. *Body composition:* If two people are the same weight, the person with a higher ration of muscle to fat will burn more calories, because muscle burns more calories than fat.

The amount of calories needed to reach and maintain a healthy weight is dependent on all the above factors. Individuals have to experiment to find the right level for them. An easy estimate of caloric needs can be found in the following equation:

(Current or desirable weight in pounds) x (A) = Daily Caloric Need
"A" stands for the individual's activity level

A = 12 if not very active
A = 15 if moderately active
A = 20 if very active
A = 25 if extremely active

Example:

A 125 pound moderately active person would need approximately 1875 calories per day; 125 x 15 = 1875 calories per day.

Remember, this is just an estimate. People who are more muscled than others, who genetically have higher metabolisms, or who are male, all may need more calories.

The best way to lose weight is slow-and-steady at about 1 to 2 pounds per week. This should be accomplished through a healthy meal plan, not a strict diet, and with exercise.

PROTEIN

4 Calories per gram
15–20% of a person's calories should come from protein.

Even though we often hear about Americans eating too much protein, your dieting daughter is more likely to skimp on protein. The average nondieting American is not fully knowledgeable about protein and consumes far too much, particularly from high fat sources. In trying to combat this, various groups such as the American Dietetic Association put out information on restricting protein. This is part of the reason why protein has gotten a bad rap. There are many myths regarding protein and therefore a common occurrence is for young female dieters to be deficient in it. Many people and especially young girls think that protein is too high in calories and fat and besides it's easier to grab a bagel than a piece of chicken. Sound familiar?

Every body cell contains protein. It is essential for life itself. The word "protein" comes from the Greek word "proteios", meaning "to take first place." Protein is essential to have in our diet everyday. Without the protein provided by food, our bodies are forced to break down vital muscle tissue to provide the protein we need. Indeed, this is what happens when your daughter does not consume enough protein. Protein is made up of amino acids. For a complete protein, all the necessary amino acids must be present.

There are two functions of protein.
1. Protein's main function is serving as a building block for body tissues and muscle. Protein is essential for growth, repair and maintenance. You need a continuous supply because cells are constantly breaking down and being replaced.
    a. Comprises the hard and insoluble coverings of the body such as hair, skin and nails.
    b. Contributes to a variety of body secretions, lubricants and fluids.
    c. Contains enzymes and hormones that regulate body functions.
    d. Plays a role in the body's immune system. It is necessary for antibody formation.
    e. Is the major component of our muscles and vital organs.
2. Protein is also a source of energy. It provides 4 calories per gram. Protein is not the best energy source. It should be used for growth and repair, while carbohydrates are used for energy. If you don't eat enough carbohydrate your protein will be used for energy. This is not a good use of protein, it should be saved for its important building and restorative function.
    a. Protein is instrumental in maintaining fluid balance in the body.
    b. Protein helps maintain the body's balance between the acid and alkaline state.
    c. Protein is the major component of our muscles and vital organs.

PROTEIN NEEDS

Our protein needs depend on our age, body size and ideal body weight (lean body mass). Throughout adult years, our needs, for the most part, remain stable.

Protein needs are not increased by the amount of stored body fat. Certain situations affect protein needs such as pregnancy and lactation, some illnesses and strenuous activity.

The ability to make and use protein depends on whether you get enough calories to fulfill energy requirements. If calories from carbohydrates and fat are too low, the body will use protein for energy instead of for building and repairing tissues. Furthermore, protein foods vary in quality with animal sources generally providing the highest quality.

Iron loss and deficiency, as well as muscle tissue loss, often result from getting inadequate or poor quality protein. Iron supplementation may be needed while on a weight loss diet, especially if animal food is restricted. Sources of iron are enriched cereals, dried fruit, beans, and some dark green vegetables.

The Food and Nutrition Board of the National Research Council has established recommended daily allowances (RDAs) for protein based on age and weight. (See the formula below). The amount of protein needed daily is a controversial subject. Some believe the RDAs for protein are not high enough. It is important to remember that we are each biochemically different and unique in our needs.

If you were to follow the RDA; The recommended daily protein allowance for an adult is calculated as follows:

$$\frac{\text{Weight in lbs.}}{2.2} = (\text{wt. in kg}) \times .8 = \text{gms of protein needed per day}$$

Example: a 128 pound woman

$$\frac{128 \text{ lbs.}}{2.2} = 58 \text{ kg} \times .8 = 46 \text{ gms per day}$$

Another way to figure out protein needs is to go by the percentage of protein necessary in a healthy diet. Since 15 to 20% of your daily caloric needs should come from protein, you can easily estimate your protein needs from your appropriate calorie level. Multiple the number of calories you need by 15 to 20%.

Example: On a daily caloric intake of 2000 calories,

2000 x .15 = 300, or 2000 x .20 = 400. This means that around 300 to 400 calories need to come from protein. Since protein is 4 calories per gram, divide 300 by 4 for a 15% protein diet and 400 by 4 for a 20% protein diet: 300/4 = 77 grams, 400/4 = 100 grams.

Remember that a 15 to 20% protein diet means your diet for the whole day. So, for example, you can have pasta, salad and a roll for lunch, just have swordfish or grilled chicken for dinner, or if you are a vegetarian have a bean burrito.

Sources: Protein is widely distributed in our food supply.

Animal Sources: meat, fish, poultry, dairy (milk, cheese, yogurt), eggs, organ meats

Plant Sources: legumes (beans, peas, lentils), grains, nuts, seeds, vegetables

Protein Quality and Usage

The ability of our body to make and use protein is based on several factors:

1. You must have enough calories, preferably from complex carbohydrates to fulfill your energy requirements, so that protein is used for growth and repair. When lowering your calories, your protein needs may rise.
2. Protein cannot be stored as a reserve in the body like fat and carbohydrate. It must be eaten daily.
3. Unless the proportions of amino acids are right, they are likely to be used inefficiently as a protein source.

It is very likely that if your daughter is dieting she may gravitate toward an almost meatless diet and may even become a vegetarian. This is common with young female dieters. It is important for you and she to know that it can be perfectly healthy to be a vegetarian but that it must be done with careful attention as the quality of protein is not the same in all sources.

The building blocks of protein are called amino acids. There are 22 possible amino acids that make up protein. Of the 22 that exist, our bodies can synthesize 13 of them. The remaining 9 of these 22 amino acids should be obtained from food everyday. They are called "essential" amino acids. Animal sources of protein provide all the essential aminoacids. Animal products are therefore considered high quality sources or complete protein. However, many animal sources of protein contain cholesterol and are often very high in fat. Some animal products are low in fat, e.g., most fish, nonfat milk, dried cottage cheese and egg whites.

Plant sources are low in one or more essential amino acids and are called low quality sources or incomplete protein. If all the essential amino acids aren't present in the proper proportion, the food is only usable to the extent of the most "limiting" amino acid. It's like assembling a document of 22 pages. If you run out of page four you can't make any more documents no matter how many of the other pages you have. When properly combined, incomplete proteins can complement one another to make a complete protein source. The generally accepted view today is that if complimentary protein foods are combined within a 24-hour period, this is sufficient to meet protein needs.

Combining Protein Sources: Plant sources can be combined to make a complete protein out of incomplete protein foods.

Protein Combinations	*Food Choices*
Grain products + peas, beans, or lentils =	Rice and bean dish Garbanzos and corn bread Lentil-rice loaf Rice and soy grits Wheat and soy bread
Milk + grain products =	Lasagna with mozzarella Yogurt and barley soup Ricotta cheese and whole- grain bread
Peas, beans or lentils + seeds =	Garbanzos, sesame vegetable sauce Tofu (or soybean curd) sesame seeds (as part of a salad) Pea soup sesame muffins

How do I know what a gram of protein is?

Many food labels will list how many grams of protein are in a serving. For your convenience the list below shows grams of protein based on an average serving, However, keep in mind that the foods listed below are not equivalent in calories or other nutrients. For example, most animal sources as well as nuts and seeds are higher in fat and calories than most plant sources.

Grams of Protein Based on Average Serving

Source	*Total Grams of Protein*
1. Chicken (4 oz.)	35
2. Turkey, light meat (4 oz.)	33.9
3. T-bone steak (4 oz.)	31
4. Halibut (4 oz.)	30
5. Swordfish (4 oz.)	28.8
6. Cottage cheese(1/2 cup)	14
7. Tofu (1/2 cup)	10
8. Lentils (1/2 cup)	8.9
9. Peanut butter (smooth style-2 tbsp.)	8

10. Milk (1 cup)   8
11. Kidney beans (1/2 cup)   7.6
12. Cheddar cheese (1 oz.)   7
13. Pasta cooked (1 cup)   6–7
14. Peanuts (1 oz.)   6.6
15. One whole large egg   6.3
16. Cashews (1 oz., approximately 18 medium size)   4.4
17. Egg white from one large egg   3.5

Remember: Foods commonly considered sources of protein may also contain large amounts of other nutrients that supply energy. The amount of *fat* contained in protein foods is of prime importance when on a weight management program. For example, T-bone steak and cheddar cheese, two foods considered high in protein, are very high in fat. T-bone steak is a whopping 82% fat and cheddar cheese is 70% fat!

FAT

9 Calories per gram
15 to 25% of your daughters diet should come from fat

As a food source, fats are notable above all else for their high energy (calorie) content. Some fat is essential, but excess fat is one of the major problems in the diet of the average American. Lowering fat, both in the diet and in the body is a healthy goal. Your daughter however, like most female dieters, may become fat paranoid and instead of trying for a low-fat diet, she may strive to have a nonfat diet. This must be discouraged. Fat has a role in our diets and in our bodies.

TYPES OF FAT

There are 3 main types of fat; *cholesterol, triglycerides and phospholipids:*

Cholesterol: This type of fat will be dealt with in a separate section that follows.

Triglycerides: Dietary fat and body fat are mostly in the form of triglycerides. This is what usually is being referred to when we use the word "fat." The term triglyceride refers to the chemical structure of the fat molecule.

Phospholipids: This type of fat is similar to triglycerides. The most common form is lecithin. Lecithin is produced in the liver and therefore has no daily requirement.

Functions of Body Fat

1. Supports and cushions vital organs; protects from injury.

2. Provides insulation; maintains body temperature.
3. Allows for regular menstrual cycle.

4. Energy source (stored body fat)

Functions of Dietary Fat

1. Provides essential fatty acids your body can't make (linoleic acid)

2. Aids the absorption of fat soluble vitamins A, D, E, and K.
3. Enhances flavor, aroma, texture
4. Increases satiety, delays hunger

Eating Fat: Consuming excess calories of any kind can lead to excess weight. Since dietary fat contains twice the amount of calories, gram for gram, as does protein and carbohydrate, an excess of dietary fat can lead to an excess of body fat. Therefore fat intake should be somewhere around 20% of total daily calories. Fat has been increasingly attacked as nutrition enemy number one, partly due to the fact that the S.A.D., or Standard American Diet, consists of 40% fat or more! Furthermore, much of the fat being consumed is saturated fat, or the unhealthy kind of fat that leads to artery blockage. (More on this later)

How do I figure out how many grams of fat a person should eat a day? Food labels are just beginning to list grams of fat and percentages of fat in each serving. However, a simple chart may make your fat detective task easier. The following chart shows you an estimated daily fat allowance based on the number of calories eaten per day. To discover how many grams of fat a day is appropriate, for your daughter or yourself just find her calorie level or your own and then move to the right stopping under the column with the % of fat you want to consume. Remember that this is approximate. One does not need to consume an exact amount of fat grams daily. There was a time when dietary tables and formulas didn't exist and people just ate naturally. A higher percent of fat in one's diet leads to higher satiety and less hunger between meals. A lower percent of fat can be used for those trying to lose weight or people with other health problems who are informed by their doctors to reduce their fat intake to such levels.

Maximum Gms. Fat/Day for Certain % Fat Diets

Daily Calories	15%	20%	25%
1,200	20 gms	26.5	33
1,500	25	33	41.5

1,800	30	40	50
2,000	33.3	44.4	55.5
2,100	35	46.5	58
2,400	40	53	66.5
2,500	41.6	55.5	69.4
3,000	50	66.6	83.3

To convert grams of fat to calories of fat, simply multiply the grams allowed by 9 cals/gm (or use ten as it is easier). This will give you the approximate amount of *calories* your daughter should be getting from fat.

Fat Allowance Example

If your daughter is eating approximately 1,500 calories/day and wants a 20% fat diet; She can shoot for 33 grams of fat/day

33 gms x 9 cal/gm = 297 calories

Out of the 1,500 calories she eats, approximately 297 of them should come from fat. Remember this does not mean only added fat, like butter, but includes fat hidden in foods such as eggs, meats, and dairy.

Kinds and Sources of Fat

1. Saturated—Mainly animal products. Also chocolate, palm oil, coconut oil and hydrogenated fats. These elevate blood cholesterol. (The more saturated a fat is, the harder or firmer it is at room temperature.)

2. Polyunsaturated—Vegetable oils, some nuts (walnut, pecan, almond). Studies indicate these tend to lower blood cholesterol. However, they have also been linked to cancer.

3. Mono-unsaturated—Most nuts, avocado, olive oil, canola oil. Mono-unsaturates have been shown in recent studies to be as good as, if not better than, polyunsaturates for both raising HDL cholesterol (good cholesterol) and lowering LDL (bad cholesterol).

Fat in Foods Can be Visible or Hidden

1. Every living thing contains some amount of fat. Animal foods, such as beef, can be as high as 50 to 70 % fat, while many plant foods have such negligible amounts as to not even be worthy of mention, such as

grapefruit that has trace amounts. What is important to understand is that fat is necessary for life.

2. All animal sources of protein contain fat unless the fat has been removed.

3. Some plant sources of protein contain significant amounts of fat such as avocados and peanuts. fat. Protein sources that do not contain significant amounts of fat are legumes and vegetables.

Visible Fats	Hidden Fats
Butter, margarine, mayonnaise, oil, fat at edge of meat, skin of chicken	• Fats inside of meats, nuts, baked products, (ie., bread), many desserts, candy, avocado, gravy, sauces, salad dressing

Fat content and labeling of food (becoming a fat detective): Check the ingredients on food labels for fat. It may be listed in disguised ways such as whole milk solids, lard, tallow, egg yolk solids, vegetable shortenings, hydrogenated oils, cocoa butter, chocolate, palm oil, coconut oil and other oils as well.

How they mislead us: Some labels like those on milk cartons, list fat content according to weight. *so,* **low fat milk may say 2% fat,** but this is only because the fat is calculated as a percentage of the total weight rather than total calories. In other words, if you weighed the milk, only 2% of the total weight comes from fat. Since there is an abundance of water in milk, (think of the quantity of powdered milk that's left after the water is removed), labeling fat content by % of weight is, of course, misleading. Who cares how much the fat in a product weighs? Consumers are interested in how many calories come from fat in the product. Determining **percent of fat as calories,** reveals that the **true figure is 32% fat!**

Here is how it works:

8 oz. of low fat milk = approximately 140 total calories
and contains 5 grams of fat.

Since each gram of fat = 9 calories per gram (9 x 5 = 45), 45 of the 140 calories come from fat, or roughly 1/3.

Therefore, low fat milk turns out to be 32% fat when calculating the fat coming from calories, not weight. Misleading isn't it!

Formula to figure out the percent of fat for different foods:

(Grams of fat) x *(9 cal/gm)*
divided by Total calories/serving

$$\frac{5 \text{ gms fat} \times 9 \text{ cal/gm}}{\text{Calories/serving}} = \frac{45}{140} = .32\ldots.\text{Or: } \textbf{32\% Fat!}$$

You can simply eyeball certain foods when shopping without going through the whole formula.

Simple example

Enrico's spaghetti sauce

60 calories/serving

1 gram of fat (you know that fat is 9 calories a gram so this sauce has **9 calories of fat**)

9 calories is so close to 10 you can see that this sauce is about 1/6 fat (10 cals out of 60)

You can do this to figure out percentage of fat, protein, or carbohydrate of any given food as long as you know the total calories per serving and the number of grams of what you wish to measure. Remember, carbohydrate and protein are only 4 kcal gm. So you would substitute a 4 instead of a 9 in the above formula. See following examples.

Food labeling examples

Figuring out percent calories from protein, fat, carbohydrate from labels.

Example A
Whole milk
Serving size: 1 cup
Calories: 160

	cal/gm	*cal of p, c or f /total cals*	*% of p,c,or f*
Protein: 8 gm	x 4 cals/gm	= 32/160	= .20 or **20% protein**
Carbohydrate: 11.5 gm	x 4 cals/gm	= 46/160	= .285 or **28.5% carbohydrate**
Fat: 9 gm	x 9 cals /gm	= 81/160	= .506 or **50.6% fat**

Example B
Häagen-Dazs Mocha Double Nut
Serving size: 4 Fl. oz.
Calories: 290

	cal/gm	*cal of p, c or f/total cals*	*% of p,c,or f*
Protein: 5 gm.	x 4 cals/gm	= 20/290	= .068 or **6.8% protein**

Carbohydrate: 22 gm.   x 4 cals/gm   = 88/290   = .303 or **30.3%**
                                                         carbohydrate

Fat: 20 gm.   x 9 cals/gm   = 180/290   = .620 or **62%**
                                                               fat

Example C
Breyer's Grand Light
Serving size.....4 Fl.oz.
Calories...........120

	cal/gm	*cal of p, c or f /total cals*	*% of p,c,or f*
Protein: 3 gm.	x 4 cals/gm	= 12/120	= 0.1 or **10 %** **protein**
Carbohydrate: 16 gm.	x 4 cals/gm	= 64/120	= .53 or **53%** **carbohydrate**
Fat: 5 gm.	x 9 cals/gm	= 45/120	= .375 or **37.5%** **fat**

Examples of Fat % in common foods:

Food	*% Fat*
Mixed nuts	75%
Hard cheese	75%
Ground beef	65%
Bread (cracked wheat)	8%
Beans (kidney, navy)	4%
Rice Brown	5%
Spaghetti	3%
Yam	2%

CHOLESTEROL

Cholesterol and fat are not the same thing. People are often confused by this. Even though cholesterol falls in the category of fats or lipids, its chemical structure is different from triglycerides or phospholipids.

Cholesterol is a vitally important substance and is produced by all animals including humans. It is, therefore, found only in foods of animal origin. It is used to perform a variety of functions such as making strong cell membranes and producing vitamin D, certain hormones, and bile acids needed for digesting fats. There is no dietary need for cholesterol because the body is capable of making all that it requires. It is generally recommended that dietary intake be limited to 300 milligrams of cholesterol a day.

Too much of a good thing, as always, in nutrition, is bad. Blood (serum) cholesterol level is a valuable estimator for early coronary heart disease. Trouble starts when too much cholesterol accumulates in the bloodstream. The cholesterol level in the blood is related to plaque development on the walls of arteries. The lower the level of blood cholesterol, the less likelihood of plaque development. Animal and human studies show that lowering cholesterol levels in the bloodstream not only prevents progression of atherosclerosis (hardening of the arteries), but lessens existing atherosclerosis.

It is important for everyone over the age of 20 to have his or her blood-cholesterol level checked at least every 5 years. If it is high, it will need to be rechecked more often. If there is a family history of heart disease, it is wise to have children screened sometime after age 2. If you have your daughter's cholesterol checked, it is important that your physician tells you the total cholesterol number, and the ratio of High Density Lipoprotein, HDL to Low Density Lipoprotein, LDL, not just whether or not the test is within the normal range. In this way, you can keep track of any changes from future or previous tests. Children ages 5 through 18 should have levels no higher than 150 mg/dl. A guide for adults would be a serum cholesterol level at or below 180 mg/dl. According to the National Cholesterol Education Program, levels of 200 to 239 are considered borderline and 240 and above indicate a high risk for heart disease.

The ratio of total cholesterol to HDL is a better predictor of heart disease risk than just total cholesterol. Some experts advise aiming for a ratio between 4.0 and 5.0. Below 3.5 is ideal. Above 7.0 the risk of heart disease doubles.

If your daughter has high cholesterol

If your daughter has high cholesterol she should see a professional who will probably tell her among other things to eat less fat, less cholesterol and more fiber. Please be aware that anorexics often have high cholesterol levels, and NOT from eating too much fat and cholesterol. When someone severely restricts their intake, their body, in desperately trying to protect them may over produce cholesterol. Additionally the liver may cease to function properly and thus not efficiently elimante cholesterol and thus cholesterol builds up. It is important that your health professional know if your daughter is restricting her food intake.

Various factors influence cholesterol levels and diet is an important one, although eating cholesterol is not the only culprit. Diets rich in fat, particularly saturated fat, tend to raise the level of blood cholesterol. In fact, studies show that saturated fat is 3 to 4 times more potent in raising blood cholesterol than dietary cholesterol itself. Saturated fat is found mostly in animal products such as meat, poultry, butter, lard and whole milk dairy products. Additionally, these foods also contain cholesterol so they give a double whammy effect. Saturated fat is also high in "tropical" plant oils such as palm kernel and coconut oil. It is also in "hydrogenated" oils, which are contained in margarine, and commercially prepared products like crackers, cookies and pastries. So, if high cholesterol is a problem it's important to figure out the cause and if appropriate, restrict not just one or two foods, but watch the intake of a variety of different foods that can contribute to high blood cholesterol levels.

Studies do show that polyunsaturated fats, and to a greater degree monounsaturates, lower blood cholesterol levels. However, don't be too hasty to buy products just because they claim to lower cholesterol. Studies also show that polyunsaturated fats increase and even double cancer rates! It's misleading to think that because polyunsaturated fats don't seem to affect cholesterol levels adversely that they are O.K. to eat. Monounsaturated fats lower cholesterol without the dangers of polyunsaturates and are a good choice. Therefore, if you are going to use fat for cooking, baking, salad dressings etc., it seems wise to use a monounsaturated fat, like olive oil.

All things considered, it is much better for someone to lower cholesterol by limiting intake of high cholesterol and high fat foods while increasing whole grains, fruits and vegetables. Increasing fiber by eating foods such as oatmeal and other whole grains has been shown to cause decreases in blood cholesterol levels, and they are foods good for you in other ways as well.

CARBOHYDRATE

4 Calories per gram
Approximately 50 to 60% of a daily diet should consist of carbohydrate.

In general, carbohydrates are a primary source of energy for the body. Carbohydrate is one of the essential nutrients required by our bodies for normal functioning. It is composed of many sugars linked together. When carbohydrates are broken down, glucose (blood sugar) is the resulting product.

NEEDS

There is no consensus for a Recommended Daily Allowance of carbohydrates. There is evidence that everyone needs at least 400 calories of carbohydrates for proper brain and nervous system functioning. In her 1992 *Encyclopedia of Food Values,* Corinne Netzer reports that approximately 45%–48% of daily caloric intake should come from complex carbohydrate sources while somewhere around 10% or under should come from simple or refined sources.

Functions

1. Carbohydrate (CHO) is a major energy source.

2. Our body tissues require a constant daily supply of carbohydrate in the form of glucose for all internal metabolic reactions to work properly.

3. Glucose is the only energy source the brain can utilize and is essential for the maintenance and normal functioning of nerve tissue.

4. Carbohydrate exerts a "protein-sparing"effect; if your daughter doesn't get enough, her body will use protein for fuel instead of for it's intended function of growth and tissue repair.

5. Carbohydrate is necessary for normal fat metabolism.

6. Carbohydrate in it's complex form provides fiber which is necessary for good health.

7. Carbohydrate in the form of fiber aids in regulating elimination, protects against cancer, provides satiety, lowers cholesterol, and regulates blood sugar.

8. Carbohydrate helps produce nucleic acids, connective tissue, and nerve tissue.

9. Many carbohydrate sources also supply protein, minerals and B vitamins.

TYPES OF CARBOHYDRATE

Just as with protein and fat, not all carbohydrates are created equal. White table sugar is carbohydrate and so is broccoli. Natural, unprocessed carbohydrates, rather than refined or empty carbohydrates, are the optimal choice. Although carbohydrates have earned a bad reputation in terms of dieting in the past, the problem arises when we eat too much of the simple refined carbohydrates and too little of the complex, more nutritious, ones. Briefly put, there are three types of dietary carbohydrate; simple, complex, and fiber:

1. Fiber is the indigestible part of carbohydrate, such as cellulose, hemicellulose and pectin, found in whole grains, beans, vegetables, and fruit.

2. Complex carbohydrates, are found in beans, grains, vegetables and fruit.

3. Simple carbohydrates are simple sugars, such as table sugar, honey, natural fruit sugars and molasses and refined, processed foods like cookies and cakes.

Fiber

Fiber is the structural component of plants which is indigestible. At least 25 gms of fiber per day are recommended. Most complex carbohydrates contain fiber which provides bulk but no calories. It is essential to have sufficient fiber in your diet to maintain optimal health.

Functions:
1. Prevents constipation.
2. Provides a feeling of fullness.
3. Aids in weight control. It takes up "space" and provides no calories. Eating foods high in fiber also prevents a certain amount of calories from being absorbed.
4. Decreases prevalence of cancer of the colon and rectum hemorrhoids, gall bladder disease, diverticulosis and irritable bowel syndrome.
5. Lowers blood cholesterol (oats, fruit, carrots, legumes).
6. Lowers blood triglycerides.
7. Helps maintain a constant glucose level (blood sugar), as it delays digestion and absorption of food. Only the soluble gels and gums (like pectin or guargum) do this, not 'fibrous' fiber.
8. Diabetes control is aided by fiber due to the blood sugar regulating effect

Complex Carbohydrates

This category of foods which includes; legumes, grains, and all other vegetables and fruits, should be the mainstay of a healthy diet making up approximately 50 to 60 % of calories consumed. Many people have used the term complex carbohydrate to refer only to starchy foods such as breads, potatoes, and pasta. All vegetables and fruits should be included in the complex carbohydrate category leaving sugars and processed foods for the simple or refined category.

As far as starch goes, when 10 or more units of sugar are linked together they make up a starch. Once eaten, these "chains" or starches must be broken down to glucose and used for energy before being absorbed. Starchy foods are important for providing vitamins, minerals, and fiber as well as calories.

It is a myth that starches should be avoided on a weight loss diet. Starches, like all other carbohydrate and protein, provide only 4 calories per gram. Complex carbohydrates, high in starch, such as kidney beans, potatoes, and pasta are excellent foods with little, or virtually no fat.

Starchy foods:

Grains   bread, crackers, cereal, rice, pasta, noodles.
Legumes   dried beans and peas, kidney, pinto, garbanzo, Lima beans.
Vegetables potato

Besides eating 4 servings of fruits and vegetables a day, a healthy diet consists of 4 to 6 servings of the following low fat complex carbohydrate choices.

Complex Carbohydrate Foods Your Daughter Should Choose From Daily

Each portion provides approximately 70 calories.

Vegetables
Beans, dried, cooked	1/3 cup
Corn on the cob	5" long
Corn (kernels)	1/2 cup
Potato, white, baked, or boiled	1–2" in diam.
Potato, sweet	1/4 cup or 21/2" long

Breads & Crackers (whole grain)
Bread, whole wheat, rye, sourdough, pumpernickel	1 slice
Pita, whole wheat	1/2 of 6" pocket
Tortilla, corn	1–6" in gram.

Grains, Cereals & Pasta
Noodles, whole wheat, cooked	1/2 cup
Oatmeal, cooked	1/2 cup
Pasta, whole wheat, cooked	1/2 cup
Rice, brown, cooked	1/2 cup
Shredded wheat	1 large biscuit or 1/2 cup spoon size
Nutri-grain	1/2 cup

Simple Carbohydrates (Refined Foods and Sugars)

Less than 10% of a daily calorie allowance should come from refined or simple carbohydrate.

Refined Carbohydrates: When we "refine" a food we break it down, separating it from its original part. Whole foods are in their natural form, not separated. Whole grains, potatoes, beans, and starchy vegetables are whole foods. Refined carbohydrates are made by processing foods to extract the starch. White flour, white rice, white bread, saltine crackers, pie crust, white noodles, dumplings, doughnuts, cream sauces etc. are all refined foods.

Simple Carbohydrates: These are found naturally as part of fruits, vegetables, milk, and honey, or in refined or processed products such as table sugar, sodas, pastries, and candy. Sugar can also be found hiding in ketchup, salad dressings, canned foods, cereal, bread, even bacon.

Problems with Refined Sugar: Refined sugar normally supplies quick, but short term energy, and supplies empty calories. To get an idea of the amount of sugar in foods see the following list.

Sugar in Foods
(Approximate amount of refined sugar in teaspoons per serving.)

Food	Serving size	Tsp. of sugar
Bran muffin (homemade)	1 muffin (2")	1/3
Iced layer cake	1 piece (1/12 cake)	9
Cereal sugar coated	1 cup	5
Cheese cake	1/12 cake	4
Coffee cake	1 piece, 3" x 3"	4 1/3
Chocolate fudge	1 piece, 1" x 1"	2 1/4
Hard candy	1 oz.	7
Vanilla ice cream	1/2 cup	4
Italian ice	1/2 cup	8
Jam	1 Tbsp.	3
Gelatin dessert	1/2 cup	4
Ketchup	1/4 cup	1/2
Apple pie	1/6 pie	5 1/3
Butterscotch pudding	1/2 cup	10
Tapioca pudding	1/2	6
Lime sherbet	1/2 cup	5 1/3
Soda cola or other sweet sodas	12 oz. can	10
Vanilla or coffee yogurt	1 cup (8 oz.)	3 1/2
Fruit yogurt	1 cup (8 oz.)	7
Chewing gum	1 stick	1/2

Below is a list of Cereals with percentage of sugar in total calories.

Cereal	% Sugar
Shredded Wheat	1.0
Corn Flakes	5.1
Cheerios	2.2
40% Bran Flakes	15.8
All Bran	20.0
Sugar Pops	37.8
Cap'n Crunch	43.3
Froot Loops	46.6
Lucky Charms	50.4
King Vitamin	58.5
Sugar Smacks	61.3

Sugar Addicts: Before you decide if you or your daughter are sugar addicts there is an important issue to clarify. When I ask most of my patients who claim they are sugar addicts what food they go in search of when they have a craving or what kinds of sugary foods do they enjoy, I mostly get answers like this; Candy Bars, Doughnuts, Pastry, Cookies, Pie, Ice cream, Cake, Chocolate. The astute observer, or any fat detective, will notice that all of these foods are high in fat.

An interesting thing about sugar craving is that often when people say they crave sugar, it is usually the fat or combination of sugar and fat they are after. People who say they are sugar addicts don't usually buy or eat jellybeans, life savers, licorice, or hard candies when they get a craving. Instead they say they want cake, pie, cookies, chocolate, or ice cream. I then point out that they are craving the fat as much as they are craving the sugar. Otherwise, life savors, etc., would do the trick. If and when someone finds themselves craving sugar, and fruit or some other healthy substitute won't do, they are much better off eating lifesavers, jellybeans, licorice, or hard candy, rather than something with both sugar and fat.

In Search of the perfect sweet—A Note on Artificial Sweeteners

Synthetic sweeteners, Xylitol, Sorbitol, Aspartame (Nutra Sweet), and Saccharin, do not normally raise blood sugar levels but there have been other harmful side-effects reported with the ingestion of large amounts of these sweeteners.

Some sensitive people *will* produce an insulin response similar to sugar when they consume artificial sweeteners. The body expects that sugar is coming and releases insulin to deal with it. Additionally, it seems that one's craving for sugar is maintained when using artificial sweeteners. Furthermore, research shows that those using Nutra-sweet often *gain weight!* A study by the American Cancer Society showed that those who used artificial sweeteners were more likely to gain weight than nonusers.

Nutra Sweet. Sweetness without calories or risk, is it possible? Millions of Americans want, and some need, a substitute for sugar. Appeasing them while satisfying the law regarding health and safety factors is a difficult task. One product to hit the sweet substitute market causing considerable controversy, is Aspartame, more commonly known as Nutra Sweet. It is produced by G.D. Searle Co., bringing in a billion dollars a year from the 100 million Americans who consume it.

Aspartame is a combination of two amino acids that are found in ordinary foods and are not sweet by themselves. Aspartame is about 180 times sweeter than sucrose but it cannot be used for cooking as it decreases in sweetness with heat. "Equal", which is aspartame in a powdered form, has about two calories per teaspoon. People with milk allergies or sensitivities should know it contains lactose (milk sugar) which makes the calories a bit higher than plain aspartame.

Those against aspartame make several points. They discuss the fact that some people (albeit rare) cannot metabolize phenylalanine (one of the amino acids in aspartame) and may suffer brain damage and even mental retardation. Some pregnant women who ingest large amounts of aspartame can expose the fetus to toxic amounts of phenylalanine. This problem affects 1,750 women of childbearing age.

Another problem is that aspartame breaks down to methanol. In fact, a petition was filed in Arizona because Nutra-Sweet in carbonated soft drinks exposed to warm climates breaks down rapidly into methanol (methyl alcohol) which is then converted to formaldehyde, a known carcinogen. The petition was denied.

Last, R.J. Wurtman reported in the *New England Journal of Medicine,* that ingesting high doses of aspartame in addition to carbohydrate will produce neurochemical changes in the brain, resulting in functional or behavioral changes. His conclusions were rejected by the FDA. In a letter to the *Lancet,* a prestigious medical journal in England, Wurtman cites three cases of healthy adults who had grand mal seizures during periods when they were consuming high doses of aspartame. He maintains that aspartame may explain previously unexplained seizures in some patients.

The FDA approved aspartame for multiple uses in 1974, but withdrew its approval when there were so many challenges and formal objections to the research data on the product. The FDA appointed a board of inquiry which upon it's review recommended that aspartame be withdrawn until further studies. The FDA disagreed and concluded aspartame to be safe.

The consumer is left to fend for him/herself. You must read and investigate the research. After all, the government said at one time that saccharin was safe, only to later discuss its implication in cancer. I recommend that anyone wanting to use artificial sweeteners, seriously consider the need for this in their diet, particularly since there is no evidence suggesting that these products aid in weight loss. Please keep in mind this information is informative. Your daughter will have to make her own choice because it will be too hard for you to dictate that she never have artificial sweeteners. But when you have the information you can supply her with knowledge and with healthier choices.

Fructose is a good alternative sweetener. It is metabolized more slowly than any other sugar and thus does not cause a rapid rise in blood sugar, resulting in an overload of insulin. Therefore, fructose is suitable for those with blood sugar problems as well as those desiring weight loss.

Appendix B

ॐ ॐ ॐ

RECOMMENDED DAILY ALLOWANCES

The Recommended Dietary Allowances (RDAs) are a set of nutrient standards established by the Committee on Dietary Allowances for the maintainance of good nutrition. The RDA are the average daily intakes of energy and nutrients considered adequate to meet the needs of most healthy people in the United States under usual environmental stresses. The following information was obtained from *Understanding Nutrition* by Eleanor Noss Whitney and Sharon Rady Rolfes.

Age Bracket	*Calories (energy units) Needed Per Day*
Infants	
0–.5 months	650
6–12 months	850
Children	
1–3 years	1300
4–6 years	1800
7–10 years	2000
Females	
11–14 years	2200
15–18 years	2200
19–24 years	2200
25–50	2200
51+	1900
Males	
11–14 years	2500
15–18 years	3000
19–24 years	2900
25–50	2900
51+	2300

Source: *Understanding Nutrition,* E. N. Whitney, and S. R. Rolfes, West Publishing Co., St. Paul MN, 1996.

Appendix C

ঌ ঌ ঌ

RESOURCES

I. Suggested Reading

A. On Eating Disorders

1. *The Body Betrayed.* Kathyrn Zerbe, American Psychiatric Press, Inc., Washington D.C. 1993.
2. *The Eating Disorder Source Book,* Carolyn Costin, Lowell House, Los Angeles, Calif. 1996.
3. *Father Hunger,* Margo Maine, Gurze Books, Carlsbad, Calif. 1991.
4. *Feminist Perspectives on Eating Disorders,* Patricia Fallon et al., Guilford Press, New York, N.Y. 1994.
5. *The Golden Cage.* Hilde Bruch, Harvard University Press, Cambridge, Mass. 1978.
6. *Males With Eating Disorders,* Arnold Anderson, Brunner/Mazel, New York, N.Y., 1990.
7. *Surviving an Eating Disorder:* Michele Siegel, et al., Harper & Row, New York, N.Y. 1988.

B. On Healthy Eating/Dieting

1. *Diets Don't Work,* Bob Schwartz, Breakthru Publishing, Houston, Texas, 1982.
2. *Encyclopedia of Food Values,* Corinne Netzer, Dell Publishing, New York, N.Y. 1992.
3. *Feeding On Dreams.* Diane Epstein and Kathleen Thompson, Macmillan, New York, N.Y. 1994.

4. *Fit or Fat* Books by Covert Bailey:

   The New Fit or Fat, Covert Bailey, Houghton Mifflin Co., Wilmington, Mass., 1991.

   Fit or Fat Target Diet, Covert Bailey, Houghton Mifflin Co., Wilmington, Mass., 1984.

   Fit or Fat Target Diet Recipes, Covert Bailey and Lea Bishop, Houghton Mifflin Co., Wilmington, Mass., 1984.

   The Fit or Fat Women, Covert Bailey and Lea Bishop, Houghton Mifflin Co., Wilmington, Mass., 1989.

5. *How To Get Your Kid To Eat … But Not Too Much,* Ellyn Satter, Bull Publishing Co., Palo Alto, Calif., 1987.

6. *Intuitive Eating,* Evelyn Tribole, St. Martin's Press, Dunmore Pa. 1995.

7. *Jane Brody's Nutrition Book,* Jane Brody, Bantam, Doubleday Dell, Des Plaines, Ill. 1989.

8. *Making Peace With Food,* Susan Kano, HarperCollins, New York, N.Y., 1989.

9. *The Nutrition Detective,* Nan Fuchs, St. Martins Press, Los Angeles, 1985

10. *Nutrition Made Simple,* Robert Crayon, M. Evans, et al. New York, N.Y. 1994.

11. *Understanding Nutrition,* Eleanor Noss Whitney and Sharon Rady Rolfes, 7th ed., West Publishing Co. St. Paul, MN. 1996.

C. On Body Image and Similar Women's Issues

1. *The Beauty Myth,* Naomi Wolf, William Morrow, New York, N.Y. 1991.

2. *Fire with Fire,* Naomi Wolf, Ballantine, Random House, New York., N.Y. 1994.

3. *Mothering Ourselves,* Evelyn Bassoff, Plume Printing, New York, N.Y., 1991.

4. *The Obsession: Reflections on the Tyranny of Slenderness,* Kim Chernin, Harper & Row, New York, N.Y.., 1981.

5. *Reviving Ophelia,* Mary Pipher, Ballantine Books, New York, N.Y., 1994.

II. EATING DISORDER ORGANIZATIONS

1. ANAD, National Association of Anorexia Nervosa and Associated Disorders, Box 271 Highland Park, Illinois 60035.
   Phone: (847) 432-8000

2. ANRED, Anorexia Nervosa and Related Eating Disorders, Inc., P.O. Box 5102 Eugene,Oregon 97405
   Phone: (503) 344-1144.

3. EDAP, Eating Disorder Awareness and Prevention

603 Stewart Street, Suite 803, Seattle Washington, 98101
Phone (206) 382-3587

4. IAEDP, International Association of Eating Disorder Professionals 123 N.W. 13th St., Suite 206 Boca Raton, Florida 33432

5. National Academy for Eating Disorders
Montefiore Medical Center, Division of Adolescent Medicine
111 East 210th St. Bronx, N.Y. 10467
Phone: (718) 920-6781

6. OA, Overeaters Anonymous
World Service Office, P.O. Box 44020, Rio Rancho, NM 87174-4020
(Look for local listing in your telephone directory.)

Endnotes

 App App App

1. Manson, JoAnn, Willett, Walter, et al. Body weight and mortality among women. *New England Journal of Medicine*, Sept. 14, 1995, no. 11. Vol. 333, pp. 677–685.

2. Source: Sixth International Congress on Obesity in Kobe, Japan. *Eating Disorders Review*, vol. 2, no. 5 Sept./Oct. 1991.

3. Zerbe, Katherine. *The Body Betrayed*. American Psychiatric Press, Washington DC, 1993, p. 250.

4. Wolf, Naomi. *The Beauty Myth*. Doubleday, New York, 1991, p.70.

5. Pipher, Mary. *Reviving Ophelia*. Ballantine Books, New York, 1994, pp. 35–36.

6. Hawkins, R.C., Turell, S., & Jackson, L.S. Desirable and undesirable masculine and feminine traits in relation to students' dietary tendencies and body image dissatisfaction. *Sex Roles*, 1983, vol. 9, pp. 705–724.

7. 33,000 women tell how they really feel about their bodies. *Glamour*, Feb., 1984.

8. *New Body Magazine*, Nov. 1987.

9. *The Body Image Trap*. Video produced by Hazelden, catalogue no. 5786H .

10. Testimony before Subcommittee on Regulation, Business Opportunities and Energy, U.S. House of Representatives Committee on Small Business, March 26, 1990.

11. *Wall Street Journal*, Feb. 1981.

12. American Psychological Association *Guidelines for the Treatment of Eating Disorders*.

13. Ref. 5, pp. 44, 61.

14. Carroll, Lewis. *Through the Looking Glass*. Random House, 1965, pp. 31–32.

15. *Glamour*, Feb., 1984.

16. Ryan, Joan. *Little Girls in Pretty Boxes: The Making and Breaking of Elite Gymnasts and Figure Skaters*. Doubleday, New York, 1995, p. 65.

17. *Ibid.*, p. 59.

18. *Ibid.*, p. 7.

19. *Ibid.*, p. 44.

20. Maine, Margo. *Father Hunger*. Gurze Books, Carlsbad, Calif. 1991.

21. Bassoff, Evelyn. *Mothering Ourselves: Help and Healing for Adult Daughters.* Penguin Books, New York, 1992, p 38.

22. *Ibid.*, p. 38.

23. Ref. 3, p. 95.

24. Chernin, Kim. *The Obsession: Reflections on the Tyranny of Slenderness.* Harper & Row, New York, 1981, pp. 176–177.

25. Ref. 4, p. 205.

26. Geist, Richard A. Therapeutic dilemmas in the treatment of anorexia nervosa: A self-psychological perspective. *Theory and Treatment of Anorexia and Bulimia,* edited by S.W. Emmett. Brunner/Mazel, New York, 1985, p. 272.

27. *Glamour* Magazine, Feb. 1984.

28. Gross, J., & Rosen, J.C. Bulimia in adolescents: Prevalence and psychosocial correlates. *International Journal of Eating Disorders ,* vol. 7, 1988, pp. 51–61.

29. Garfinkle, P., Molodofsky, M., & Garer, D., Prognosis in anorexia nervosa as influenced by clinical features, treatment and self-perception. *Canadian Medical Association Journal,* vol. 117; 1977, pp. 1041–1045.

30. *Diagnostic and Statistical Manual of Mental Disorders.* American Psychiatric Association, Washington, D. C., 1994.

31. Ref. 4, p. 205.

32. Ref. 30, pp. 544–545. Used with permission.

33. Ref. 30, pp. 544–550. Used with permission.

34. Ref. 30, p. 731. Used with permission.

35. Ref. 30, p. 550. Used with permission.

36. Epstein, Diane, & Thompson, Kathleen. *Feeding on Dreams.* Macmillan, New York, 1994, p. 10.

37. Ref. 24, pp. 46, 47.

38. Ref. 36, p. xvii.

39. *Ibid.*, p. xvii.

40. *Ibid,* p. 49.

41. Pritikin, Nathan. *The Pritikin Permanent Weight Loss Manual.* Bantam Books, New York, 1981.

42. Diamond, Harvey, & Diamond, Marilyn. *Fit for Life.* Warner Books, 1985.

43. *Ibid.* p. 6.

44. Katahn, Martin. *The Rotation Diet.* Norton, New York, 1986, p. 19.

45. Bailey, Covert. *Fit or Fat.* Houghton Mifflin, New York, 1977.

46. Bailey, Covert. *The Fit or Fat Target Diet.* Houghton Mifflin, New York, 1984.

47. Bailey, Covert, & Bishop, Lea. *The Fit or Fat Target Diet Recipes.* Houghton Mifflin, New York.

48. Bailey, Covert, & Bishop, Lea. *The Fit or Fat Woman.* Houghton Mifflin, New York.

49. Bailey, Covert, *The New Fit or Fat,* Houghton Mifflin, New York, 1991.

50. Sears, Barry. *Enter the Zone.* HarperCollins, New York, 1995.

51. Hammer, L. D., Kraemer, H. C., Wilson, D. M., Ritter, P. L., Dornbusch, S. M. (1992). Standardized percentile curves of body mass index for children and adolescents. *American Journal of Diseases of Children,* 145:259–263. (38)

52. Satter, Ellyn. *How to Get Your Kid to Eat ... But Not Too Much.* Bull Publishing, Palo Alto, Calif., 1987, p. 375.

Bibliography

ॐ ॐ ॐ

Andersen, Arnold. *Males with Eating Disorders.* New York: Brunner/Mazel, 1990.

Bailey, Covert. *Fit or Fat.* New York: Houghton Mifflin, 1977.

Bailey, Covert. *The Fit or Fat Target Diet.* New York: Houghton Mifflin, 1984.

Bailey, Covert. *The New Fit or Fat.* New York: Houghton Mifflin, 1991.

Bailey, Covert. *The Fit or Fat Woman.* New York: Houghton Mifflin, 1993.

Bailey, Covert & Bishop, Lee. *The Fit or Fat Target Diet Recipes.* New York: Houghton Mifflin, 1989.

Bassoff, Evelyn. *Mothering Ourselves.* New York: Penguin Books, 1992.

The Body Image Trap. Videotape. Produced by Hazelden, catalog no. 5786 H.

Brody, Jane. *Jane Brody's Nutrition Book.* New York: Bantam Books, 1981.

Brown, Catarina & Jasper, Karin. *Consuming Passions.* Toronto: Second Story Press, 1993.

Bruch, Hilde. *The Golden Cage: The Enigma of Anorexia Nervosa.* Cambridge, MA: Harvard University Press, 1978.

Carroll, Lewis. *Through the Looking Glass.* New York: Random House, 1965.

Cash, Thomas & Pruzinsky, Thomas. (Eds.). *Body Images: Development, Deviance, and Change.* New York: Guilford Press, 1990.

Chernin, Kim. *The Obsession: Reflections on the Tyranny of Slenderness.* New York: Harper and Row, 1981.

Corbin, Cheryl. *Nutrition.* New York: Holt, Rinehart, & Winston, 1981.

Crayhon, Robert. *Nutrition Made Simple.* New York: M. Evans, 1994.

Diagnostic and Statistical Manual of Mental Disorders. (4th ed.). Washington, DC: American Psychological Association, 1994.

Diamond, Harvey & Diamond, Marilyn. *Fit for Life.* New York: Warner Books, 1985.

Eating Disorders Review. Report on the 6th International Congress on Obesity in Kobe, Japan. Vol. 2, No. 5, 1991.

Epstein, Diane & Thompson, Kathleen. *Feeding on Dreams.* New York: Macmillan, 1994.

Fallon, Patricia, et al. *Feminist Perspectives on Eating Disorders.* New York: Guilford Press, 1994.

Freud, Sigmund. The Ego and the Id. In J. Strachey (Ed. and Trans.), *The Standard Edition of the Complete Psychological Works of Sigmund Freud* (Vol. 19, pp. 3–66). London: Hogarth Press, 1961. (Original work published 1923)

Garfinkle, P., Molodofsky, M., & Garer, D. Prognosis in Anorexia Nervosa as Influenced by Clinical Features, Treatment, and Self-Perception. *Canadian Medical Association Journal, 117,* 1041–1045, 1977.

Geist, Richard A. Therapeutic Dilemmas in the Treatment of Anorexia Nervosa: A Self- Psychological Perspective. In S. W. Emmett (Ed.), *Theory and Treatment of Anorexia and Bulimia.* New York: Brunner/Mazel, 1985.

Gross, J. & Rosen, J. C. Bulimia in Adolescents: Prevalence and Psychosocial Correlates. *International Journal of Eating Disorders, 7,* 51–61, 1988.

Hammer, L. D., Kraemer, H. C., Wilson, D. M., Ritter, P. L., & Dornbusch, S. M. Standardized Percentile Curves of Body Mass Index for Children and Adolescents. *American Journal of Diseases of Children, 145,* 259–263, 1992.

Hawkins, R. C., Turrell, S., & Jackson, L. S. Desirable and Undesirable Masculine and Feminine Traits in Relation to Students' Dietary Tendencies and Body Image Dissatisfaction. *Sex Roles, 9,* 705–724, 1983.

Kano, Susan. *Making Peace with Food.* New York: Harper & Row, 1989.

Katahn, Martin. *The Rotation Diet.* New York: Norton, 1986.

Krueger, David. *Body Self and Psychological Self.* New York: Brunner/Mazel, 1989.

Latimer, Jane. *Living Binge Free.* Denver, CO: Living Quest, 1994.

Levenkron, Steven. *Treating and Overcoming Anorexia Nervosa.* New York: Charles Scribner, 1982.

Maine, Margo. *Father Hunger.* Carlsbad, CA: Gurze Books, 1991.

Manson, JoAnn, Willett, Walter, et al. Body Weight and Mortality Among Women. *The New England Journal of Medicine, 333* (11), 677–685, 1995.

Natow, A. & Heslin, J. *The Fat Counter.* New York: Pocket Books, 1989.

New Body Magazine. November, 1987.

Null, Gary & Null, Steve. *Protein for Vegetarians.* Memphis, TN: Pyramid, 1974.

Nutritive Value of American Foods in Common Units. *Agriculture Handbook.* No. 456.

Orbach, Susie. *Fat Is a Feminist Issue, I.* New York: Berkley Books, 1978.

Orbach, Susie. *Fat Is a Feminist Issue, II.* New York: Berkley Books, 1982.

Pipher, Mary. *Reviving Ophelia.* New York: Ballantine Books, 1994, pp. 35–36.

Pritikin, Nathan. *The Pritikin Permanent Weight Loss Manual.* New York: Grosset & Dunlap, 1982.

Roth, Geneen. *Breaking Free from Compulsive Eating.* New York: New American Library, 1984.

Ryan, Joan. *Little Girls in Pretty Boxes: The Making and Breaking of Elite Gymnasts and Figure Skaters.* New York: Doubleday, 1995.

Satter, Ellyn. *How to Get Your Kid to Eat . . . But Not Too Much.* Palo Alto, CA: Bull, 1987.

Sears, Barry. *Enter the Zone.* New York: HarperCollins, 1995.

Schauss, Alexander, Friedlander, Barbara, & Meyer, Arnold. *Eating for A's.* New York: Pocket Books, 1991.

Siegel, Michele, et al. *Surviving an Eating Disorder.* New York: Harper & Row, 1988.

Striegel-Moore, R. H., Silberstein, L. R., et al. A Prospective Study of Disordered Eating Among College Students. *International Journal of Eating Disorders, 8,* 99—509, 1989.

Testimony Before Subcommittee on Regulation, Business Opportunities and Energy, U.S. House of Representatives Committee on Small Business, March 26, 1990.

Wall Street Journal, February, 1981.

Wolf, Naomi. Hunger. In Patricia Fallon et al. *Feminist Perspectives on Eating Disorders.* New York: Guilford Press, 1994.

Wolf, Naomi. *The Beauty Myth.* New York: William Morrow, 1991.

Wolf, Naomi. *Fire with Fire: The New Female Power and How to Use It.* New York: Fawcett, 1994

Woodman, Marion. *Addiction to Perfection.* Toronto: Inner City Books, 1982.

Yates, Alayne. *Compulsive Exercise and the Eating Disorders.* New York: Brunner/Mazel, 1991.

Zerbe, Kathryn. *The Body Betrayed.* Washington, DC: American Psychiatric Press, 1993.